I0748405

CORMAC MCCARTHY'S NEOLIBERALISM

But they counted our life a pastime,
and our time here a market for gain:
for, say they, we must be getting every way,
though it be by evil means.

—*The Wisdom of Solomon*

CORMAC MCCARTHY'S NEOLIBERALISM

A Breakdown in Mercantile Ethics

EDITED BY BRIAN JAMES SCHILL

The University of Tennessee Press / Knoxville

First Edition.

An earlier version of chapter 4, "Human Become Coin: Neoliberalism, Anthropology, and Human Possibilities in *No Country for Old Men*" by Jonathan and Rick Elmore, was published in *The Cormac McCarthy Journal* 14, no. 2 (2016): 168–85.

An earlier version of chapter 5, "'In what direction did lost men veer?': Late Capitalism and Utopia in Cormac McCarthy's *The Road*" by Casey Jergenson, was published in *The Cormac McCarthy Journal* 14, no. 1 (2016): 117–32.

Chapter 7, "Diamonds, drugs, and the digital age: Global capitalism in Cormac McCarthy's *The Counselor*" by Lydia R. Cooper, is reprinted in full by permission of the Taylor & Francis journal *Critique—Studies in Contemporary Fiction* 59, no. 4 (2018): 445–58.

Library of Congress Cataloging-in-Publication Data

NAMES: Schill, Brian James, editor.
TITLE: Cormac McCarthy's neoliberalism : a breakdown in mercantile ethics / edited by Brian James Schill.
DESCRIPTION: First. | Knoxville : The University of Tennessee Press, 2025. | Includes index. | Summary: "From his first southwestern novel *Blood Meridian* to his Ridley Scott-directed screenplay *The Counselor*, American author Cormac McCarthy spent his career both caricaturing and commenting upon neoliberalism as an economic, political, and cultural project. Editor Brian Schill and his contributors explore McCarthy's response to neoliberal capitalism and the Pulitzer Prize-winner's status as a "neoliberal writer" himself. This volume covers the bulk of McCarthy's published writings, including his two new novels *The Passenger* and *Stella Maris*, and documents how and to what effect McCarthy's fiction confronts the politics and ethics of neoliberalism-and why McCarthy is more prescient in his analysis of political economy than previously explored in scholarship" — Provided by publisher.
IDENTIFIERS: LCCN 2024050945 (print) | LCCN 2024050946 (ebook) | ISBN 9781621909378 (hardcover) | ISBN 9781621909385 (kindle edition) | ISBN 9781621909392 (adobe pdf)
SUBJECTS: LCSH: McCarthy, Cormac, 1933-2023—Criticism and interpretation. | McCarthy, Cormac, 1933-2023—Political and social views. | Neoliberalism. | LCGFT: Literary criticism.
CLASSIFICATION: LCC PS3563.C337 Z63525 2025 (print) | LCC PS3563.C337 (ebook) | DDC 813/.54—dc23/eng/20241120
LC record available at https://lccn.loc.gov/2024050945
LC ebook record available at https://lccn.loc.gov/2024050946

To Elias, Ezra, and Evelina, who continue to believe in both an alternative and a more egalitarian future.

CONTENTS

FOREWORD

David Holloway

Brian James Schill is surely correct when he suggests, in his Introduction to this book, that insufficient attention has been paid to Cormac McCarthy's status as a chronicler of the neoliberal era. The arc of McCarthy's mature career, from *Suttree* onwards, maps so precisely to the chronology of creative destruction and crisis marking neoliberalism as a historically distinct mode of accumulation. Simultaneously, McCarthy's passing in 2023 coincides with what feels like a decisive moment, as regimes of neoliberal governance buckle in the global ferment of populist authoritarianism let loose by decades of "accumulation by dispossession"—David Harvey's resonant phrase for the predatory logic of neoliberal capital that updates, following Rosa Luxemburg, Marx's concept of "primitive accumulation" for the breaking up of feudal agriculture by the enclosure and expropriation of common land in Britain during the Middle Ages.[1]

Part of what makes Harvey's use of Marx significant is his suggestion that cycles of wholesale expropriation, far from occurring only as a precondition for modes of primitive capitalism, can be seen recurring throughout capitalist history, and with particular ferocity in neoliberalism. Viewed retrospectively within this frame, the keystone text in McCarthy's corpus increasingly appears to be *Blood Meridian, or the Evening Redness in the West* (1985), a crucial novel of the neoliberal era, centrally concerned as it is with the contiguous and simultaneous irruption of multiple eras of primitive accumulation.[2] The landscapes of Southern Texas and Northern Mexico during the period in which *Blood Meridian* is set were a virtual laboratory of New World primitive accumulation, as a Spanish-Mexican society structured around aristocratic assumptions about land and labor was ripped apart in the violent inauguration of a new capitalist order, where "the coming of barbed wire represented an enclosure movement that displaced people and left them landless," as "displaced Mexicans, who had formerly worked on the great landed estates were reduced to [the status of] wage laborer."[3] The fencing of the land in the "Epilogue" to *Blood Meridian*, then, closes the novel with an image that fuses the genesis of capitalism in the American Southwest with the deeper history of capitalist enclosure that precedes it, recasting each of those periods synchronically as pure gothic horror, while also referring us forward, unavoidably, to the indelible present of the novel itself—the 1980s—the decade in which the political economy of the US entered a period of neoliberal accumulation by dispossession as profound and far-reaching as the capitalist transformation of the Southwest in the nineteenth century. Read as such today and refracted retrospectively through the catastrophic history of neoliberalism—born in the traumatic breakdown of corporatist Fordism, crashed in the financial crisis of 2007–08, polarized by the immiseration of its new precariat and the vertiginous wealth of its global elite, menaced by the crypto-fascisms its own crises have finally produced—the preternatural chaos of *Blood Meridian* feels like nothing less than a moment of cataclysmic secular prophecy, a vivid presentiment of disastrous neoliberal futures to come.

The conundrum this poses for critics, of course, is that such a reading is essentially poetic. McCarthy is not writing *about* neoliberalism in *Blood Meridian*—not in any conventionally realist or allegorical sense—any more than his retreat into private narrative spaces voiced as pure hallucinogenic subjectivity in *The Passenger* or *Stella Maris* is *about* neoliberalism's privatization of the commons or its hyper-individualization of social relations. Even at its most mimetic, McCarthy's relationship with neoliberalism largely resides in what is left unsaid and what remains absent, the gothic undertow of his language working instead by suggestion and implication, by allusion to contents that remain relatively repressed but that may be glimpsed or intuited in shadowy form as half-felt half-presences pressuring the action: a parade of material ghosts bundled together in some indecipherable but dreadfully palpable way, pervading the narrative without necessarily becoming either properly conscious or fully unrepressed in the text. One synecdoche for this might be the *source* of the case of money that Llewelyn Moss retrieves from the massacre at the beginning of *No Country for Old Men* (2005), the object around which the narrative orbits, without which there is no plot and no novel. The place where the money trail ends—the place, we might say, where the narrative therefore effectively begins, as the case first changes hands and is embodied as investment capital—is the securitized "missing" floor,[4] as Carson Wells calls it, at the top of a corporate skyscraper in Houston, whose views over the city to the lowlands and the bayou beyond reconfigure the imperial gaze of nineteenth century landscape painting as the provenance of corporate power. In *No Country for Old Men*, that is, the primeval gangsterism we see in the streets begins with and articulates, in a very literal sense, a void: the missing corporate floor whose influence thus becomes immanent—if not sublime—in the text, even as the floor itself remains "missing."

One response to this critical conundrum might perhaps be found in Mark Fisher's description of neoliberalism as a cultural condition as much as a structure of political economy. The references to Fisher's *Capitalist Realism* in several of the essays in this collection open intriguing possibilities as to how we might think about McCarthy as a writer of, as well as "about," neoliberal capitalism, not least because the palpable feeling of crisis that haunts McCarthy's mature work is so reminiscent of the qualities that Fisher ascribes to styles of capitalist realism. In contemporary dystopian cinema, Fisher suggests, catastrophe "is neither waiting down the road, nor has it already happened. Rather, it is being lived through," insofar as its causes are so opaque and detached from the present "as to seem like the caprice of a malign being; a negative miracle, a malediction which no penitence can ameliorate." Such a blight, Fisher continues, "can only be eased by an intervention that can no more be anticipated than was the onset of the curse in the first place."[5] Seeking, here, to summarize one indicative form of what he means by capitalist realism, it hardly needs pointing out that Fisher's own style is almost parodically reminiscent of Cormac McCarthy's. As are the contents of James Ellroy's neo-noir, where Fisher finds a "fixation on the luridly venal," a "hyperbolic insistence on cruelty, betrayal and savagery,"[6] in a neoliberal worldview which shares with American hip-hop, for example, a presumption that authenticity, or fidelity to the Real, is grounded in acceptance of corruption and perpetual exploitation, in a world made up only of winners and losers, "a kind of super-identification," as Fisher puts it, "with capital at its most pitilessly predatory."[7]

Capitalist Realism is perhaps best known for baldly reworking the proposition that no qualitatively different way of organizing our material life now feels possible, because one hallmark of neoliberal capital is that it "seamlessly occupies the horizons of the thinkable."[8] The implications of this for critics exploring Cormac McCarthy's relationship with neoliberalism are far-reaching. For if Fisher's observation that capitalist realism is a cultural condition as much as a set of genres or styles, because its mimesis cleaves so closely to the neoliberal world it accepts as ontology and reproduces as truth, it might then be possible to posit McCarthy's own mature prose as itself a kind of super-identification with neoliberal capital and to describe it, too, as a mode of capitalist realism. It is certainly tempting to take Fisher's riffing on Deleuze and Guattari, in his description of neoliberal capital "metabolizing and absorbing anything with which it comes into contact," and reapply this to McCarthy's signature styles—particularly his high style, with the totalizing power it has always displayed to remake anything upon which it is trained in its own portentous image, in iterative acts of poetic violence, moments of creative literary destruction, a stream of aesthetic expropriations and enclosures of people and ideas and things.[9] If McCarthy's writing might be described in this way, as another form of capitalist realism, it is not so great a leap also to ascribe an analogous experience to one possible set of reader-responses to his prose, in the feelings of inevitability or inescapability his language can induce: in the spiraling sentences in whose length and complexity the reader can feel simply locked, the irrefutable density of the words on the page, the reaching of narrators and protagonists for universal truths, all of which make the prose itself feel ontological, immovable, carceral, an avalanche of language in which the reader may feel (and may derive pleasure from feeling) simply lost or overwhelmed.

Another implication of this is that the frame Schill presents to the reader in his introduction—"wherein the author is simultaneously a diagnostician and symptom of the pathology in question"—may pertain equally to authors of literary criticism; particularly so, perhaps, when a collection of essays assessing the relationship between neoliberalism and literature is institutionally framed by the cultural condition (as Fisher might have it) of the neoliberal university. How is literary criticism even possible, one might ask, if among its many uncountable colonialisms neoliberal capital has also colonized the academy? What questions can criticism even ask, and what forms might it meaningfully take, if the neoliberal ground on which it is now built means that critique, as such, is always already incorporated or erased?

Breakdown in Mercantile Ethics answers these questions emphatically, not only by showing how McCarthy's language engages the material and ideological realities of neoliberalism, but also by presenting readers with the gaps, aporia, traces of suture, and moments of rupture, into which both literature and literary criticism can still insert themselves to illuminating effect. It is worth dwelling on this because the idea that the act of reading cannot help but involve a reconfiguring of the familiar world draws us away from the limiting effects that a purely symptomatic historical reading might otherwise bring to McCarthy's relationship with neoliberalism. In collision with the historical sensibilities and political experience of readers and critics, the capitalist realism of these novels and plays does not simply reflect or transcribe the world mimetically or metaphorically: rather, it transmogrifies the world, so that reading becomes an exercise in estrangement, a series of encounters with the Real in which a world we may not otherwise be able to escape or transcend is reworked to look odd, alien, threatening and uncanny, transparent, provisional, and ideological—a vital job for literature and criticism in any era, and an indispensable one in our own.

Notes

1. David Harvey, *The New Imperialism* (Oxford: Oxford UP, 2005). See also Rosa Luxemburg, *The Accumulation of Capital* (1913; repr. London: Routledge and Kegan Paul, 1951); and Karl Marx, *Capital*, vol. 1 (1867; repr. London: Penguin, 1990).

2. David Holloway, "Creative Destruction, Primitive Accumulation and the Imagination of Catastrophe in Cormac McCarthy's *Blood Meridian*" in *Profils Américains* 17, eds. Christine Chollier and Edwin T. Arnold (Montpellier: Université Paul-Valéry, 2004), 109–25.

3. William G. Robbins, *Colony and Empire: The Capitalist Transformation of the American West* (Lawrence: Univ. Press of Kansas, 1994), 30.

4. Cormac McCarthy, *No Country for Old Men* (London: Picador, 2005), 142.

5. Mark Fisher, *Capitalist Realism: Is There No Alternative?* (2008; repr. Alresford: Zero Books, 2022), 2–3.

6. Ibid., 11.

7. Ibid., 12.

8. Ibid., 8.

9. Ibid., 6.

ACKNOWLEDGMENTS

In addition to the authors contained herein, Lydia Cooper in particular, this anthology owes its existence to the words, efforts, and support of the following individuals and groups: Sharon Carson, Robin David, David Deacon, Steven Frye, Joe Leiss, Dianne Luce, Stacey Peebles and everyone at the Cormac McCarthy Society (CMS), Thomas Wells and everyone at the University of Tennessee Press (especially Maliea Ruby and Jonathan Boggs), Aaron Wentz, Joshua Wynne, Scott Yarbrough, everyone offering thoughtful questions about "Cormac McCarthy's neoliberalism" both online and at various CMS conferences, and anyone reading these words now.

Thanks.

INTRODUCTION
ALL PLACES ARE THE WRONG PLACE

Brian James Schill

"I didnt even want to take this job."

Such were the anxious last words of the second of two Hotel Eagle clerks murdered in Eagle Pass, Texas, in 1980 in Cormac McCarthy's *No Country for Old Men* (2005). At issue is not the notion that the clerks were simply in the wrong place at the wrong time, McCarthy implies in his bleakest of books, countering the Eagle Pass sheriff's assessment that the first clerk fell into "about as bad a piece of luck as you could have." It's that for subjects ambling across the United States of America in the latter half of the twentieth century, luck has nothing to do with it: all places are the wrong place. In the same conversation in which he expressed this desperation for work, the nameless clerk confessed—to the ex-Army Colonel and future corpse Carson Wells, whose corporate employer, the Matacumbe Petroleum Group, is as invested in heroin as hydrocarbons—less a desire than a *need* to accept any gig available in an increasingly volatile economy where real wages in almost every industry have declined, public services too have dried up, corporations and their federal sponsors run the show, and inflation and privatization have made things like higher education and healthcare luxury goods. Wells simply shrugs. "You need to relax," says the bounty hunter, waving away the clerk's distress. "They're not coming back. I can pretty near guarantee it."[1]

Despite his confidence, Wells is at this moment himself on the cusp of failing his effort to protect the novel's pseudo-protagonist, Llewelyn Moss, from both clerks' killer, the scrupulous and spectral Anton Chigurh, who of course does come back. Caught unawares by his fellow assassin, whose own employer had arranged a cash-for-narcotics trade with Matacumbe, Wells would go on to price out his own life, offering Chigurh a mere $14,000 cash money to walk away. "It is [a good payday]," Chigurh humors Wells. "It's just in the wrong currency."[2] The conflict between these parties—in what amounts to a class war that directly involves not only extralegal narcotraffickers but well-heeled private corporations, the Mexican and American governments (likely including the American Central Intelligence Agency [CIA][3]) and hungry job-hunters on both sides of the border—is the event that provides Moss, a Vietnam veteran and arcwelder, the once-in-a-lifetime opportunity to make his and his Walmart cashier spouse Carla Jean's wage slavery a thing of the past. Stealing more than $2 million from the dope runners—which is to say, from Chigurh, corporate America, and the CIA—Moss, as even he expected, triggers a catastrophic series of events that produces more than a dozen bodies, including his wife's and his own.

Failing to prevent the ultraviolence plaguing his unassuming patch of American dirt and failing in the end to apprehend Chigurh and better protect his community, Terrell County Sheriff Ed Tom Bell throws in the towel. Not only Chigurh and Wells, thinks Bell after the fact, but Moss and Matacumbe, the nineteen year old he'd sent to the gas chamber, the teenage runaway murdered alongside Moss, and the two middle schoolers who accept Chigurh's literal blood money in exchange for a vow of silence: *all* of these actors appear to him as some "new kind" of human subject, as "somethin we really aint never even seen before." So it is that Bell tells his wife, Loretta, he's clocking out. The job's dangers notwithstanding, Bells says, the couple is still "six thousand dollars in debt over this job," despite decades of honest public service work. Does the lawman hope to get out "while he's ahead?" Loretta asks with a smile, meaning while he's alive. "And I said no mam I just aim to quit," responds Bell bitterly. "I aint ahead by a damn sight. I never will be." Unable to pay down his debts to either his creditors or the taxpaying public, never mind his failure to match wits and weapons with Chigurh, Bell calls it a career, dreaming at novel's end that he has lost the currency that his father gifted him and lamenting how the American people are "being bought with our own money. . . . There is fortunes bein accumulated out there that they dont nobody even know about. What do we think is goin to come of that money?"[4]

As this sketch of McCarthy's twist on the crime thriller makes clear, *No Country* is a novel whose personalities are not so much obsessed with the acquisition and loss of wealth than desperate to survive an America that, by the 1980s, has made of them what Judith Butler once called "abject subjects" and forced them to engage in a direct and often fatal—or, to use a tired appellation, Hobbesian—competition with each other as a matter of course.[5] Regardless of their social position, that is, each of these various assassins, veterans, and service industry workers, cops and kids, day laborers and petroleum executives, are unable to escape the event horizon of a political economy that, since at least the 1970s, has pulled them into a subjectivity that forces them to think less about the common good, less about either the past or the future, than about themselves as investment portfolios *in situ* in a zero-sum game whose market position at every moment rises and falls in inverse proportion to that of their competitors. If *No Country* and several of McCarthy's late novels, plays, and screenplays are any indication, the author's own answer to Bell's question is this: violence, depravity, precarity, the permanence of crisis, and the dissolution of magnanimous citizens, local communities, and nation-states themselves. These are the only things "goin to come" of a political economy where human beings have been reduced to lowing animals—thus Chigurh's cattle gun—and/or to self-interested enterprises in a highly competitive and increasingly privatized and deregulated global marketplace where both government and the public sphere have wisped away like so much cigar smoke alongside the preponderance of social relations.

All of this, Bell tells a news reporter, is a product of the "breakdown in mercantile ethics" that has made each of the parties with whom he interacts incapable of thinking beyond their own short-term self-interest, of imagining a future where their bodies and souls are not capital investments, of cultivating a constitution or ethic outside of market logic.[6] Indeed, far from being "just" a crime thriller or a reflection on desire, ethics, and justice along the Texas-Mexico border, *No Country* is arguably the diagnosis of a condition much more material in scope. That condition, the writers contributing to this book argue, is the global event of neoliberalism, which emerged in the West formally as a collection of organizing principles even before the Second World War, a set of official policies, institutions, and legal codes by the 1970s, and as the only game in town across the social, economic, cultural, ontological, and political registers by the turn of the century. To wit, the better one comes to understand the history, theory, and practice of neoliberalism the harder it becomes *not* to see Chigurh, with his flat affect, "faintly exotic" mien, and almost autistic commitment to economic reason and the violence required to enforce that reason—plus a bad haircut—as anything but neoliberalism anthropomorphized.[7] And not only *No Country*: the essays herein demonstrate that beyond "late capitalism" as a too-broad signifier, neoliberalism—a more precise term signifying a cultural logic that Wendy Brown argues "names a historically specific economic and political reaction against Keynesianism and democratic socialism, as well as a more generalized practice of 'economizing' spheres and activities heretofore governed by other tables of value"[8]—has been central to Cormac McCarthy's literary project since at least *The Gardener's Son* (1977) and through his final novels *The Passenger* and *Stella Maris* (2022).

Consider *No Country*'s immediate predecessors. After articulating "all American cowboy" John Grady Cole's flight from Texas in the wake of the state's increasing capitalization and the loss of his family ranch in *All the Pretty Horses* (1992), McCarthy ends his National Book Award-winning Border Trilogy with the same cowboy dead in the alley behind a Mexican brothel—"lost in the rain in Juárez" as Bob Dylan once put it[9]—as the New Mexican ranch that had been his employer too is crushed by the treads of the American military-industrial complex.[10] Mourning the death of his protégé, Billy Parham survives his own economization only to end up homeless in a neoliberal hellscape as the century turns. "There was no work in that country anywhere. . . . In the spring of the second year of the new millennium he was living in the Gardner Hotel in El Paso Texas and working as an extra in a movie," writes McCarthy of Billy's seventy-eighth year,

> When the work came to an end he stayed in his room. There was a television set in the lobby and men his age and younger sat in the lobby in the evening in the old chairs and watched television but he cared little for it and the men had little to say to him or he to them. His money ran out. Three weeks later he was evicted. He'd long since sold his saddle and he set forth into the street with just his AWOL bag and his blanketroll. . . . A week later he was somewhere in central Arizona. . . . He sat beneath a concrete overpass and watched the gusts of rain blowing across the fields.[11]

This somber development, McCarthy predicted in 1998, is the likely result of the expansion of a political economy the author had earlier described as increasingly "natural" to the Mexican prison that held John Grady years before: "no more than a small walled village and within it occurred a constant seethe of barter and exchange in everything from radios and blankets down to matches and buttons and shoenails and within this bartering ran a constant struggle for status and position. Underpinning all of it like the fiscal standard in commercial societies lay a bedrock of depravity and violence where in an egalitarian absolute every man was judged by a single standard and that was his readiness to kill."[12]

By ending his trilogy in the year 2002, with Billy penniless and out of options, McCarthy was not simply articulating the horror that was the Southwest's mid-century neoliberalization or literary fiction's inability to challenge its own capitalization; he was describing, yes, the events that had engulfed most of Mexico and the American Southwest since at least the fifteenth century, and, more cogently, the world *as it was* at the moment of the novel's composition and publication in the 1990s. Nowhere is this fact more evident than in McCarthy's characterization of John Grady's lover, Magdalena. About halfway through *Cities of the Plain* (1998), John Grady, comforting Magdalena in a motel room as she conveyed to him in painful detail the trauma that had been her life to that point, breaks down in tears at his lover's origin story. "She was from the State of Chiapas and she had been sold at the age of thirteen to settle a gambling debt," wrote McCarthy of the ill-fated, epileptic prostitute with whom John Grady had fallen immediately in love in the first pages of the trilogy's last installment. "She had no family. In Puebla she'd run away to a convent for protection. The procurer himself appeared on the convent steps the following morning and in the pure light of day paid money into the hand of the mother superior and took the girl away again."[13]

For readers accustomed to a stylist known for expounding upon the arid majesty of the northern Mexican landscapes bordering the United States—Sonora, Chihuahua—the geographic reference was as much a clue to the author's own neoliberal moment as it was a snapped wire. Why reference the southern state of Chiapas? Because, as Neil Harvey tells it, territory traditionally held by Indigenous Mexicans in Chiapas and other states in the Mexican south had been contested over for the course of several centuries, often with a violence—waged by Spanish imperialists, the Mexican and American governments, and American and European corporate interests—that was slowly making its way north. As the Indigenous population lost access to its lands and corporate capitalism spread, many sought work on the coffee and cacao plantations of the southwest corner of Chiapas specifically only to end up as indentured servants.[14] "Others were forcibly taken to mahogany lumber camps, or *monterías* on the eastern edges of the Lacandon forest, where they were held in virtual slavery," continues Harvey of the long-simmering conditions that produced not only Magdalena and the poverty that has plagued Chiapas for decades but the "numerous clashes [that] occurred in the 1950s and early 1960s" as Indigenous persons with communal rights to ancestral territory (*comuneros*) fought to protect their land from the managers of government-owned land who sought to annex the territory to monied developers.[15]

As if to provide context to David Harvey's notion that neoliberalism is, effectively, a class war waged from above, McCarthy, in the opening *Cities* scene, elaborates on Neil Harvey's scholarship by describing the socioeconomic divides governing the lives of his mostly working-class American characters and their antagonists who, although beginning their lives in places like Chiapas, were now—having followed the money—just a river away from the United States in Ciudad Juárez. Emphasizing La Venada's often overweight prostitutes, whose garish makeup was "cracked like sizing" and who, "in their shabby deshabille," looked up at John Grady and his crew "from the shabby sofas where they sat," McCarthy establishes early on the wide gulf separating the sex workers at La Venada—whose "black greasepaint" lined "their dark indian eyes"—from those of The White Lake, whose "hostess in evening attire" takes clients' hats and whose working women "lounged on sofas of red damask and gold brocade" wearing "negligees and floorlength formal gowns and sheath dresses of white satin or purple velvet that were split up the thigh and they wore shoes of glass or gold and sat in studied poses."[16] This latter scene, populated by "mostly welldressed Mexicans with a few Americans dressed in flowered shirts of an intemperately thin cloth," was the social space away from which Billy had warned John Grady, arguing "It's real expensive. . . . It aint no place for a cowboy."[17] Such scenes flank the ranch hands' many anxious conversations about the imminent takeover of their employer's land by the federal government, a notion that prompts Billy to assert to John Grady that "Anyway this country aint the same. Nor anything in it. The war changed everthing. I dont think people even know it yet." How did the war change America? wonders John Grady reasonably. "It just did. It aint the same no more," repeats Billy without elaborating but thinking likely of the new capitalism then emerging. "It never will be."[18]

Set in the 1950s, all of this is but prologue to the violence that would erupt in Chiapas and across Mexico from the 1970s to the 1990s simultaneous to the various energy and economic crises in the West and the growing debate over "globalization" and internationally binding policy pacts like the North American Free Trade Agreement (NAFTA). Hailed by its advocates in the business and political classes as ushering in a radical new era of international prosperity—"The Clinton administration would blow an historic opportunity if it doesn't go all out and win congressional approval of the North American Free Trade Agreement," chuffed Malcolm Forbes Jr. in his own magazine in 1993, rolling his eyes at the "Fear-mongering opponents [who] preposterously prey upon unfounded anxieties that this deal will impoverish us"[19]—NAFTA was supposed to be the rising tide that lifted all boats. Instead, the project produced not only higher levels of unemployment in and emigration from Mexico in the three decades since its passing, but increased violence on both sides of the border and throughout the country.[20]

It also produced something else in the 1990s: several well-organized resistance organizations that went very public, very quickly, both before and after the agreement's authorization. The most successful of these was Rafael Sebastián Guillén Vicente's—Subcomandante Marcos—*Ejército Zapatista de Liberación Nacional* (EZLN) in Chiapas, which formalized its opposition to neoliberalism, and NAFTA in particular, the day the agreement took effect on January 1, 1994. Marcos's "Zapatistas" understood that, Forbes's cynicism notwithstanding, the trade deal would dehumanize whole populations by binding them to volatile and antidemocratic markets and a chronic precarity of being—"jobs" yes, but not stable, gainful, or dignified employment—at the same time as it militarized nations against their own increasingly impoverished, humiliated, and angry citizens, undermining both peace and prosperity in the process. "Since the beginning, the fee that capitalism imposes on the southeastern part of this country makes Chiapas ooze blood and mud," thundered Marcos in 1992 as McCarthy prepared to publish *All the Pretty Horses*. "Millions of women, millions of youths, millions of indigenous, millions of homosexuals, millions of human beings of all races and colors, participate in the financial markets only as a devalued currency, always worth less and less, the currency of their blood turning a profit."[21] History, we now know, has validated Marcos, who went on to argue—in advance of the 1997 murder of some forty unarmed Indigenous peasants by an anti-EZLN militia in the Chiapan village Acteal—that "National repression is a necessary premise of the globalization neoliberalism imposes. The more neoliberalism advances as a global system, the more numerous grow the weapons and the ranks of armies and national police. The numbers of the imprisoned, the disappeared, and the assassinated in different countries also grows," including in the US.[22]

Such violence was prophesied by not only Marcos but McCarthy, whose *Cities*, revised alongside the development of NAFTA and its policy adjuncts in the 1990s, today serves as a bitter rejoinder to the economic compact between the US and Mexico. Marcos's questions prefigure McCarthy's trilogy, which was likewise asking: What are the effects of neoliberalism on the human community? How does a global marketplace change the individual subject's spiritual and political reason? What new kinds of ontology have emerged since the last great war, since Los Alamos and Bretton Woods? This is all to say that *Cities of the Plain*, as a capstone on the Border Trilogy, makes little sense to a contemporary reader outside of its neoliberal timestamp, outside a political economy that has deregulated industry, enabled international capital flight, and undermined worker protections in the US and abroad (ranchers and Indigenous persons included), outside the growth in human trafficking and new forms of international sex slavery in particular, outside of the financialization of the economy and the entrepreneurialization of human capital, and outside the swelling of immigration globally and the growth of income inequality on both sides of the Mexican-American border, all of which in the end make most human enterprises either stateless or dead, and often both.

In sum, the Border Trilogy's unfolding simultaneous to neoliberalism's long codification in the 1980s and 1990s serves to illustrate the degree to which the contemporary reader of a novel like *Cities* cannot help but recall not only the nightly news but her direct experience of neoliberal capitalism in the West, of her own economization, whatever her social status. By originating Magdalena's life and exploitation in Chiapas in the 1930s and 40s, and thus increasing the likelihood that Magdalena was herself an Indigenous girl—in noticeable contrast to John Grady's affection for the highborn and patently Europeanized Alejandra in *Horses*—McCarthy was not simply signaling familiarity with a then-current debate over NAFTA and a Zapatista rebellion in Chiapas so much as doing for a wide array of readers in America what Michel Foucault, with some conceit, insisted his own books on a variety of eighteenth and nineteenth century institutions were doing: inscribing a "history of the present" via a novel that although set in 1952 and 2002 is really describing the world as it was becoming in 1998, and as it is today.

Neoliberalism: A Very Brief History

None of this is to suggest that McCarthy had NAFTA or Subcomandante Marcos explicitly front-of-mind as he finalized *Cities*, or that free trade, globalization, and multinational capitalism in the 1990s were intentional, one-to-one targets of the novel. McCarthy is hardly so formulaic as to intend such a specific reading of, say, *The Gardener's Son*'s antagonist, James Gregg, as the harsher neoliberal equivalent of his father William's earlier, and ostensibly "better," *laissez-faire* capitalism. Even so, the writers cited below and those contributing to this volume demonstrate that in telling the story of Ed Tom Bell and John Grady Cole, of Robert McEvoy and Lester Ballard, of Llewelyn and Carla Jean Moss and the counselor, McCarthy has, for decades, been telling the story of neoliberal America. The contributors to this book, in fact, make an excellent case that an honest reading of McCarthy's *oeuvre* all but *requires* a consideration of the neoliberal reason that since the 1970s and 1980s has produced the author himself and his audience, and the increasingly choppy sea through which both were and are navigating.

Because the term neoliberalism is so slippery though, finding itself used in often inexact ways by journalists and politicians, activists and scholars, a more precise definition here is in order. Building upon and outpacing the eighteenth and nineteenth century's *laissez-faire* liberalism of David Hume, Adam Smith, John Stuart Mill, and Jean-Jacques Rousseau, *neoliberalism* should be understood as a series of market-oriented theories, practices, discourses, and policies that tend to be framed in one of two overlapping ways. One being an ideologically salient *theory*—or "rationality" to quote Wendy Brown—envisioning an expansion of human freedom and transformation of individual human subjects and society almost exclusively through the proliferation of market mechanisms; the second being a series of on-the-ground policies, practices, and programs—undertaken by local legislators, international economists, and institutional bureaucrats—that advance competitive, market-based private interests and private property ownership in particular and look to rebrand government itself as an entity whose sole purpose is to enable markets and, when necessary, discipline market operations with force. Although many observers both for and against such prescriptions have asked whether the word "neoliberalism" can even be said to hold meaning today, it will be utilized in this book not only because the concept's first advocates used it, even before the Second World War, but because as a signifier it still communicates something more specific and novel than terms like "late-capitalism" or "globalization" vis-à-vis the production, distribution, and analysis of commodities, cultural texts, and subjectivities.[23]

Coming into its own in the 1970s, then, neoliberalism's birth and evolution look something like this: In the wake of extreme socioeconomic volatility early in the previous century (culminating in the stock market crash of 1929 and the Great Depression) and, eventually, the second of *two* World Wars and a Russian Revolution that had likewise disrupted the world economy, a collection of American and European economists, businessmen, and legislators—which is to say, elites—began exchanging ideas as early as the 1930s concerning the saving of capitalism from both itself and from democracy, the populist and emancipatory gyrations of which had also shown a capacity for disrupting markets. Although classical liberalism had already posed, for the governing of subjects, the market, and the "man of exchange" *homo oeconomicus* (coupled imperfectly with *limited* democracy), as a replacement for the monarchies and aristocracies, colonies and empires that were, by the nineteenth century, already in retreat, this cohort of twentieth century thinkers saw that the market had not, in fact, limited the emerging constellation of nation-states enough. *Laissez-faire* had not prevented social democracy and the intervention of Keynesian welfare economics, had not prevented (and in fact perhaps enabled) the rise of communism and fascism, had not prevented the social unrest that reached an apex across the globe in the 1960s. Even more inexcusable was the fact that liberalism had failed to exploit states—most of which had been too hands-off—to their full potential as custodians of the free market.

First deploying the term "neoliberalism" at the Walter Lippmann Colloquium in Paris in 1938—named for the American thinker whom, Noam Chomsky reminds us, gave the world the concept of "manufacturing consent"[24]—this group of thinkers theorized how to reinvent government in a way that would better enable a deregulated (global) market economy and individual enterprise broadly at the same time as it depoliticized populations, giving elites more direct control of government and the global economy. Following the Second World War—and the establishment of the International Monetary Fund (IMF) and General Agreement on Tariffs and Trade (GATT), which later became the World Trade Organization, in Bretton Woods, New Hampshire—the group codified its mélange of views in the late 1940s after founding a club, the Mont Pèlerin Society, dedicated to the new liberalism whose inaugural membership included Austrian economist Ludwig von Mises, his student Friedrich August von Hayek, German economist Wilhelm Röpke, University of Chicago economists Milton Friedman and George Stigler, and philosopher of science Karl Popper. Assembling in the Swiss village of Mont Pèlerin in 1947, Hayek and crew penned the Society's "Statement of Aims," which fretted how "Over large stretches of the Earth's surface the essential conditions of human dignity and freedom have already disappeared" as a direct result of "the growth of a view of history which denies all absolute moral standards and by the growth of theories which question the desirability of the rule of law" and "by a decline of belief in private property and the competitive market."[25]

For these thinkers, the global poisoning of free thought by the twin evils of fascism and socialism in the twentieth century signaled a "road abandoned," as Hayek put it, a broad departure from individuality, choice, and freedom writ large in lieu of their opposites.[26] Even ostensibly "free" nation-states like the US and its allies had built up far too many protectionist walls around themselves since the turn of the century—subsidies, tariffs, welfare programs, and minimum wages—that jiggered the international market on goods and labor and disrupted humans' enterprising spirit and the freedom of both entrepreneurs and capital. None of this was needed, argued Hayek, insofar as societies themselves typically produce a natural and "spontaneous" order that governments disrespect to their own peril.[27] The antidote to such poisons was a renewed emphasis on a type of political economy that expanded and protected markets, better challenged labor organizing, limited government intrusion in markets, and freed individuals to pursue their own economic self-interest at the same time as it depoliticized, even "de-democratized," and privatized entire societies.

That is to say, while not anti-statists as such, Hayek, Mises, and their advocates sought the "dethronement of politics" in domestic and international affairs alongside a belief in what Quinn Slobodian calls a "militant globalism," looking to use law and economics as buffers to officious government on the one hand, and, on the other, as a way of actively instrumentalizing government on behalf of global markets.[28] After all, "*Laissez-faire* was never more than a rule of thumb," quipped Hayek late in his career. "Although it is conceivable that the spontaneous order which we call society may exist without government, if the minimum of rules required for the formation of such an order is observed without an organized apparatus for their enforcement, in most circumstances the organization which we call government becomes indispensable in order to ensure that those rules are obeyed."[29] Government, in other words, was not the enemy, but a useful tool that when used correctly could bring about more and better market *and* social order. In fact, the imperial and/or authoritarian state hardly concerned Hayek or Mises insofar as such states better "encouraged" adherence to rules beneficial to markets. Mises in particular fretted less about political authoritarianism than an "interventionist government that appealed to 'the people' for its legitimacy. His state could find its legitimacy only in its defense of the sanctity of private property and the forces of competition," Slobodian wrote, adding that for many neoliberals the authoritarian nation-state "could be useful insofar as it provided services of stabilization (which would often include restrictions to migration) and cultivated legitimacy in the political sphere. But like democracy, it also bore the risk of tipping into excess. Thus, it needed to be constrained just as democracy did."[30]

So it is, Friedman argued after Hayek that the expansion of both political and economic freedom for individuals meant separating political and economic power. Government should neither busy itself with economic planning or regulating increasingly international industries because such activities suggest that government believes it can know the desires and needs of not only citizens but industry, that it can *know* the world economy in its totality. Because it cannot, the state should state exist almost exclusively to set the rules of the game and act as the "umpire" for the players—and enforce the smooth functioning of free markets, serving as the disciplinarian when necessary. "These then are the basic roles of government in a free society: to provide a means whereby we can modify the rules, to mediate differences among us on the meaning of the rules, and to enforce compliance with the rules on the part of those few who would otherwise not play the game," Friedman wrote in *Capitalism and Freedom* (1962), glossing over his unapologetic defense of forcing a very specific game upon possibly nonconsensual players and the notion that modifying the rules of that game meant modifying them on behalf of private and corporate interests almost exclusively.[31]

Leaving the organization of societies to Hayek's spontaneous order rather than those short-sighted political institutions and their agents would produce a certain "unanimity without conformity" within societies, as Friedman put it, where the free individuals participating in free markets best approximates a "natural" consensus of community thought and action, without the coercion of the state.[32] Natural law, in fact, was central to the neoliberal imaginary.

Since competition, which had replaced mere exchange in the marketplace, was the product of Nature herself and came to be through the spontaneous order that societies generate, argued Hayek, opposing free and open international markets and competition, as did socialism, meant opposing Nature herself.[33] Along these lines, the market's often self-correcting regulation and spontaneous order, early neoliberals thought, could be aided and expanded by the steadfast collection and rigorous analysis of economic data from across industries by agencies like the National Bureau of Economic Research in the US, founded in 1920, or the European Economic Community (later the European Union). The market's production of this world of numbers, this "world of [price] signals" as Slobodian put it, gave economics something of an oracular quality, elevating it to the level of the natural sciences, as a verifiable source of knowledge of the world and the conduct of biological life within it. Any business or government that then dismissed not just markets but economic analysis, that refused to engage in econometrics, was too dishonoring Truth, Nature, and Reason as categories.[34]

Eventually abandoning the idea that more and better data alone could help anticipate and/or prevent market fluctuations—in no small measure because 1) a sublime world economy truly was beyond representation, and 2) this starry-eyed valorization of science, data, and research smacked of the dialectical materialism they abhorred—the neoliberals took a more proactive stance. Understanding that economic nationalism among states was obstructing economic growth and contributing to ongoing global volatility, these neoliberals set about designing a sort of overlapping double world: strong nation-states, which maintained local culture but enforced local law and the participation of citizens in competitive markets, overlain with more nimble and interdependent international economic institutions, which encouraged the international flow of capital via the limitation of economic nationalism. "We cannot hope for order or lasting peace after this war if states, large or small, regain unfettered sovereignty in the economic sphere," chirped Hayek in *The Road to Serfdom* (1944) as his colleagues set about advocating for the endowment of not only corporations but capital itself with rights to things like the freedom of speech and cross-border movement. "What we need and can hope to achieve is not more power in the hands of irresponsible international economic authorities but a superior political power which can hold the [local] economic interests in check and in the conflict between them can truly hold the scales, because it is itself not mixed up in the economic game."[35]

Even as this ideology gained traction after the Second World War, this new governmentality flourished only slowly as postwar deficits and international development required massive public spending and a certain degree of economic nationalism, particularly in postwar Europe. For this reason, neoliberals often squabbled over the best solution to problems like decolonization in the Global South. Worth noting at this point is the fact that Hayek, Friedman, and their allies were aided by the emerging "deep state," whose advocates on both sides of the Atlantic set about sponsoring, establishing, and coordinating a variety of cultural initiatives in the arts designed to propagandize populations on the superiority of the American and Western European way of life—free enterprise, open markets, individualism, and expressionist aesthetics—in the face of the Soviet collectivism and realism.[36] As Frances Stonor Saunders and others have documented, from the late 1940s to 1967, the CIA-sponsored Congress for Cultural Freedom (CCF), for example, established or funded literary and political magazines (*Encounter*, The *Paris Review*, *Der Monat*, *Preuves*) proffering Western perspectives, filtered money to nonprofit foundations (the Rockefeller, Farfield, and Ford foundations) who directed grant funding to academics, writers, painters, and musicians most likely to toe the ideological line, financed international conferences (e.g., 1949's Cultural and Scientific Conference for World Peace in New York) looking to undermine the Soviet system, and arranged foreign tours for American musicians (e.g., the Boston Symphony Orchestra in Europe). All of this, coming as it did in the wake of decolonization and Bretton Woods, was designed to both advertise and export American neoliberalism without seeming to do so explicitly (and without the overt use of force). While there is no space here to pursue the question, the degree to which McCarthy's own work—which was supported by the Rockefeller Foundation and excerpted in CCF-financed publications like the *Yale Review* and the *Sewanee Review*—was caught up on this propaganda effort is worth exploring.[37]

Percolating for decades, Hayek's and Friedman's ideas began flowering finally west of Europe in the wake of Lyndon Johnson's Great Society, which triggered an exasperated reaction from the US Chamber of Commerce in 1971 for what eventual Supreme Court Justice Lewis F. Powell Jr. called, in a sharp letter to the Chamber, the long and multi-pronged "assault" on America's enterprising spirit. "We are not dealing with sporadic or isolated attacks from a relatively few extremists or even from the minority socialist cadre. Rather, the assault on the enterprise system is broadly based and consistently pursued," Powell lamented of even modest attempts at social democracy in the US. "The overriding first need is for businessmen to recognize that the ultimate issue may be survival—survival of what we call the free enterprise system, and all that this means for the strength and prosperity of America and the freedom of our people."[38]

Sensing that the time was right for a counteroffensive against not only Franklin Roosevelt's but Johnson's various "socialisms," Powell and his ally Richard Nixon couldn't help but notice the remarkable business opportunity that then presented itself. The 1970 election of socialist Salvador Allende as President of Chile horrified many Western governments, business leaders, and intelligence agencies, all of whom who were knee-deep in the Cold War and were by now well acquainted with neoliberal economic thought generally and the US Chamber of Commerce position on free enterprise specifically as a necessary antidote to Soviet communism. Allende's election was particularly galling to many American businessmen and bureaucrats given that they had both invested heavily in the Andean nation and financed the education and training of Chilean economists—the "Chicago Boys"—at Friedman's University of Chicago since the 1950s.[39] Seeing in Allende's election a threat to the international market in his own hemisphere—and America's investments in the resource-rich nation—Nixon and his Secretary of State Henry Kissinger sought to "make the [Chilean] economy scream,"[40] in part by cutting off credit to Chile and pressuring other states and agencies like the IMF to curtail or deny bank loans requested by the Allende government and/or freeze its assets. "I don't see why we need to stand by and watch a country go Communist due to the irresponsibility of its own people," quipped Kissinger at the time, tapping the ash from his cigarette and certainly aware that he was advocating for government interference in what was supposed to be a spontaneous, natural market order.[41] As Chile's economy crumbled, Chilean general Augusto Pinochet launched a bloody, CIA-backed military coup in 1973 that killed Allende and his advisors. Soon reopening Chile to foreign investment and getting its goods back on the world market, with American assistance, Pinochet hosted visits from both Friedman and Hayek—the latter of whom had already admitted that if his choice was between authoritarianism or democracy he preferred a "liberal dictator to a democratic government lacking liberalism."[42]

Shepherded along by what was coming to be known as the "Washington Consensus" in policy circles, the Chilean economy did grow under Pinochet and in many ways outperformed the rest of the South American economy in the 1970s. Recognizing this "market correction" as a sort of coming out party for their life's work, Friedman, Hayek, and their associates cautiously cheered the validation they took from the Chilean case study—never mind the prolonged and repeated economic recessions that hit the world economy in the late-1960s and 1970s—suddenly finding themselves in demand as a multinational cohort of economists and legislators moved forward on the overt, if inconsistent, application of the Mont Pèlerin Society's previously marginal policy ideas. With Ronald Reagan in the US and Margaret Thatcher in the UK soon leading the way, the neoliberalization of the American and British economies proceeded at an astounding pace in the 1970s and thereafter as cities (e.g., New York in 1975) were essentially handed over to private interests and states themselves adopted austerity budgets and became formal market enterprises wherein previously state-based functions like education, healthcare, and national security were increasingly privatized.[43]

Ruminating on all this in the late-1970s, French philosopher Michel Foucault was one of the earliest observers to see the technocratic set of practices, discourses, and processes of this resurgent liberalism as the reification of a new "governmentality" in the service of a new subjectivity, one which essentially reversed *laissez-faire* and demanded that governments intervene *on behalf of markets exclusively*, cultivating the norming of competition and the "veridiction" of markets as the North Star of human civilization. In this way, Foucault argued, markets emerged for neoliberals and all human subjects as not one but *the* site of Truth and Knowledge and thus the model to be generalized throughout society.[44] And as a new type of governance emerged out of this novel epistemology, so did a new type of human subject, the new *homo oeconomicus*, who serves not merely as a man of exchange but as his own (self-regulating) revenue-generating enterprise and as a unit of "human capital" who could too be quantified as a data point and an investment, as could each of his choices and experiences: commodities purchased, education attained, lifestyles cultivated, relationships produced, religious beliefs professed, love received (or not) as a child or an adult—it is all *economic* information for the unit of human capital who doubles as a living "abilities-machine." "What constitutes this investment that forms an abilities-machine?" asked Foucault before coining the neologism "biopolitics" to describe the effects of this new reason:

> We know that the number of hours a mother spends with her child, even when it is still in the cradle, will be very important for the formation of an abilities-machine, or for the formation of human capital, and that the child will be much more adaptive if in fact its parents or its mother spend more

> rather than less time with him or her. This means that it must be possible to analyze the simple time parents spend feeding their children, or giving them affection as investment which can form human capital. Time spent, care given, as well as the parents' education—because we know quite precisely that for an equal time spent with their children, more educated parents will [raise] a higher human capital than parents with less education—in short, the set of cultural stimuli received by the child, will all contribute to the formation of those elements that can make up a human capital.[45]

For Foucault, in other words, neoliberals had developed not only a new type of analysis and a new "legal interventionism" in the economy, but a new analytical object: the human-as-enterprise wherein not only commercial data but even human experience and traditionally private affairs were markets to be penetrated and shaped by market principles, their analysts, and their enforcers.[46] "The *homo-oeconomicus* sought after is not the man of exchange or man the consumer; he is the man of enterprise and production," added Foucault, thinking perhaps of the American Enterprise Institute, which had been founded in 1938 in opposition to Roosevelt's New Deal and whose Council of Academic Advisers at one time included Friedman. "This means that what is sought is not a society subject to the commodity-effect, but a society [of entrepreneurs] subject to the dynamic of competition. Not a supermarket society, but an enterprise society."[47]

Worth noting at this point is that despite having emerged out of the Enlightenment's classical understanding of liberalism, the politics of neoliberalism as an economic and cultural ideology were and remain a bit muddled. Many of the self-identified "neoliberals" noted thus far were liberal only in the economic sense, nurturing elsewhere more traditionally conservative biases. This is why someone like Nixon could govern as a conservative, pandering to a White working-class demographic while also supporting neoliberal economic policies that tended to benefit the business class first and foremost. "The change in the meaning attached to the term liberalism is more striking in economic matters than in political," admitted Friedman in 1962. "Because of the corruption of the term liberalism, the views that formerly went under the name are now often labeled conservatism. But this is not a satisfactory alternative."[48] The term nonetheless stuck, dissolving in the process the old left-right binary in economic matters. As this unsatisfactory term took root, it was adopted by both major parties in the US such that neoliberal thinking helped produce the aforementioned Washington Consensus wherein all major political parties in the developed world defer to Washington, the World

Bank, and IMF on global economics and agree that there is, today, zero debate to be had over economic policy. Neoliberalism, which functions as a sort of keystone, keeping the left and right sides of the stonemason's archway aloft, is the consensus view among all "serious" legislators of any party.

Armed with a formidable rhetorical arsenal then—there is "no alternative," "there is no such thing as society but only individuals"[49]—Thatcher was especially effective. Combatting high inflation through a combination of austere state budgets, higher interest rates, and reduced national employment, the Prime Minister sapped the power of organized labor broadly, literally undermining the British coal and automobile industries, privatized formerly public corporations like British Telecom and British Airways, and converted public tenements into private housing—all while at least attempting to dismantle the English welfare system.[50] In the US, Reagan likewise deregulated industry, broke an air traffic controllers' union strike, lowered corporate taxes, and oversaw one of the largest transfers of public wealth to private accounts in history, as what had been a 78 percent individual income tax rate on the wealthy was cut to 28 percent.[51] He did all of this while likewise cutting federal budgets and bolstering American military capacity to help maintain and/or open international markets by force, including in Latin America. Reagan's successors have all followed suit, trying to compel competitive market economies in Panama, Haiti, Bolivia, Iran, Afghanistan, Iraq, and the Horn of Africa—all of which was accomplished by an increasingly privatized US Army, which became necessary after Nixon abolished military conscription in what reads, retroactively, as an explicitly neoliberal policy move.

Years before George W. Bush's Afghanistan and Iraq adventures, though, it must have felt to Bill Clinton in the 1990s as if there truly was no alternative to neoliberalism—at least if one wanted to maintain the support of the business class that had helped elect him and his "third way" allies like England's Tony Blair. In seemingly trying to over-identify with his predecessors, Clinton "reformed" the American welfare system to the detriment of most of its recipients, further deregulated industry—in particular the nation's telecommunications system—and formalized NAFTA, which paved the way for later multinational trade agreements around the world, including the Central America Free Trade Agreement (CAFTA) and the Regional Comprehensive Economic Partnership (RCEP) agreement among the nations in the Asia-Pacific region. Along the way, new technologies and legislation enabled the "financialization" of the economy, wherein financial tools and services enabled the international exchange of debt, speculative earnings, derivatives, currency valuations, and equity. For example, the 1999 repeal of the Glass-Steagall Act of 1932 in the US, which for six decades had forced the separation of commercial banking from investment banking, allowed the finance sector to take on an increasingly prominent role in a postindustrial economy that was growing despite producing fewer and fewer durable goods for consumption or export.

This last development was especially problematic, argues Wendy Brown, in so far as the broad financialization of the economy, when combined with the emerging subjectivity Foucault described, produced an "economized" society in which market logic—which had already penetrated spaces, like parenting, dating, and spirituality, that were heretofore protected from such rationality—was producing humans who were little more than an assemblage of financialized, rent-seeking enterprises. "*Homo oeconomicus* as human capital is concerned with enhancing its portfolio value in all domains of its life, an activity undertaken through practices of self-investment and attracting investors," wherein nearly all human thoughts and actions are "increasingly configured as strategic [economic] decisions and practices related to enhancing the self's future value," writes Brown, recalling the ubiquitous injunction by the market that contemporary subjects "market themselves" or build their "personal brand" in an effort to enhance their social position and thus generate and wield economic influence.[52] So it is, Brown says, in an inversion of Nixon's—via Friedman—tongue-in-cheek quip, "we are all Keynesians now,"[53] that today "we are everywhere *homo oeconomicus* and only *homo oeconomicus*."[54]

Feeling the effects of this militant globalism—of the increased cost of higher education and healthcare, and the hemorrhaging of manufacturing jobs to the Global South (whose takers are in every case paid far less than their American counterparts), of shrinking retirement accounts and fragmented labor unions, of the loss of ancestral lands and public space to multinational developers, of the financialization of the human body and conversion of human beings into investment portfolios—a multiplicity of groups opposing "globalization" generally, and neoliberalism specifically, had organized across the planet as the century turned: Chiapas in 1994, Seattle in 1999, Genoa in 2001, Tahrir Square, Tunisia, and Wall Street in 2011, and Standing Rock in 2016. Agitating against austerity and exploitation, against unemployment and the commodification of self and the privatization of nature (seeds, water, genes), and against the growth in income inequality and desertification of the planet were the Zapatistas in Mexico and Greenpeace in Canada, anarchists in Sweden and the American Federation of Labor-Congress of Industrial Organizations (AFL-CIO) in the US, plus dozens of religious associations and Indigenous people's movements. "Today human beings in almost every corner of the world sell their labor to multinational corporations, often for less than a dollar an hour, in return for the chance to chase the images of wealth and status those corporations use to tantalize them," protested members of the "ex-workers collective" CrimethInc. in 2001 in an echo of Subcomandante Marcos. "The wealth that their labor creates is sucked out of their communities into the pockets of these companies, and in return their unique cultures are replaced by the standard-issue monoculture of Western consumerism."[55]

In a grim irony, much of the econometric data itself demonstrates that the grievances EZLN, CrimethInc., and their allies on the political Left and Right aired were, and remain, *en pointe.* Among other economists, Thomas Picketty has documented in painful detail, over several publications, both how income inequality in the US has grown significantly since 1980 and purchasing power has declined markedly.[56] So it is that home ownership has, ironically, *dropped* in the US since 2001—in large part as a result of the Great Recession in 2008–2009—meaning that four decades of neoliberalism has produced *fewer* owners of private property across society rather than more.[57] Accordingly, adds the US Bureau of Labor Statistics, as income inequality has increased and property ownership declined, labor union membership plummeted, with overall union participation dropping by 50 percent between 1983 and 2023, resulting in less capacity for laborers to demand wages or health benefits that match inflation.[58] Finally, a raft of clinical studies over the past two decades has verified prophecies by Freud and Foucault, Deleuze and Guattari concerning the "madness" and "schizophrenia" that accompany late capitalism.[59]

Furthermore, despite Friedman's insistence that the imposition of a free market, buttressed by negotiated contract relations, has "been accompanied by a major reduction in" discrimination against racial, ethnic, or cultural minorities, the rise of *homo oeconomicus* has actually produced heightened racial animus in several arenas.[60] To speak not of the multiplicity of studies documenting how neoliberal economic policies have caused considerably more damage to poorer, and often Browner, communities than those populated by middle- and upper-class Whites, Joshua Inwood argues that the Republican Party's "Southern Strategy" that emerged in the 1970s alongside neoliberalism actually increased racism by capitalizing on White resentment of declining economic opportunity in the American South—caused in part by neoliberalism's stagnation of wages and movement of jobs out-of-state—and shifting the blame to immigrants and the social and political demands made by racial minorities in the wake of the civil rights movement.[61] As Inwood quotes Lee Atwater, former advisor to Ronald Reagan, the key to appealing to working-class White voters in the US when your own policies are exacerbating their plight is to simply shift voter attention to the "unreasonable" demands of minority groups and the poor—without seeming to do so: "So you say stuff like 'forced bussing,' 'states rights,' and all that stuff. At this point, you're getting so abstract now, you're talking about cutting taxes, by this time you're talking about all these economic things, and the by-product of them is, blacks get hurt *worse* than whites," Atwater told one interviewer of Reagan's own Nixonian strategy. "If it is getting this abstract, and that coded, then we're doing away with the [accusation of racism], because obviously sitting around saying 'we want to cut taxes' is much more abstract than even the bussing thing, and a hell of a lot more abstract than [saying] 'nigger, nigger.'"[62] Once political discourse reaches this level of abstraction, Inwood continues, policymakers' attempts to implement additional neoliberal policies and programs often proceed unchallenged, at least by most White voters of all classes.

All of this is to say that from White Southerners in the US organizing against migrant labor in their communities—having misunderstood the socioeconomic context for the explosion of immigration to the US from the Global South since at least the 1980s—to White South Africans seeing their apartheid regime *endorsed* by neoliberals, including Röpke and Friedman, neoliberalism itself has objectively contributed to racial antagonism across the globe. Friedman, for example, went on the record in 1976 to oppose universal suffrage in Zimbabwe (formerly Rhodesia) on the grounds that it would produce a "drastically lower level of living and opportunity for the masses of black Rhodesians" when international markets disciplined the nation—withdrawing investments—for taking political and socioeconomic equality seriously.[63] Like it or not, Friedman was correct in this assessment of how markets would respond to such efforts by local leaders.

We should not be surprised, then, that two decades into the twenty-first century, argues Brown, neoliberalism has hamstrung democracy as an institution in massive and myriad ways. Replacing the language of justice and political self-determination, never mind the belief in the common good in itself, with the language of business and self-promotion—quarterly earnings, investment opportunities, and "jobs numbers", public-private partnerships and branding, engagement, winning, and trending—the independent citizen, who no longer has a non-commercial public sphere in which to gather or debate policy, is vanishing under neoliberal governance, replaced by the individuated human enterprise who is always-already a self-interested investment portfolio, concerned not so much with *liberté, egalité,* and *fraternité* but herself and her market position in the hyper-competitive global marketplace. Neoliberalism "transforms the democratic promise of shared rule into the promise of enterprise and portfolio management at the individual and collective level," Brown explains. Such governance "converts the classically modern image of the nation comprising diverse concerns, issues, interests, points of power, and points of view into the nation on the model of Wal-Mart," wherein legislators are "team leaders" and citizens are at best mere "guests" or "customers" whose entire lives are oriented toward economic growth within and for the corporate body.[64] And when the consumer has finally exhausted her usefulness to the enterprise—and note neoliberalism's elision of the often gendered character of the now-financialized and economized worlds of domestic labor and the service sector[65]—she is dismissed without ceremony, retaining an identity as neither consumer nor citizen.

The sum of these parts, as Peter Sloterdjik noted long ago, is that the dominant attitude we human capitals inevitably assume within such a structure is cynicism, which, as a new collective unconscious, has reached the level of ideology itself.[66] As opposed to the traditional take on ideology formulated by Marx—a version of the Christian's "for they know not what they do" wherein the subject is an unwitting "victim" of a false consciousness that shapes her response to, and action in, the world—cynicism is the subject's shoulder-shrugging acceptance of her complicity in a structure she knows to be unjust and unethical but into which she feels forced and incapable of changing. That is to say, when a human enterprise finds herself trapped in a financialized, corporate environment at all times and exploited by private interests as a means only, rather than an end, when her very life hinges upon her ability to monetize her personal equity—apartment, automobile, body—because there are no longer either stable (benefitted) career prospects or welfare programs in the volatile "gig" economy, when democratic institutions themselves are no longer capable of addressing public needs or complaints because they too have been corrupted by market logic, then the human abilities-machine has no choice but to assume a cynical posture toward the state, the economy, and other abilities-machines, who are of course in the same situation. Such cynicism is assumed in advance as *de rigueur*, as the attitude adopted everywhere, all the time because the subject, ironically, has little choice in the neoliberal economy and sees little, if any, reason to expect change. After all, "there is no alternative."

Neoliberalism's Cormac McCarthy

All of this was old news by the new millennium, of course, as much as all of it was a result, to greater or lesser degrees, of the neoliberalization of the world economy that was taking shape just as McCarthy was coming into his own as an artist. Likewise, the notion that McCarthy's work is both influenced by and, in direct and indirect ways, commenting upon political economy is nothing new. Around the turn of the century, Robert Jarrett explored cultural exchange in McCarthy and Christine Chollier described the ways in which markets—or the refusal of them—figure into most of McCarthy's narratives.[67] David Holloway, whose *The Late Modernism of Cormac McCarthy* (2002) effectively changed the conversation around McCarthy and political economy, too argues that *Cities of the Plain* marked a turning point for an author who, over the course of several novels, tried to develop a "late modernism"—in the aesthetic, political, and ideological sense—in order to engage and perhaps escape the contradictions of a political economy which well before 1980 was showing signs of universal domination of not only the human subject but art as a category.[68] Performing an explicitly dialectical reading of McCarthy's corpus to that point, Holloway, whose method paved the way for this study, explores how McCarthy utilizes a revised modernist aesthetic in order to demonstrate how language as a representational strategy might still be capable of transcending material conditions, how literature might carve out an autonomous, nonmarket space in an economy that, Fredric Jameson and others have noted, has expressly moved to obliterate the "semiautonomy of the cultural sphere."[69] Like modernism, though, says Holloway, the success of McCarthy's efforts in this regard had, to that point, been debatable at best. For even if McCarthy was successful in diagnosing the pathologies and contradictions of a political economy that has commodified and "economized" men, women, and children, has fragmented communities, and has generated often apocalyptic violence, his own narratives tend to suggest that the time for challenging such a political economy in a serious way may have passed us by. The *Cities* epilogue is a case in point. Examining in detail the long exchange between Billy and the storytelling drifter he meets under a highway overpass, Holloway suggests that McCarthy's attempt at crafting an aesthetics of representation in fiction that functions as its own form of criticism of political economy ultimately fails to escape the object of its critique. "The storyteller from the epilogue—in positing the disappearance of McCarthy's own narrative—is offered to us as something like a figure for authorship itself," says Holloway, "or, more specifically, a figure for authorship as it is conceived within the limitations of our own historical moment: self-canceling, denuded of hermeneutic agency or effectivity, always on the point of reinscription within whatever structures it might seek to understand or oppose."[70] By the end of the trilogy, in other words, McCarthy appears to have come to accept the fact that the shape of the world, as the drifter tells Billy, "was forced in the void at the onset and all talk of what might otherwise have been is senseless for there is no otherwise."[71] According to Holloway, that is, McCarthy's fatalism here is an open admission, at the end of a 1000-page trilogy and its astounding predecessor, *Blood Meridian, or the Evening Redness in the West* (1985), that his own attempts to broach the "limits of contemporary aesthetic practice . . . pushing against the barriers of the mode of intellectual production in which McCarthy finds himself situated" have, like Sheriff Bell, failed.[72] So it is that the Border Trilogy, despite its aesthetic achievement, says Holloway, "confirms the impossibility of an authentic alternative to neoliberal capitalism."[73] Or, as the *Cities* storyteller puts it sharply, speaking not to Billy but McCarthy directly, "Those stories which speak to us with the greatest resonance have a way of turning upon the teller and erasing him and his motives from all memory."[74]

This is hardly the end of the story, though. For Holloway, McCarthy escapes the deadlock posed by neoliberalism's colonization of art, language, and discourse via what the *Blood Meridian* narrator calls an "optical democracy" that, in the desert at least, renders "nothing more luminous than another and nothing more enshadowed," including humankind and that most human of inventions, the free market.[75] In advocating for this perspective, wherein neither man nor mineral, flora nor fauna outrank any other phenomena, McCarthy is explicitly repudiating anthropocentrism and the conspicuous ecological, political, and socioeconomic horrors of late capitalism. In other words, says Holloway, McCarthy's use of language "converts itself back into a force of being-for-itself that goes to work against the inertia of the commodity world."[76] It does so by transcoding, as Jameson puts it, optical democracy from an ontology of the desert to an aesthetic strategy in a neoliberal landscape that all but dares the market to publish, to sell, what the writer has produced. The legendary "unfilmablility" of *Blood Meridian*, and, to a lesser degree, the nightmarish Tennessee novels serve as cases in point, as does Sheriff Bell's passing reference to those children of neoliberalism—the punk rockers—who, "with green hair and bones through their noses speakin a language they couldnt even understand," in the late 1970s and early 1980s could be heard back-talking the Name of the Father in all its forms: parents, schools, churches, cops, and capitalism around the anglophone world.[77] Optical democracy as an ideological strategy thus "reiterates the possibility of language itself as praxis or political 'other,'" says Holloway, which "restores to view that cleavage between aesthetics and the world upon which earlier modernisms depended" and which, unlike modernism, provides language, art, and the artist herself an opportunity to "[transcend] or momentarily overcome" their commodification.[78]

Later critics mining the political economy of McCarthy's fiction include: Jonathan Imber Shaw, who uses the Latin American conflicts in the 1980s to argue that reading *Blood Meridian* through the Salvadoran civil war contextualizes and expresses Americans' cultural and socioeconomic anxieties concerning the Latinx "other" during the Reagan era; Raymond Malewitz, for whom McCarthy's embedding the "misuse value" of the objects of capital into his novels signals his attempt to develop alternatives to capitalism; Stephen Tatum, who sees in *No Country* a Mexican drug ballad, or *narcocorrido*, that sings of the effects neoliberalism has on Mexican and American communities; Nicholas Monk, who follows Holloway in describing how modernism proper—the cultural analogue of capitalism—constitutes "the social and political hegemony . . . from which McCarthy's characters are in flight," from Arthur Ownby and Cornelius Suttree to John Grady Cole and the man and his son in *The Road*; Dan Sinykin, who shows how *Blood Meridian* contextualizes Reagan's "morning in America" rhetoric as an attempt to distract from what has actually been a sunsetting of American Empire, including of capitalism and the violence that capitalism's slow decline will continue to produce; and John Mark Robison's tracing of coins in *Blood Meridian* and noting how the kid's/man's dream of the coldforger producing "specie current in the markets where men barter" and of which "is the judge" signals Holden's ultimate suzerainty.[79] It is likely Holden's profile, says Robison, which is being stamped on the coins that all subjects will be forced to use as currency in a globalized market economy.[80]

As useful as each of these readings are—Holloway's in particular—they tend to generalize their analyses through the use of terms like "late" or "multinational" capitalism and/or "market economy," occasionally "globalization"; very rarely do the studies noted above cite neoliberalism as a new and specific phase of capitalism, let alone define and contextualize the concept in detail. As such, these analyses often fail to articulate how the evolution of capitalism since at least the Second World War has produced a very different political economy and human subjectivity than was the case in, say, the early and middle twentieth century American context, but which was McCarthy's direct experience and shaped his own labor and the products of that labor and their reception in the late twentieth and early twenty-first centuries. Building upon these critiques, then, the essays in this book (whose authors have in some cases written about McCarthy in the neoliberal context elsewhere[81]) argue that to gloss over neoliberal political economy specifically while reading Cormac McCarthy is to opt out of a deeper material and epistemological understanding of the author's decades-long intellectual project: its increasingly commodified conditions of production and its reception by an increasingly capitalized, economized, and financialized reader. Ignoring, for example, the fact that *Child of God* was published the same year that the Chicago Boys facilitated a murderous coup in Chile (and thus serves retroactively as a sort of literary rendering of the neoliberal moment's own antisocial necrophilia), to bracket neoliberalism in a reading of something like *Stella Maris* is to miss an opportunity to contextualize the low-hanging fruit of Alicia's matriculation to the University of Chicago as a teenager, where she would have been a student simultaneous to the faculty appointments of both Hayek and Friedman, is to miss the fact that her predilection for topos theory and her father's nuclear activities overlaps with McCarthy's interest in the complexity theory that was effectively invented by Hayek—the subject of this book's conclusion.

For even McCarthy's minor works bear the stamp of an uncomfortable interest in the new capitalism rapidly emerging in the 1970s—or at least the murky transition then underway from old regime to a new, financialized market economy. Consider *The Stonemason* (1994). The drama following a multigenerational family of black masons in early-1970s Kentucky is easily the author's most explicitly "political" narrative, focusing as it does on labor politics, economic justice, generational divides, and the problems of race and religion in an era of energy crises, stagflation, and Watergate. Indeed, the drama's not so much polemic as pedantic tone led many prospective directors and critics initially interested in the notion of McCarthy on stage to instead offer some version of Edmund Wilson's review of Vladimir Nabokov's translation of Pushkin's *Evgeni Onegin*: "One . . . suspects that his perversity here has been exercised in curbing his brilliance; that—with his sado-masochistic Dostoevskian tendencies . . . he seeks to torture both the reader and himself."[82] Commenting, for instance, on the play's "surprisingly amateur" class consciousness, on how the play's "theme of personal, familial, and professional integrity is so overtly, even ponderously *stated*," Peter Josyph, in an exasperated—almost insulted—review, wrinkled his nose at how leading man Ben Telfair's monologues assume the tone of the worst finger-wagging presbyters, adding "there is no mistaking the message" in McCarthy's moralizing, for which its author "can never again be charged with nihilism."[83] Or, as Edwin Arnold put it more charitably, after documenting how some Arena Stage actors in 1992 felt the play "reinforced prevailing racist views of dysfunctional black family life," *The Stonemason* was really, in the end, just "a case of good intentions gone awry."[84]

Such critics are not wrong. *The Stonemason* is architecturally problematic, ethically overwrought, and impractical as stagecraft, to the degree that its author may have done harm both to his own cause and that of the Black community he sought to animate. It has never been staged as published for good reason, and readers have very little incentive to laud what easily can be read as a pretentious fit of self-indulgence by a stylist who went too far in telling a story that is not his to tell. Even so, the very factors that have to date doomed the play—the project's lofty aspirations and boldness of vision, its attempt to engage more directly with its characters' socioeconomic and political realities, its refusal to undersell itself—are simultaneously what make it a compelling analytical object. McCarthy's effort to reach beyond his grasp and to explore the material lives of a working class family whose background differs greatly from his own is to be commended both as a refusal to condescend to what was by the 1990s his growing middle class audience looking perhaps for more romantic, commercial western fare and as a strategic attempt to drop into a market economy a fragile art-bomb that was *designed to detonate*. Does McCarthy try too hard when he gives Ben lines like, "He whom the firmament itself has not the power to puzzle. Gazing into your soul beyond bone or flesh to its utmost nativity in stone and star and in the unformed magma at the core of creation"?[85] Yes. Does the play, in the end, fail to break new theatrical ground? Sure. And in so doing it fails better, to resurrect Samuel Beckett, than McCarthy's earlier detours into writing for stage and screen—*The Gardener's Son*, *Whales and Men*—which are likewise "impossible" and more explicit in their political economy than the author's published novels.

Indeed, even if McCarthy misfires in dramatizing the lives of black workers whose constructions were, by the 1970s, being dismantled by the same economy that was still excluding those workers from possessing those buildings, he did so by seeking to stage a vision of an America "where all boundaries—of familiarity, belief, place, body, and identity—can and will be used against you, where they will be torn up and plowed under," as Greil Marcus once put it, speaking of David Lynch's *Lost Highway* (1997).[86] In this way, in exploring the dismantling of the *community* that built America—not only the titular stonemason himself, Edward "Papaw" Telfair, but his debt-ridden son, Big Ben, fawning grandson Ben ("I always wanted to be like [Papaw]," Ben gushes in the first act), and workers of all backgrounds—*The Stonemason* is the story of neoliberalism's *un*building of America, whose own unstagability reflects the play's point about the effects of neoliberalism on both art and a disintegrating America.[87]

Several scenes in the play's third act drive this point home. Searching for his missing nephew, Soldier, Ben—who by this point has twice referenced Marx and once Hegel—catches up with Jeffrey, one of Soldier's fellow former Nighthawks gang members. Unsatisfied with Jeffrey's answer to the question of Soldier's whereabouts, Ben asks the teen what became of the old gang. "They aint no more Nighthawks. Aint no more clubs," snaps Jeffrey:

> Just a bunch of freelancers out roguing and doin drugs. These young bloods are all strung out, man. You understand what I'm tellin you? Fourteen year old. Twelve. You leanin all over me bout some young dude got killed. Shit. It's just brother against brother.[88]

After Jeffrey accuses Ben of living in the past, of being "swallowed up" by history for romanticizing his grandfather's ways, Ben asks his interlocutor who—when brother against brother is the norm—is running the show. "It look to you like somebody *runnin* it?" spits Jeffrey. "Everbody over sixteen the same age to me. And I feel like I'm a hundred."[89] Defeated, Ben returns home only to be asked by his own father for a $6,000 loan. When his son refuses, Big Ben, who by then had admitted to his son that black contractors like him are forced to underbid jobs every day just to survive, disappears, reappearing later in the play only to put a pistol to his jaw in his bedroom.

In the end, Papaw too gives up the ghost finally, at age 102, and Soldier is discovered dead by Ben in a cheap motel room with a needle in his arm.

The play's technical and cultural problems notwithstanding, all of this is much more moving than melodramatic for the critic who considers not only the characters' context—wherein the same President Nixon who enabled White racism sends, without irony, a letter to congratulate a black centenarian on this birthday in order to invite him to lay the cornerstone at the groundbreaking of a new *bank*—but that of the playwright who, in the 1980s and 1990s, was himself living through the effects of not only Nixon's, but Reagan's and Clinton's variegated neoliberalisms. All of this—the contractor who underbids his own labor only to commit suicide, the teenager dead of heroin, Nixon, a black family's failed effort to restore its ancestral home—is the product of neoliberalism, implies McCarthy in what remains his most cogent, polemic writing. In a clever bit of metacommentary, *The Stonemason* shows readers an author rummaging through the "ruins of neoliberalism," as Wendy Brown put it, gathering up the misshapen pieces of American civilization—unhewn stones and American folktales, welfare reform and Nixon's war on drugs, Robert Johnson, James Baldwin, and King James—in an effort to rebuild a (working) class consciousness, a living structure held together not by Portland cement but by "the warp of the world," as Ben says of his grandfather's handiwork: "For true masonry is not held together by cement but by gravity. . . . By the stuff of creation itself."[90] Like Papaw, McCarthy here refuses to concede to clinker and limestone, trusting instead that God "has laid the stones in the earth for men to use and he has laid them in their bedding planes to show the mason how his own work must go. A wall is made the same way the world is made."[91] Or unmade. So it is with McCarthy's first published play.

Cormac McCarthy's Neoliberalism

Or is it? Given McCarthy's predilection for exploring political economy across media, the most significant question that arises for readers and scholars of McCarthy is the degree to which the author can, as human capital himself writing in the neoliberal era, be seen as a producer of anything but commodities, can be anything but a shill in an economy where art itself has been not only commodified, but weaponized by the state. In other words, if it is true that neoliberalism has universalized the market and financialized even the artist, where and how (if at all) do McCarthy's novels either reiterate or reject the assumptions and machinations of a neoliberal reason that shaped the conditions of their production and consumption? The answers to such questions matter—including Holloway's conclusion that even if optical democracy works as a way of resisting the commodification of art, "it is important to note that by the end of the Border Trilogy optical democracy appears to be a waning form"[92]—insofar as our answers determine how readers should interpret not just McCarthy's preoccupation with political economy in his fiction but especially his shift from a high-styled literary modernism to a punchier "commercial" screenwriting style later in his career and his chronic residence at the venture capital-, defense-, and tech industry-financed Santa Fe Institute (SFI).

McCarthy's various aesthetic strategies aside—the alternately Faulknerian and Hemingwayesque sentences, the mythic and dialogic voice, emphasis on ultraviolence and the cultural taboo, attention to the materialism of his characters' actions, and his creation of an often phantasmagoric world reminiscent not so much of Faulkner or Hemingway as Flaubert's *The Temptation of St. Anthony*—many critics begin their answers to the above questions by noting the author's own "materialism" and his intentionally spartan lifestyle and highly "physical" writing process, all of which have become the stuff of legend. "We lived in total poverty," one of the author's former spouses, Anne DeLisle, told *New York Times* writer Richard Woodward, who himself noted that for "nearly eight years [the couple] lived in a dairy barn outside Knoxville." "We were bathing in the lake," DeLisle continued of her former husband's asceticism and exclusive use of an old Olivetti typewriter for composing. "Someone would call up and offer him $2,000 to come speak at a university about his books. And he would tell them that everything he had to say was there on the page. So we would eat beans for another week."[93] Woodward later adds that McCarthy "has spent most of his adult life outside the ring of the campfire," detailing the author's refusal of the "gig economy" that, by the 1970s, was encouraging artists to brand themselves as personalities over and above their creations (at least insofar as CIA money was drying up). "It would be hard to think of a major American writer who has participated less in literary life. He has never taught or written journalism, given readings, blurbed a book, granted an interview. None of his novels have sold more than 5,000 copies in hardcover. For most of his career, he did not even have an agent."[94] Or, as McCarthy himself had put it in a letter to the

Paris Review-affiliated Larry Bensky in 1962, he and DeLisle were living "on what might be described as below subsistence" and spent their days "walking, reading, and talking to strangers."[95]

The result of this ethic is a body of work that, despite the ubiquity of the marketplace by at least the author's third novel, genuinely seems to be trying to resist commodification and economization, as much as it serves as a commentary upon an evolving political economy that saw the 1970s as the last decade when any non-trust-funded artist of any medium in the United States could actually survive on the occasional royalty check and odd-job. This ethic is why many critics of McCarthy who question McCarthy's politics and aesthetics conclude that the author, despite his position as a financialized, SFI-adjacent neoliberal subject in a totalizing market economy, provides readers with strategies for confronting, resisting, and even escaping neoliberal hegemony. Even if the McCarthy object-novel is a commodity, argues Nicholas Monk for example, it is one that nonetheless undermines the commodification of both art and the human subject. McCarthy's writing "escapes . . . counsels of despair that suggest that the dialectic of modernity renders a work of art wholly and without exception just another plank in the edifice of neoliberal hegemony," says Monk, adding that readers who recognize the novels' refusal of commodification come to a certain political consciousness, understanding the author's prompt that "any commodity that contains the communicable expression of an idea that exposes the process, destroys its own existence as [just] a commodity."[96]

Nicholas Brown's thorough discussion of the autonomy of art is instructive here. Basing his analysis on Kant's definition of art as something that is "purposive without a purpose" (an object that has, at the moment of production, use value for neither its producer nor its consumer), Brown posits that in the neoliberal era the "autonomy" of the art object—as something that can, at the ontological level, even exist independent of the totalizing market economy—is paradoxically both in doubt and demonstrably true.[97] Against Holloway's argument that *Cities of the Plain* is McCarthy's admission of defeat; against Jameson's pessimism and the fatalism embedded in Theodor Adorno's claim that "The autonomy of works of art . . . is tendentially eliminated by the culture industry, with or without the conscious will of those in control"; against *The Baffler* founder Thomas Frank's notion that "The anointed cultural opponents of capitalism are now capitalism's ideologues," which is "Why Johnny can't dissent," Brown suggests that works of art somehow do exist in a social space, and that some of them even offer poignant and productive critiques of the socioeconomic status quo in ways formal and informal, explicit and implicit.[98] Calling the "useless" work of art the "internal, unemphatic other to capitalist society," Brown argues that what identifies works of art as autonomous today is their need for interpretation, a need typically lacking in raw materials and consumer services, retail and wholesale products of all makes and models: the automobile or Stetson hat, the brisket and the Formica table upon which it is served, the housekeeping or tax return service—and any advertisements designed to promote them—all possess automatic use and exchange values for both producer and consumer, and harbor little need for "interpretation."[99] Not so for the work of art, even if that work *resembles* a commodity. "If works of art were commodities like any other, desires represented by the market would be subject to analysis and elucidation, but interpretation of the work itself would be a pointless endeavor," Brown insists:

> If a work of art is not only a commodity—if a moment of autonomy with regard to the commodity form is analytically available, if there is something in the work that can be said to suspend its commodity character—then it makes entirely good sense to approach it with interpretive tools. Since its form is a matter of intention, it responds to—indeed demands—interpretation.[100]

This too was Adorno's point in the late 1960s as he was drafting his aesthetic theory. Grudgingly admitting that "art's autonomy remains irrevocable," Adorno nonetheless still saw signs that its autonomy was flagging as, in the neoliberal era, "society became ever less a human one."[101] Even so, in calling the artwork an afterimage of reality, Adorno notes that the best art preserves and heightens the tensions inherent in the societies in which paintings or musical compositions or novels are produced. Works of art are "real as answers to the puzzle externally posed to them," he continues:

> The unsolved antagonisms of reality return in artworks as immanent problems of form. This, not the insertion of objective elements, defines the relation of art to society. The complex of tensions in artworks crystallizes undisturbed in these problems of form and through emancipation from the external world's factual facade converges with the real essence.[102]

Such antagonisms of reality—such tensions of form and content—are certainly heightened in McCarthy, as the examples identified in this introduction suggest. This is obviously part of what makes the author's novels so consistently compelling as works of art.

Also compelling, though, is Nicholas Brown's skepticism of the mature Cormac McCarthy. Writing how *The Road* "certainly has the feel of a work," Brown argues that because the novel doesn't do much to undermine its own genre form, "on closer examination, the McCarthyan sentence looks less like the modernist will to style as a mode of coherence than like a kind of decorative gingerbread."[103] For even if we accept that art retains a level of autonomy today, if we accept that McCarthy sought for decades to recuperate neoliberalism's possession and economization of the narrative act and/or discourse as such—producing "anticommodities" with no obvious use value and that both expose the underside of, and antagonisms within, neoliberal capitalism and demand interpretation—how should we interpret the fact that by the 1980s and thereafter McCarthy was all-in on developing his narratives for Hollywood, drafting copy with an eye to its potential on-screen appeal?[104] How should we take the fact that even if he identifies the problems of neoliberalism in his texts, his characters time and again refuse to explore alternatives to neoliberalism and/or time and again fail to escape it? How should we take his decision to maintain a senior fellowship with the Santa Fe Institute, whose parade of predominantly private sector patrons include neoliberal and/or libertarian capitalists and their monied foundations, never mind the American military-industrial complex: Citibank, the US Department of Defense, Sun Microsystems, Google, Charles and David Koch, Morgan Stanley, Raytheon, Boeing, foreign currency market speculator and "financial manager" Jeffery Epstein, and the John Templeton Foundation?[105]

At the risk of making too fine a point, the last example on the donor list above openly admits that as an organization it remains "grounded in the ideas of classical liberal political economy" and that it uses its resources to finance "education, research, and outreach projects to promote individual freedom, free markets, free competition, and entrepreneurship."[106] So it is that Charlie Gere's commentary is here worth quoting at length. "The recognition of complexity as an area of research worth funding was explicitly bound up with the emergence of post-Fordist capitalism," says Gere:

> The Santa Fe Institute itself was funded by Citibank with the expectation that its research might contribute to the bank's capacity to understand and

> manage the complexities of globalized capital. Much of the work done in the Institute has been and continues to be concerned with the application of complexity to economics. To some extent complexity theory represents a kind of scientific legitimation of the ideology of neo-liberalism.[107]

Indeed, SFI would likely not even exist without the blessing of either neoliberalism or "complexity" as ideological injunctions, which the SFI has, in turn, been immodest in helping promote and multiply; and it is unlikely the organization would have been so open to McCarthy's partnership and residence were his works not in some way aligned, even unintentionally, with their mission and vision.

On this last, readers would do well to recall that McCarthy's decades-long commitment to the institute—founded by a collection of former Manhattan Project physicists—has from its founding made complex systems science a "first among equals, or at least the polestar, in a remarkably wide ranging, raucous, and searching conversation," as Bryan Giemza put it.[108] As I argue later in this book, though, it is difficult for the historian of neoliberalism who ruminates on McCarthy to forget that complexity, as a subject of interdisciplinary study and a mystification of political economy, was "founded" in part by none other than Friedrich Hayek, who dedicated considerable time and ink to the study of complexity in global economics. By the 1960s, in fact, not long after publishing an odd treatise on psychology that wonders why humans make the choices they do, Hayek offered the world "The Theory of Complex Phenomena," which notes that in so far as the analysis of complexity overlaps with the study of spontaneous order in socioeconomic structures, the study of "complexity" as a category *just is* the study of where and how to deploy physics in the service of market economics.[109]

For historian of science Erik Baker, this pedigree—combined with the fact that dozens of SFI researchers have over the years produced papers with titles like "Money as Minimal Complexity," "The multiplex structure of interbank networks," and "Network geometry and market instability"[110]—means that the Institute has, since 1984, produced not only complexity science but neoliberalism *qua* ideology. "The key political accomplishment of corporate and libertarian financing for the human sciences at SFI has not been the creation of a well-codified and easily weaponizable ideology—an *ism*—but rather the creation of a new social world populated by a new political subject: the SFI *libertarian*," writes Baker, explaining how longtime SFI economist

Brian Arthur once openly admitted that part of his job at SFI was helping his colleagues in their "rediscovering [of] Austrian economics." "The history of SFI illustrates . . . that this transformation [to neoliberal political economy in the West] *was not a spontaneous process* or a product of a shifting zeitgeist but was deliberately encouraged by a right-wing funding infrastructure."[111] Such a fact has gone mostly unacknowledged by both McCarthy and many McCarthy scholars, including Giemza, who, despite a thoughtful analysis of science in McCarthy's fiction, treats SFI with a notable lack of skepticism. After lauding SFI's commitment to economist and leadership "guru" Warren Bennis's "Great Groups" theory of social change, Giemza notes SFI's modest $14.4 million endowment (FY20) as proof that "SFI arguably punches well above its financial weight" before glossing the organization's reliance on the defense, tech, and finance industries for its operating budget.[112] None of what Giemza says is untrue; however, notable is his relative silence concerning the atomizing and fragmenting economics—the neoliberalism—embedded deep in this architecture, which profoundly affects the production and consumption of the emergent complexity systems science that captured so much of Cormac McCarthy's late fiction, never mind the production and consumption of literary fiction itself.

Given this frame—wherein the author is simultaneously a diagnostician *and* symptom of the pathology in question—the analyst's primary task becomes determining the degree to which McCarthy is here playing the game as opposed to being played by it. This gaming, the writer's slow shift in both form and content, which peaked perhaps in *The Road* and *The Counselor* but is still evident in *The Passenger* and *Stella Maris*, began not only as neoliberalism was becoming the global cultural and political dominant but seems to have been triggered in part by McCarthy's affiliation with SFI-adjacent researchers in the 1980s. Put another way, scholars pondering Cormac McCarthy's neoliberalism must ask where and how the SFI—and perhaps the CIA-funded foundations and literary journals that supported McCarthy's early work—colonized the author's thought and prose at the same time as neoliberalism was colonizing the globe. This is where Nicholas Brown's skepticism of *The Road* finds its footing. Because for Brown, after one compares *The Road* not only to other modernisms (e.g., Hemingway, Joyce, Wallace Stevens, Kafka) but other eschatologies (from Beckett's *Waiting for Godot* and *Worstword Ho* to Camus's *The Plague* to the films of George Romero or George Miller), "we are left with a book that overpaints its generic postapocalyptic narrative with portes cochères, 'gelid' motor oil, and lyrical descriptions of fish rather than . . . exploiting a generic form whose constraints must be acknowledged and overcome rather than merely elevated stylistically."[113]

That is to say, instead of suspending and transcending the commodity form or challenging power, *The Road* is arguably a pure commodity that merely restates, if beautifully, the old chestnut that, as Fredric Jameson or Slavoj Žižek or Mark Fisher all quipped, it is easier to imagine the end of the world than the end of capitalism.[114] Recognizing, of course, that these two "ends" may be one and the same, McCarthy, in *The Road*, doesn't challenge but seems to accept neoliberalism's—and especially Margaret Thatcher's—suggestion that there *is* no alternative to the current SFI-sponsored political economy, that radioactive decay, the commodification of life itself, and a certain neofeudalism are the future of humankind. As such, works like *The Road*, *The Passenger*, *The Counselor*, and even *No Country* ultimately serve readers a main course of Fisher's "capitalist realism" with a generous helping of Sloterdijk's cynicism-as-ideology. This is not a verdant post-capitalist world or a new literary style, not the bleak but still critically engaged worlds of *Suttree*, *Blood Meridian*, or the Border Trilogy—but a fashionably gray positivism and/or somewhat aloof lapsarianism wherein fathers and sons stumble their hopeless way through Wendy Brown's ruins of neoliberalism, populated not by flora and fauna but cannibals and corpses.[115]

Although *The Counselor* and its cognates do *identify* the frayed social fabric and decline in traditional morality—the "breakdown in mercantile ethics"—that seems to have accompanied neoliberalism's forced competition and commodification of life, McCarthy's leading men and women routinely *stop* at this glancing identification, having internalized it seems Thatcher's maxim and thus never speculating on collective pathways *out* of the cultural and moral senescence, social fragmentation, and ecological collapse wrought by political economy. In these and other ways is McCarthy's fiction exceedingly "neoliberal." This is not, of course, to curse ranch-hands' or psychiatric inpatients' failure to organize against cannibals and cartels, state psychiatrists and federal bureaucrats; it is to note that McCarthy, as a writer, seemed disinclined to wander down that road himself, even as a thought experiment, having come to believe, in the wake of literary naturalism's emphasis on determinism and scientific objectivism, his own rhetoric on the impossibility of either political organizing, social change, or any viable alternative to the status quo. For even when McCarthy does locate his protagonists in a (radical) community of allies—as in *Suttree* or *The Passenger*—these harried men and women ultimately *abandon* their comrades, rejecting the revolutionary subjectivity implicit to the Knoxville or New Orleans underclass—of prisoners, wage slaves, fishermen, or inpatients—in order to go-it-alone, and often die alone, rather than confront their ubiquitous and invisible adversary, which is of course neoliberal reason and its agents, as part of an amalgamated class. "A car had stopped for Suttree, he'd not lifted a hand. Let's go, said the driver," McCarthy writes on the final page of his longest novel, whose antihero leaves Harrogate and J Bone, Michael, Trippin Through the Dew, and Joyce on their own to fight jailers, juries, psychiatrists, and social workers. "Behind them the city lay smoking, the sad purlieus of the dead immured with the bones of friends and forebears."[116] Only the most naïve optimist would refuse to acknowledge that these characters' bones (save Suttree's) are likely to be found soon among such purlieus.

Certainly this is part of neoliberalism's strategy: convincing the subject that *The Road*, *Snowcrash*, *Mad Max*, *The Children of Men*, *The Hunger Games* or "The Walking Dead" are the future—and that resistance is futile. Such narratives are too often simply communiqués within a larger propaganda system contributing to Lippmann's manufacture of consent and designed to remind human capitals of the truth of Voltaire's *Candide* that despite its horrors ours is already the best possible world. This is not to say that all zombie films or crime novels are always-already reactionary; progressive versions of such narratives, those which imagine alternatives, do exist. *The Road* and its descendants, however, generally offer readers no avenue for egress from the horrors they stage, no hint of collective problem-solving or the revolutionary potential of collective action in the face of existential sociopolitical or ecological problems—just isolation and death. McCarthy's late works, in other words, often require less *interpretation* than their predecessors, serving as so much bait in an effort to do the opposite of what we know art is capable of doing. Rather than evoking a sense of transcendence or the sublime or challenging power and staging the possibility of things we are usually told are impossible, the novel instead crushes the reader with at times overwrought illustrations of what Hannah Arendt called the banality of evil and the inevitability of the social, political, and environmental collapse already underway. Insofar as McCarthy helps chaperone these developments into the imaginations of increasingly economized readers of literary fiction or financialized filmgoers in the twenty-first century, he buttresses a cultural narrative, an ideology, and a political economy that have joined forces to convince us all that there is no alternative to either neoliberalism or apocalypse.

Imagining an Alternative

This does all sound hopeless. The broader point of this book, however, is that such a reading is actually *less* bleak than much of McCarthy's fiction—particularly his late work. If nothing else, the authors in this book—many of whom still convincingly read in McCarthy the *resistance* to neoliberalism—continue to believe in an alternative. But whether or not McCarthy believed this himself by the twenty-first century, and whether or not his work really reinforces or rejects neoliberalism, are the questions. This book is a modest attempt to explore some answers to those questions. To that end, the reader will note in the chapters that follow that the manifestation of neoliberal reason more broadly in the 1970s and thereafter means that this book will necessarily focus on McCarthy's middle and late works—from *The Gardener's Son* (ca. 1976) through his last novels. That said, the Tennessee novels do make an appearance.

Arguing that McCarthy's first screenplay stages a class antagonism designed to rob human capitals of their agency, Jordan Dominy calls the film broadcast of *The Gardener's Son* on the American Public Broadcasting Service (PBS) in 1977 a "parable" in the tradition of the Nazarene that "shows the dire consequences of emphasizing individual profit at the expense of community and common interests." Following Dominy, both Lydia Cooper and Julian Caradec take on the Border Trilogy and its subsequent novels to suggest that McCarthy's interest in transactional relations, the use and exchange value of humans and animals, and the documentation of ownership in the neoliberal economy colors each of his works around the turn of the century. Caught up in this interest, both writers argue, are a series of searching questions—be they about the origins of biodisaster, an impending socioeconomic collapse, or the nature of reality—that compel readers to seek out their own answers to important questions of political economy. For both Caradec and Cooper, McCarthy's reluctance to psychologize or make use of his characters' interiors—focusing instead on their actions and their use of *things*—signals a certain commodification of language itself in the neoliberal era. Following the Elmore brothers' important reading of *No Country for Old Men* as McCarthy's attempt to anthropomorphize neoliberal anthropology, Casey Jergenson and Christine Chollier provide complementary readings of *The Road* as the critique of neoliberal capitalism. Cooper and Vernon Cisney, respectively, then tackle McCarthy's screenplay *The Counselor* and its analogues, to show how the critique of neoliberalism McCarthy first screened in the late 1970s via *The Gardener's Son* continued well into the twenty-first century. Finally, I close out the book with an extension of this introduction by asking how effective McCarthy's critique of neoliberal capitalism, such as it is, can be when the author himself remained, for decades, deeply committed to an institution—the Santa Fe Institute—whose primary product was less complexity science than neoliberal ideology itself. More specifically, McCarthy's decades-long chasing of Hayek serves as a symptom of McCarthy's inability to escape the shadow of the neoliberal structures that he, intentionally or not, helped reinforce even as he undertook a decades-long archaeology of neoliberal reason. The author's last two novels, *The Passenger* and *Stella Maris* (2022), provide evidence of this inability.

It is a robust debate, full of opposing arguments on and analyses of a wide variety of texts. Only time will tell where and how the loss of one of America's greatest authors in 2023 will affect both his reception and the scholarship of his often polarizing works. Even more, the 2024 revelation by *Vanity Fair* of McCarthy's relationship with a teenager in the 1970s further complicates his legacy as a "product" of neoliberal reason insofar as the revelation raises a host of questions about McCarthy's personal and political choices in the 1970s, particularly as they revolved around his interpersonal relationships.[117] That is to say, the debate over Cormac McCarthy's "neoliberalism" doesn't end with this book, which was well into its development when news of McCarthy's passing and, later, the affair in question broke. If anything, my hope is that America's loss of one of its most remarkable writers means that the critique of McCarthy's political economy can now proceed more rapidly and effectively hereafter.

Notes

1. Cormac McCarthy, *No Country for Old Men* (New York: Alfred Knopf, 2005), 145, 136.
2. Ibid., 173.
3. See Alfred W. McCoy, *The Politics of Heroin: CIA Complicity in the Global Drug Trade* (Brooklyn: Lawrence Hill Books, 1991), 41–44, 387–95.
4. McCarthy, *No Country*, 3, 46, 296, 303, 309.
5. Judith Butler, *Bodies that Matter: On the Discursive Limits of "Sex"* (New York: Routledge, 1993), 3.
6. McCarthy, *No Country*, 304.
7. Ibid., 112.
8. Wendy Brown, *Undoing the Demos: Neoliberalism's Stealth Revolution* (Princeton: Princeton UP, 2015), 21.

9. Bob Dylan, "Just like Tom Thumb's Blues," *Highway 61 Revisited*, Columbia Records LP CL2389, 1965.

10. Cormac McCarthy, *Cities of the Plain* (New York: Knopf, 1998), 3.

11. Ibid., 264–65.

12. Cormac McCarthy, *All the Pretty Horses* (New York: Knopf, 1992), 182.

13. McCarthy, *Cities of the Plain*, 139.

14. Neil Harvey, *The Chiapas Rebellion: The Struggle for Land and Democracy* (Durham: Duke UP, 1998), 50.

15. Ibid., 49, 60.

16. McCarthy, *Cities of the Plain*, 5, 3, 55, 66–67.

17. Ibid., 66, 59.

18. Ibid., 78.

19. Malcolm S. Forbes Jr., "Fact and Comment," *Forbes*, Whale Media Holdings, 13 Sept. 1993: 25–26.

20. See the World Bank's entry for "Mexico" online for historical trends in Mexico for unemployment, violence, poverty, GDP, and emigration through 2023, accessed 1 July 2024, https://data.worldbank.org/country/mexico.

21. Subcomandante Marcos, "A Storm and a Prophecy—Chiapas: The Southeast in Two Winds" in *Our Word Is Our Weapon*, ed. Juana Ponce de Leon (New York: Seven Stories Press, 2001), 23.

22. Marcos, "Tomorrow Begins Today," in ed. Ponce de Leon, *Our Word Is Our Weapon*, 109–10.

23. See Wendy Brown, *Undoing the Demos*, 20, where neoliberalism is called "a loose and shifting signifier." See also Quinn Slobodian, who in *The Globalists: The End of Empire and the Birth of Neoliberalism* (Cambridge, Mass.: Harvard UP, 2018), posits the arguable meaninglessness of the term (2); and Rajesh Vengopal, who calls neoliberalism a "controversial, incoherent, and crisis-ridden term." See Vengopal, "Neoliberalism as a concept," *Economy and Society* 44, no. 2 (2015): 165–87.

24. Noam Chomsky and Edward Hermann, *Manufacturing Consent: The Political Economy of the Mass Media* (1988; repr. New York: Pantheon, 2002), lix.

25. "Statement of Aims," Mont Pèlerin Society, 1947, accessed 1 July 2024, https://www.montpelerin.org/Statement-of-Aims.html.

26. F. A. Hayek, *The Road to Serfdom* (1944; repr. Chicago: Univ. of Chicago Press, 2007).

27. F. A. Hayek, *Law, Legislation, and Liberty*, vol. 1, *Rules and Order* (Chicago: Univ. of Chicago Press, 1973), 35–54.

28. Slobodian, *Globalists*, 13–16, 104–5.

29. Hayek, *Rules and Order*, 62, 47.

30. Slobodian, *Globalists*, 33, 15.

31. Milton Friedman, *Capitalism and Freedom* (1962; repr. Chicago: Univ. of Chicago Press, 2002), 24–25.

32. Ibid., 23.

33. See Hayek, *Rules and Order*, 39–40.

34. Slobodian, *Globalists*, chap. 2.

35. Hayek, *Road to Serfdom*, 231–32.

36. See Frances Stonor Saunders, *The Cultural Cold War: The CIA and the World of Arts and Letters* (1999; repr. The New Press, 2013), chs. 3, 12, 15, 16.

37. For CCF funding of literary magazines that excerpted McCarthy, see Saunders, *Cultural Cold War*, 280, 284; Joel Whitney, *Finks: How the CIA Tricked the World's Best Writers* (New York: OR Books, 2016); and Dianne C. Luce, *Embracing Vocation: Cormac McCarthy's Writing Life, 1959–1974* (Columbia: Univ. of South Carolina Press, 2023), 78–81.

38. Lewis F. Powell Jr., "Attack on American Free Enterprise System" (1971), *The Powell Papers*, Washington and Lee University School of Law Scholarly Commons, accessed 1 July 2024, https://scholarlycommons.law.wlu.edu/powellmemo/1.

39. David Harvey, *A Brief History of Neoliberalism* (Oxford: Oxford UP, 2005), 8.

40. Peter Kornbluh, "Chile and the United States: Declassified Documents Relating to the Military Coup," 11 Sept. 1973. National Security Archive, "Electronic Briefing Book No. 8," The George Washington University, accessed 1 July 2024, https://nsarchive2.gwu.edu/NSAEBB/NSAEBB8/nsaebb8i.htm.

41. Lois Hecht Oppenheim, *Politics in Chile: Socialism, Authoritarianism, and Market Democracy* (Cambridge: Westview/Perseus, 2007), 59, 91.

42. Hayek quoted in Bruce Caldwell and Leonidas Montes, "Friedrich Hayek and his visits to Chile," *Review of Austrian Economics* 28, no. 3 (2015): 261–309.

43. Harvey, *A Brief History*, chap. 2 and 3.

44. Michel Foucault, *The Birth of Biopolitics: Lectures at the Collège de France 1978–79*, trans. Graham Burchell (London: Palgrave Macmillan, 2008), 130–32, 145.

45. Ibid., 229.

46. Ibid., 167, 229–30.

47. Ibid., 147.

48. Friedman, *Capitalism and Freedom*, 6.

49. Harvey, *A Brief History*, 40, 82.

50. Ibid., chap. 3.

51. Ibid., 52.

52. Brown, *Undoing the Demos*, 33–34.

53. Harvey, *A Brief History*, 13.

54. Brown, *Undoing the Demos*, 31.

55. CrimethInc. Ex-Workers' Collective, *Days of War Nights of Love: Crimethink for Beginners* (Salem: CrimethInc. Free Press, 2001), 65–66.

56. Thomas Picketty, *Capital in the Twenty-First Century*, trans. Arthur Goldhammer (Cambridge: Belknap/Harvard, 2013), 24, chap. 7–12. Picketty demonstrates the lie of Friedman's claim in *Capitalism and Freedom* (169) that "capitalism leads to less inequality than alternative systems of organization and that the development of capitalism has greatly lessened the extent of inequality."

57. "Quarterly Residential Vacancies And Homeownership, First Quarter 2024," U.S. Census Bureau, release number: CB24-62, 30 April 2024, accessed 1 July 2024, https://www.census.gov/housing/hvs/files/currenthvspress.pdf. In Fargo, N.D., for example, the percentage of housing units that were owner-occupied between 2018 and 2022 was a dismal 44.2 percent. See also "QuickFacts: Fargo city; North Dakota; Cass County, North Dakota; North Dakota," U.S. Census Bureau, accessed 1 July 2024, https://www.census.gov/quickfacts/fact/table/fargocitynorthdakota,casscountynorthdakota,ND/PST045222.

58. "Union Members—2023," U.S. Department of Labor, Bureau of Labor Statistics, 23 Jan. 2024, accessed 1 July 2024, https://www.bls.gov/news.release/pdf/union2.pdf.

59. See Anna Zeira, "Mental Health Challenges Related to Neoliberal Capitalism in the United States," and *Community Mental Health Journal* 58 (2022): 205–12; and Stephen Nkansah-Amankra, et al., "Disparities in health, poverty, incarceration, and social justice among racial groups in the United States: A critical review of evidence of close links with neoliberalism," *International Journal of Health Services* 43, no. 2 (2013): 217–40. On the "prophecies" in question, see Sigmund Freud, *Civilization and Its Discontents*, trans. James Strachey (1929; repr. New York: W. W. Norton, 1961); Michel Foucault, *Madness and Civilization*, trans. Richard Howard (1961; repr. New York: Vintage, 1965); and Gilles Deleuze and Felix Guattari, *Anti-Oedipus: Capitalism and Schizophrenia*, trans. Mark Seem (1972; repr. London: Penguin, 2009).

60. Friedman, *Capitalism and Freedom*, 108.

61. Joshua F. J. Inwood. "Neoliberal racism: the 'Southern Strategy' and the expanding geographies of white supremacy," *Social and Cultural Geography* 16, no. 4: 407–23, accessed 1 July 2024, https://doi.org/10.1080/14649365.2014.994670.

62. Ibid., 9.

63. Slobodian, *Globalists*, 178, ch. 5.

64. Brown, *Undoing the Demos*, 211.

65. Ibid., 99–107.

66. Peter Sloterdjik, "Cynicism: The Twilight of False Consciousness," trans. Michael Eldred and Leslie A. Adelson, *New German Critique* 33 (1984): 190–206.

67. See Robert Jarrett, *Cormac McCarthy* (London: Twayne, 1997); and Christine Chollier, "'I aint come back rich, that's for sure,' or the questioning of market economies in Cormac McCarthy's novels" in *Myth, Legend, Dust: Critical Responses to Cormac McCarthy*, ed. Rick Wallach (Manchester: Manchester UP, 2000), 171–76.

68. David Holloway, *The Late Modernism of Cormac McCarthy* (Westport: Greenwood Press, 2002).

69. Fredric Jameson, *Postmodernism, Or, the Cultural Logic of Late Capitalism* (New Haven: Duke UP, 1990), 48.

70. Holloway, *Late Modernism*, 21.

71. McCarthy, *Cities of the Plain*, 285.

72. David Holloway, "'A false book is no book at all': the ideology of representation in *Blood Meridian* and the Border Trilogy" in *Myth, Legend, Dust: Critical Responses to Cormac McCarthy*, ed. Rick Wallach (Manchester: Manchester UP, 2000), 185–200.

73. Holloway, *Late Modernism*, 21.

74. McCarthy, *Cities of the Plain*, 277.

75. Cormac McCarthy, *Blood Meridian, or the Evening Redness in the West* (1985; repr. New York: Vintage, 1992), 285.

76. Holloway, *Late Modernism*, 121.

77. McCarthy, *No Country*, 295.

78. Ibid., 137, 165.

79. McCarthy, *Blood Meridian*, 322–23.

80. See Jonathan Imber Shaw, "Evil Empires: *Blood Meridian*, War in El Salvador, and the Burdens of Omniscience," *The Southern Literary Journal* 40, no. 2 (2008): 207–31; Raymond Malewitz "'Anything Can Be an Instrument': Misuse Value and Rugged Consumerism in Cormac McCarthy's *No Country for Old Men*," *Contemporary Literature* 50, no. 4 (2009): 721–41; Stephen

Tatum, "'Mercantile Ethics': *No Country for Old Men* and the Narcocorrido," in *Cormac McCarthy: All the Pretty Horses, No Country for Old Men, The Road*, ed. S. Spurgeon (London: Continuum, 2011): 77–93; Nicholas Monk, *True and Living Prophet of Destruction: Cormac McCarthy and Modernity* (Albuquerque: Univ. of New Mexico Press, 2016), 5; Dan Sinykin, "Evening in America: 'Blood Meridian' and the Origins and Ends of Imperial Capitalism," *American Literary History* 28, no. 2 (2016): 362–80; and John Mark Robison, "The Authority of Currency in Cormac McCarthy's *Blood Meridian*," *The Cormac McCarthy Journal* 15, no. 1 (2017): 30–45.

81. For early articles exploring neoliberalism in Cormac McCarthy, see: Lydia R. Cooper, "Diamonds, drugs, and the digital age: Global capitalism in Cormac McCarthy's *The Counselor*," *Critique: Studies in Contemporary Fiction* 59, no. 4 (2018): 445–58; David Deacon, "'Some Unholy Alloy': Neoliberalism, Digital Modernity, and the Mechanics of Globalized Capital in Cormac McCarthy's *The Counselor*," *European Journal of American Studies* 12, no. 3 (2017), accessed 1 July 2024, http://journals.openedition.org/ejas/12364; Jordan Dominy, "Cannibalism, Consumerism, and Profanation: Cormac McCarthy's *The Road* and the end of capitalism," *The Cormac McCarthy Journal* 13, no. 1 (2015): 143–58; Jonathan and Rick Elmore, "'Human Become Coin': Neoliberalism, Anthropology, and Human Possibilities in *No Country for Old Men*," *The Cormac McCarthy Journal* 14, no. 2 (2016): 168–85; Casey Jergenson, "'In what direction did lost men veer?': Late Capitalism and Utopia in *The Road*," *The Cormac McCarthy Journal* 14, no. 1 (2016): 117–32; and Simon Schleusener, "The Dialectics of Mobility: Capitalism and Apocalypse in Cormac McCarthy's *The Road*," *European Journal of American Studies* 12, no. 3 (2017), accessed 1 July 2024, http://journals.openedition.org/ejas/12296. See also Dan Sinykin, *American Literature and the Long Downturn: Neoliberal Apocalypse* (Oxford: Oxford UP, 2020).

82. Edmund Wilson, "The Strange Case of Pushkin and Nabokov," *The New York Review of Books*, 15 July 1965, NYREV, Inc., accessed 1 July 2024, https://www.nybooks.com/articles/1965/07/15/the-strange-case-of-pushkin-and-nabokov.

83. Peter Josyph, "Older professions: the fourth wall of *The Stonemason*" in ed. Rick Wallach, *Myth, Legend, Dust*, 119–40.

84. Edwin Arnold, "Cormac McCarthy's *The Stonemason*: the unmaking of a play" in ed. Rick Wallach, *Myth, Legend, Dust*, 149.

85. McCarthy, *The Stonemason* (New York: Vintage, 1994), 112.

86. Greil Marcus, *The Shape of Things to Come: Prophecy and the American Voice* (New York: Farrar, Straus and Giroux, 2006), 107.

87. McCarthy, *Stonemason*, 6.

88. Ibid., 75.

89. Ibid., 74–75.

90. Ibid., 9–10.

91. Ibid.

92. Holloway, *Late Modernism*, 169.

93. Richard Woodward, "Cormac McCarthy's Venomous Fiction," *New York Times Magazine*, 19 April 1992, 28–40, accessed 1 July 2024, www.nytimes.com/1992/04/19/magazine/cormac-mccarthy-s-venomous-fiction.html.

94. Ibid.

95. Luce, *Embracing Vocation*, 26.

96. Monk, *True and Living*, 181.

97. Nicholas Brown, *Autonomy: The Social Ontology of Art Under Capitalism* (New Haven: Duke UP, 2019).

98. See Theodor Adorno. "Culture Industry Reconsidered," trans. Anson G. Rabinbach, *New German Critique* 6 (1975): 12–19; and Thomas Frank, "Why Johnny can't dissent" in *Commodify Your Dissent*, eds. Thomas Frank and Matt Weiland (New York: Norton, 1997), 35.

99. Brown, *Autonomy*, 9.

100. Ibid., 8.

101. Theodor Adorno, *Aesthetic Theory*, trans. and ed. Robert Hullot-Kentor (1970; repr. London: Continuum, 2002), 1.

102. Ibid., 5–6.

103. Brown, *Autonomy*, 93.

104. For McCarthy's transition to writing for the screen, see Stacey Peebles, *Cormac McCarthy and Performance: Page, Stage, Screen* (Austin: Univ. of Texas Press, 2017).

105. For analyses of the political economy of SFI, see Ciarán Dowd, "The Santa Fe Institute" in *Cormac McCarthy in Context*, ed. Steven Frye (Cambridge: Cambridge UP, 2020), 33–44; Erik Baker, "The ultimate think tank: The rise of the Santa Fe Institute libertarian," *History of the Human Sciences* 35, no. 3–4 (2022): 32–57; and Fabrizio Li Vigni, "The failed institutionalization of 'complexity science': A focus on the Santa Fe Institute's legitimization strategy," *History of Science* 59, no. 3 (2021): 344–69.

106. "Individual Freedom & Free Markets," John Templeton Foundation, accessed 1 July 2024, https://www.templeton.org/funding-areas/individual-freedom-free-markets.

107. Charlie Gere, *Digital Culture* (London: Reaktion Books, 2002), 147.

108. Bryan Giemza, *Science and Literature in Cormac McCarthy's Expanding Worlds* (New York: Bloomsbury Academic, 2023), 8.

109. F. A. Hayek, "The Theory of Complex Phenomena," *Studies in Philosophy, Politics, and Economics* (London: Routledge, 1967), 22–42.

110. See Preadeep Dubey, et al., "Money as Minimal Complexity," *Games and Economic Behavior* 108 (March 2018): 432–51; Leonardo Bargigli, et al., "The multiplex structure of interbank networks," *Quantitative Finance* 15, no. 4 (2015): 673–91; and Areejit Samal, et al., "Network geometry and market instability," *Royal Society Open Science* 8, no. 2 (Feb. 2021), accessed 1 July 2024, https://doi.org/10.1098/rsos.201734.

111. Baker, "The ultimate think tank," 34, emphasis added.

112. Giemza, *Science and Literature*, 15.

113. Brown, *Autonomy*, 94–95.

114. Mark Fisher, *Capitalist Realism: Is There No Alternative?* (2008; repr. Hampshire: Zero Books, 2014), 2.

115. For a similar critique of *The Road* in this regard, see David Holloway, "Mapping McCarthy in the Age of Neoconservatism, or the Politics of Affect in The Road," *The Cormac McCarthy Journal* 17, no. 1 (2019): 4–26.

116. McCarthy, *Suttree* (1979; repr. New York: Vintage, 2010), 471.

117. Vincenzo Barney, "All the Pretty Little Horses," *Vanity Fair* 67, no. 1 (2024): 84-142.

1
THE CONTRADICTORY COMMUNITY OF *THE GARDNER'S SON*

Jordan J. Dominy

Near the end of both the film and the published screenplay of Cormac McCarthy's *The Gardener's Son* (1976), a photographer takes a portrait of Robert "Bobby" McEvoy the morning of his hanging. As McEvoy turns to leave the photographer's storefront, the photographer asks if he can make copies of the portrait to sell, stating he would share his profit on a "fifty-fifty basis" with the condemned man's family. At first Bobby does not respond to the offer. But as he exits the studio he turns and tells the enterprising photographer, "I dont give a big rat's ass. If people are dumb enough to buy em. Dont you let my family know where the money come from."[1] Bobby's reaction urges the audience to consider why he would not want his family to know where their share of the profits originate: does he wish for his father and younger sisters to be oblivious to the source of the remuneration so it seems that some force for good in the universe is working in their favor? Is he ashamed that he resorted to selling his image to satisfy the morbid infatuation that "dumb" people may have with men destined for the hangman's noose? Does he feel a disappointment in himself for finally caving to a social and financial system that had deprived him of agency and is prepared to take his life in exchange for exercising that agency? Or is this Bobby's final act of agency within an increasingly commercial society that more and more seems to be taking away individuals' autonomy?

This brief exchange illustrates that in *The Gardener's Son*, as in many works in Cormac McCarthy's *oeuvre*, the reasons for many characters' actions are scarcely delineated in dialogue. Rather, his characters express motives and rationales through simple acceptances or refusals, physical actions, and the relationships they build with others and their communities. This recurring trope in McCarthy's work, when combined with the fact that he and his collaborator, the film's director Richard Pearce, were working with historical figures and events as source material, help show how this first screenplay by McCarthy is part of a general commentary upon neoliberalism that the author develops over the course of his career. Bobby McEvoy never states the reasons why he shoots and kills James Gregg, the son of the renowned southern industrialist, William Gregg, the founder of the Graniteville, South Carolina, textile mill where he and his family have worked; nor does he state why he does not want his family to know where the proceeds of the sale of his photograph comes from when the funds are delivered.

Even so, mining *The Gardener's Son* for McEvoy's motivations reveals McCarthy's prescient recognition of the challenges surrounding the emerging neoliberal order as it stood in the 1970s. This is to say, writing about the resistances to and contradictions within industrial capitalism as they manifested in an American mill community in the nineteenth century allowed McCarthy to explore the significance of neoliberal capitalism a century after James Gregg's murder. The greatest of these contradictions—the one between the capitalist's need for profit and the desire for philanthropic goodwill (or to at least *appear* philanthropic)—reveals how the Gregg family ownership of the mill deprives its workers of agency in ways both direct and indirect. These antagonistic relations between management and workers at the mill emerge as part of McEvoy's motivation, becoming the seeds from which American neoliberal capitalism eventually sprouts.

Considered within the larger scope of Cormac McCarthy scholarship, *The Gardener's Son* has received relatively little attention. This should not be surprising given that, firstly, McCarthy is better known in the wider literary world as a novelist. Secondly, *The Gardener's Son* was first broadcast as part of the American Public Broadcasting System (PBS) anthology series *Visions* in 1976. Although it garnered multiple Emmy nominations, the film appears not to have enjoyed wide availability since then, and a published version of the screenplay did not appear until 1996 (with some variance from the film version of the narrative). Much of the published scholarship on *The Gardener's Son* has, in fact, used archival material to establish and examine the differences between the shooting and published scripts, as well as to consider how Pearce's research with McCarthy influenced early drafts of the screenplay.[2] Dianne Luce, for example, connects *The Gardener's Son* to *Child of God* (1973) through Pearce's admission that McCarthy's third novel "had been the one that struck me."[3] Indeed, as Luce posits, specific details of *Child of God* would likely have been striking to Pearce if he was reading the novel while developing a film about James Gregg's murder.[4]

For his part, historian Broadus Mitchell, in a 1928 biography that mostly praises William Gregg and his accomplishments, explains as an afterthought that Gregg's son, James, was killed in cold blood by a ne'er-do-well "bad boy" named Robert McEvoy, who had lost a leg as a boy after falling off some train cars on which he had been playing.[5] Later, after the mill shooting, he attempted to escape to Columbia, South Carolina, via rail car dressed in women's clothing and a wig. Unfortunately for Bobby, a telegraph from an alert train conductor led to the boy's apprehension upon arrival. After his conviction and hanging, Bobby's father surreptitiously exhumed and reburied his son's body for fear that "doctors would disinter it to dissect the brain."[6] These are the similarities, Luce observes, that Pearce would have found between McEvoy and the actions and fate of Lester Ballad, who is finally captured after attacking a man while wearing a frightwig, loses a limb in the attack, and after his death becomes a cadaver at the state medical college with his "head sawed open and the brains removed."[7]

Stacey Peebles builds upon these points to identify one especially important similarity between Ballard and McEvoy:

> For both Ballard and McEvoy, motivation is an important question. Ballard may be a murderer, arsonist, and necrophiliac, but he's also a child of God—so why does he do those things? [. . .] McEvoy is similarly enigmatic, and the furthest [Broadus] Mitchell takes his speculation is that his murder of James Gregg was merely the act of a "bad boy" who acted for no apparent reason.[8]

Peebles goes on to show evidence that the historical Bobby McEvoy would have had a reasonably clear motivation for killing James Gregg. Despite Mitchell's favorable view of William Gregg, other historians, including Tom E.

Terrill (who consulted with Richard Pearce on his background research) show instead poor working conditions at the mill and conflict between the Greggs and their laborers, including a strike against a wage cut and a petition among workers to commute McEvoy's death sentence. Both of these efforts were futile.[9]

Historical accuracy notwithstanding, there is confusion among characters in *The Gardener's Son* regarding identifying any motivation for McEvoy's murder of the younger Gregg. Bobby's sister Martha says several times she does not know why Bobby did it; Mrs. Gregg believes it was out of ingratitude; and other characters claim it was out of Bobby's grief in losing his mother. Consequently, this misunderstanding means readers must carefully consider what becomes a discussion of the value of human life in an increasingly financialized society that tosses aside the common good as it grows more focused on competition and the individual accumulation of wealth.[10] This consideration makes McCarthy's first screenplay and the context provided by its pre-neoliberal source material worthy of more critical attention.

William Gregg, Silent Character

Some of the most consequential evidence to aid the reader's understanding of the screenplay's emphasis on agency, wealth, and value in a community comes in the form of the screenplay's silent character, William Gregg. The particular story of Bobby McEvoy may be the focus of the action in *The Gardener's Son*; however, William Gregg's vision for an industrialized southern United States is a significant contributor to the creation of the conditions that breed the conflict driving the screenplay's plot. In other words, these details about the historical William Gregg's upbringing, introduced by McCarthy, serve as a foundation for an understanding of the work as an early critique of neoliberalism.

In the "Cast of Characters" in the published version of the screenplay, McCarthy describes William Gregg as "a ghost lying in the bed" whose funeral is held within the first eighteen pages of the screenplay and the first eighteen minutes of the film.[11] Some readers, such as J. Douglas Canfield, associate the limited visibility of the elder Gregg with the figure of the absent father, one who also appears with some frequency in McCarthy's fiction.[12] Whatever the case, William Gregg's figure looms large in *The Gardener's Son*, both in the narrative and in the screenplay's historical context, as an iteration of the silent character trope: the writers' choice of presenting the businessman yet not allowing him to speak for himself is an invitation for readers to look more closely at this dying father of American industry, the historical William Gregg.

At his graveside, a speaker—described by McCarthy as "Perhaps one of the stockholders"[13]—eulogizes Gregg as "a guiding force in the lives of nearly every one of us" and as "an example of the virtue of hard work" who benefited the people in his life by providing income via jobs at his mill and a nice, safe town with homes, schools, churches, and (implied by his status as a likely stockholder) dividends.[14] In parts of the monologue omitted from the film, this speaker even muses upon the late Gregg's upbringing:

> He himself was born in indigent circumstances and was thrown upon his own resources at an early age. By force of his own character, by the habits of energy and industry and perseverance, he acquired for himself a fair share of the world's wealth and some of its honors. But the crowning glory of his life and the true benefactors of his labors are here in the community which he established.[15]

But such platitudes are mere mythmaking. The historical William Gregg did not come from "indigent circumstances," and Mitchell does not indicate that Gregg's childhood was spent in poverty. On the contrary, Gregg seems largely to have been set up for success from an early age. He was born on the Virginia frontier in 1800, and his mother died when he was young. So was he cared for by a neighbor until the age of ten, at which time he became apprentice to his uncle, a very successful watchmaker in Alexandria, Virginia.[16] Soon into the apprenticeship, this uncle opened one of the earliest cotton textile mills in Georgia. Although this mill failed to endure the economic conditions precipitated by the War of 1812, it nonetheless left an impression on young William Gregg, who went on to become, in his biographer's words, "the father of the cotton manufacture in the cotton States."[17] After further apprenticeship watchmaking and silversmithing during his youth, Gregg opened a successful shop in Columbia, where he expanded into mercantile trade and engaged in direct trade with Europe. Illness led Gregg to retire from his business in Columbia, but he used his "unemployed funds" to purchase an interest in the Vaucluse Manufacturing Company. In 1838, he returned to business as a jeweler in a lucrative firm in Charleston, then one of the wealthiest cities in the nation.[18] These opportunities and wealth as a young man enabled Gregg to observe textile manufacturing both as an apprentice in his uncle's factory and then later as a *laissez-faire* capitalist seeking consultation on how to bring the industry to the agrarian south. If "thrown upon his resources at an early age," as his eulogist states, William Gregg's resources were fine apprenticeships and early exposure to the manufacturing business for which he became famous.

Another significant comment from the eulogist, also omitted from the film, is that all of Gregg's achievements "seem created almost by magic."[19] This suggestion is not far from the truth, and it belies some misdirection on the part of this supposed stockholder. Gregg received the charter for the Graniteville Manufacturing Company in late 1845 and raised—or contributed from his own wealth—all three-hundred thousand dollars of capital investment for the charter authorized within two years.[20] Indeed, his biographer observes that Gregg did not draw a salary from the company during the first five years of its operations, though he oversaw its construction and operation as the president elected by shareholders: "It is true that [Gregg] was a rich man with leisure to give to any project that took his interest, and certainly all he performed for Graniteville was done *con amore*."[21] This fawning description of Gregg's work organizing the Graniteville company and its shareholders resonates with the fictional shareholder's graveside panegyric. Graniteville's mourners are meant to understand Gregg's legacy in the manner of Broadus Mitchell's presentation: as a selfless labor of love for the people of South Carolina, who were provided with gainful employment and a sense of purpose through the businessman's energies. This mythologizing overlooks, of course, the fact that Graniteville's mills and its mill town are the product of investment capital by Gregg that will earn him and his fellow shareholders great wealth, even if he declines a salary for work. This portrayal makes investing, to people who do not understand it, seem like a kind of sorcery—a sort of "magic"—especially to the poor whites who abandoned their farms to come live and work at the mills, selling their labor to Gregg in exchange for hourly wages. Because the mill's employees have little or no money, let alone capital, though, the question of how the owners of the mill became wealthy in the first place was likely a mystery to them. Nor would they have understood how Gregg made his fortune in mercantile trading. This type of wealth creation is not far off from how Karl Marx sardonically describes the capitalist creation of value by putting money, rather than hands, to work: "By virtue of being value, it has acquired the occult ability to add value to itself. It brings forth living offspring, or at least lays golden eggs."[22] To succeed, such a capitalist enterprise as Gregg's needs a population to persuade that selling their labor—their agency—is an opportunity for financial success and independence.

Given the historical record and Pearce's and McCarthy's thorough review of it as they developed *The Gardener's Son*, readers with access to that same historical record, whether about William Gregg himself or about the growth of manufacturing in the United States in the nineteenth century, might judge this shareholder to be an unreliable source. What, then, does his misdirection show? First, it reveals that competing social realities are the backdrop against which the drama of *The Gardener's Son* plays out. Capitalists such as William Gregg understand that their true labor is accomplished by their hard work and investments, and overseeing the mill *pro bono* for a period was no labor of love but a hedge to help ensure the success of the investment. It also accomplishes the cultivation of a benevolent persona that survives after his death as the stockholder's comments indicate. Secondly, this embellished tale of Gregg's success is an important part of the myth of what would become neoliberalism: every individual has the same freedom to work, grow, and persevere as they see fit, and that hard work in a competitive market economy will be rewarded, almost inevitably. For William Gregg's mill at Graniteville to be successful and productive, he had to cultivate a benevolent "garden of industry," and part of that cultivation was propagating industriousness and entrepreneurship as virtues that aided the common good, as producing the wealth that is the reward for this ethic. With that consideration, the shareholder's eulogy draws an indirect comparison between the laborers attending the funeral and the mill's founder. It also makes a veiled comparison between James Gregg and the "*band of filthy and ragged people . . . nearly all bare-footed*" who arrive at the mill seeking work after the funeral.[23] They wish to use their freedom, just as the young "indigent" elder Gregg did, to work and earn a living. But with nothing to offer the migrants by way of work, the younger Gregg turns them away. And Bobby McEvoy watches him do it.

Diligents and Indigents

Indeed, this up-by-your-bootstraps version of neoliberal mythmaking that "originates" with the death of William Gregg—and is continued by the dewy eulogist, Gregg's wife, and the workers migrating to Graniteville—is inseparable from late capitalism's injunction that individuals and only individuals are responsible for their success or failure in a competitive market economy.

The Gardener's Son includes statements and actions from Mrs. Gregg and the younger Gregg, James, that provide a more complete picture of how much of a contradictory figure William Gregg was even within a nineteenth century industrial milieu that, by the time the viewer is seeing his exploits on American television in 1977, has morphed into neoliberal capitalism. Indeed, the contradictions broached by James Gregg and his mother arguably emerge out of the conflict of old and "new" capitalisms. In one particular scene, a disagreement between Mrs. Gregg and her son reveals the incongruities that must be reconciled between capitalists who see themselves as either serving and/or building a community versus those who are out simply to turn a profit. Appearing in the film after Bobby McEvoy has worked at the mill and overheard James Gregg send away the aforementioned job-seekers, this scene is not in the published screenplay but is worth describing at length.[24]

In a cemetery, while placing fresh flowers at her late husband's monumental tombstone, Mrs. Gregg also visits and places fresh daisies at a more modest grave marker a few paces away. The marker bears only the inscription "THE LITTLE BOY / 1855." According to Mrs. Gregg, this is the marker for a child who was put off the train at Graniteville because he was very sick. The boy died before he could provide his name, and it is implied that Mrs. Gregg saw to it that he was provided the grave and marker at the cemetery. The juxtaposition of the unknown boy's modest tombstone and the massive marker for William Gregg indicates the cognitive dissonance that Mrs. Gregg must negotiate. This material separation is softened, though, by Mrs. Gregg's assiduous care for both graves.

The scene progresses as James approaches in a horse-drawn carriage and uses his mother's attention to the unknown boy's grave as an opportunity to comment on human nature—and his new approach to business. He draws a parallel between his mother's attention to the dead boy and her steadfast support of his father's famous commitment to the common man. James asks for and receives an explanation for how the boy came to be buried in the cemetery, never making it to a destination that Mrs. Gregg imagines had a family waiting for him. This explanation does not satisfy James. He conjectures that the boy "probably run off from somewhere" and his death twenty years ago shows it wasn't the Civil War that changed people: "People say it was the war. But it was the same before the war. People wandering up and down the country, eat up with hookworms, god knows what else. . . . Inbred, their eyes grown together. . . . Come down here expect us to put them to work. Raise the children up in habits of industry."[25] Although Mrs. Gregg balks at her son's characterization of the people who come seeking work at the mill, James is unrelenting, telling his mother that the poor believe the mill town is just a "dosshouse" and that the Greggs have no obligation to accommodate *anyone*. "The world is made up of indigents and diligents," the younger Gregg says:

> You can't help the indigent. The more you do for 'em, the weaker he gets. The diligent don't need your help. And they say the good Lord must have loved the poor 'cause he made so many of them. I think he just kept trying to see if one of the squint-eyed sons of bitches would get off his ass and do some work.[26]

Mrs. Gregg, already in disagreement with her son's characterization of the struggling families who come to the mill seeking work, expresses offense at her son's language, especially on cemetery grounds. She states that she will walk home rather than ride with James in the carriage. Then James takes her arm, rather forcefully, pleading that she accept the ride home. Even after his mother relents, stepping up into the carriage, James continues his diatribe against the workers flocking to the mill, relating the story of a family that "didn't have a pot to piss in nor a window throw it out of. . . . And they worked for about two weeks and then they left. You know what they said? They said they didn't like the water. Habits of industry. Good god." Mrs. Gregg replies, "Your father put a good deal of store in the common people. They made this company. He believed that this place could be a garden. A garden of industry. The people only needed the opportunity to work." The scene closes with James having the last word: "I know what he believed. It's alright."[27]

James Gregg's crude comments to his mother, and his ostensible disagreement with his father's ethic, are telling. On the face of it, his words dehumanize the population of workers that the mill relies on. They show that he does not believe all people deserve basic dignity on the basis of their human existence. Instead, their worth and usefulness depends on whether or not they work to further *his* enterprise. Also, his comments seem to be a clear dismissal of the "habits of industry" that are important to the capitalist mythos cultivated by William Gregg. James Gregg is more than content to dispense with any notion that there is any magnanimity in his enterprise. His first responsibility is to his shareholders, after all. On the other hand, it seems Mrs. Gregg does afford dignity to the poor, and not just based on their potential as workers. Even so, further focus on the specifics of James Gregg's comments bring the less *laissez-faire* than *neoliberal* myth to the surface.

James Gregg does not believe people are shaped by the conditions in which they find themselves: "People say it was the war. But it was the same before the war." Based on the anecdotal story of the boy buried in the cemetery and his experience with poor rural whites seeking work at the mill, the younger Gregg paints with broad strokes a society in which those human capitals willing to work become healthy, productive, and wealthy while the shiftless, lacking the entrepreneurial spirit, idly meander through life disease-ridden and prone to incest. Within his worldview, success or lack thereof is not connected at all to any social or material conditions, such as a deadly military conflict that crippled the economy of the southern states or the extant wealth that Mrs. Gregg points out James was born into. By his use of the word "dosshouse," James shows his belief that people are not seeking work at the mill but simply the lodging associated with employment. Furthermore, he believes that these conditions are ordained: there will always be plenty of poor people because of either the Christian God's love for them or his experiment to see if any of them would eventually become industrious laborers to support Gregg's or other capitalists' enterprises.

James's final argument in this regard is to note how the family that quit the factory after two weeks because "they didn't like the water." He dismisses this group as people who cannot learn the "habits of industry" because they are so sensitive to what he believes to be an inconsequential difference between the quality of the water at Graniteville and the water in the region from which the family emigrated. However, the younger Gregg is unable (or unwilling) to account for the trauma that a mill town would have inflicted upon a family used to the agrarian life. Tom E. Terrill explains:

> Industrial work required a sharp break in the work life and sometimes even in the life expectations of the farmers who migrated to Graniteville. There they found time measured in hours and minutes and less subject to the seasonal fluctuations they had known on the farm. They lost their prerogative to decide how to spend their workdays. Although their work pace was slow by modern standards, they had to work indoors in rooms that were hot, extremely noisy, full of lint that could reduce visibility to six feet, and often filthy from expectorated tobacco.[28]

It is not simply that the family "didn't like the water" in the city, which was very possibly less clean than the rural water to which the migrants were accustomed. They suffered a profound loss of agency and were no longer able to control their daily routines, working conditions, and downtime. Conforming to such expectations for work was required of workers for the mill to operate at maximum profitability and efficiency, and this work was a condition of taking up residence at Graniteville. In light of such radical changes in their day-to-day life, this particular family more than likely felt that such demands were not worth the new environment. However, they dared not articulate this sentiment to an authority figure. James Gregg's subsequent unwillingness to respect the dignity of people he describes as so poor they do not "have a pot to piss in," whose poverty is in fact exacerbated by James's own actions and the economic rationality he has internalized, leads to a conundrum wherein even entrepreneurial and hard-working individuals who ask for modest necessities like clean air or drinking water elicits scorn from the capitalist who comes to see such individuals as the shiftless, socially immobile "indigents" whom he will neither suffer nor abet.[29]

Garden of Industry or Garden of Dignity?

Nearly as significant as the son's comments are the mother's actions (or inactions). Was Mrs. Gregg's desire to walk home from the cemetery rather than riding with her son an expression of her disagreement with his language, or did it signal disagreement with his opinion of the people working in the mill or who seek work at the mill? Or his new understanding of the businessman's (and market's) role in society? Whatever it is she takes as the greatest affront, she still accepts James's offer, not resisting when he grabs her arm to help her into the carriage. There is considerable subtext within this dynamic: does James want his mother to ride home because of her status as a wealthy widow? Or does his insistence on this point reveal a patriarchal social dynamic in which he insists he is correct in matters facing the public sphere, such as industry and labor? Perhaps at the root of her disagreement with her son and its contradictory valences are Mrs. Gregg's emphasis on what she believes to be the good that her late husband's enterprise accomplished. She insists on honoring such accomplishments within even the domestic sphere, which she articulates at the peril of seeming oblivious to such an act's inconsistencies: "[William Gregg] believed that this place could be a garden. A garden of industry." This line, absent from the published screenplay, is an obvious reference to the title and raises questions about who is the eponymous gardener. For Mrs. Gregg, the gardener is clearly her husband. However, Luce in "The First Screenplay" argues that the title, especially in light of Mrs. Gregg's comment, invites comparison between the younger Gregg and Robert McEvoy as the eponymous gardener's son of the novel: one the son of the gardener of industry, the other son of a literal mill gardener, and both figurative sons of the biblical first gardener, Adam.[30] This connection rhymes with the capitalist mythos invoked by the stockholder's claim that William Gregg was born and grew out of indigent circumstances and worked his way to the top of a market economy. Adam, as the first gardener of humanity, had no material wants before being cast out of Eden and cursed to work. And so, simultaneously, Adam is mythologized as the father of both humanity and industry, the shared and therefore equitable starting point for all persons spiritually and, by inference, materially.

This split between the spiritual and the material is the most salient contradiction in Mrs. Gregg's worldview that helps readers and viewers see how she is both generous to workers and resentful of their assertions of agency. She demonstrates this in the cemetery scene where Mrs. Gregg, herself a gardener tending to a plot of humans, cultivates some notion of equality between the anonymous boy and her wealthy husband in spite of the differences between the size and ornateness of their markers. She reveals this contradiction more clearly at the beginning of *The Gardener's Son* through her involvement in the amputation of Bobby McEvoy's leg. Given that Dr. Perceval's and Mrs. Gregg's interaction begins with her indication that there has been no change in her husband's condition, and that the doctor inquires about "that boy in the village" whose condition Mrs. Gregg described as "urgent," the thinly veiled subtext is that Mrs. Gregg summoned the doctor not to reevaluate her husband's condition but rather to see to the ailing Bobby.[31] In a portion of their conversation about the catatonic William Gregg, omitted from the film but retained in the published screenplay, Mrs. Gregg declares "He hated sickness." Dr. Perceval responds, "I guess he despised any kind of idleness," which Mrs. Gregg confirms: "Yes. Wouldnt tolerate it."[32] Mrs. Gregg's characterization of her husband's intolerance of idleness has a deep tradition in the United States that dates back to colonial times via the fabled Puritan work ethic and Benjamin Franklin's popular *Poor Richard's Almanack*. Mitchell explains in his biography of William Gregg that he closely supervised his workers and their families to ensure their industriousness. Children between ages six and twelve were required to attend the company-provided schools, and Gregg enacted temperance rules in Graniteville to keep the workforce sober and forbade dances to limit frivolous idleness.[33] Of the rules and attention to order that William Gregg held over his workers, Mitchell writes,

> Gregg and Graniteville were identical terms. He made the place out of hand, and it reflected, in every department of its life, his affectionate care. There have been mill men in the South since who, while no less despotic over their communities, have been less benevolent. . . . The subjects over whom he ruled in his little kingdom were economically as weak as he was strong, and yet no hint of exploitation ever entered his consciousness.[34]

The chapter that this passage opens in Mitchell's biography is entitled "A Benevolent Despotism," no less. This hatred of sickness and idleness survives into the twentieth and twenty-first century US as a labor milieu with long hours, little to no paid sick leave, and often stagnant wages. All of this is often the norm for many contemporary workers, remaining in the US even as the COVID-19 global pandemic began in 2020.

McCarthy could not have foreseen such events while working on *The Gardener's Son* in the 1970s. Nevertheless, if the screenplay demonstrates anything it's that the evergreen branches connecting productivity with virtue and idleness and sickness with immorality in American culture were as palpable in the nineteenth century as the 1970s. This frame gives readers-viewers cause to scrutinize Mrs. Gregg's own motivations, especially her concern over Bobby McEvoy's well-being. Presumably, the McEvoys received word that Dr. Perceval would be calling to evaluate Robert's leg, given that Martha McEvoy notifies her parents upon spotting the doctor's carriage traveling toward Kalmia, the Gregg's estate near Graniteville. They do, however, seem surprised when Mrs. Gregg accompanies Dr. Perceval for the visit, which suggests that Mrs. Gregg does not have a reputation for mingling with the masses. Mrs. Gregg spurns Mrs. McEvoy's hospitality, saying after Martha receives instructions to heat the kettle, "Please dont trouble yourself Mrs. McEvoy. I only came to see about the boy," eventually telling Mrs. McEvoy not to bother providing refreshment a second time.[35] After the bedridden Bobby swears at Dr. Perceval, Mrs. Gregg visits his bedside, assuring the doctor and the McEvoys that Bobby would not behave the same way with her.[36] In the course of Bobby and Mrs. Gregg's conversation, the former consistently denies that sepsis has made his recovery without amputation impossible. There is, however, an arc to Mrs. Gregg's commentary. After Bobby declares he would rather be dead than give up a leg, she states, "No one has the right [to say this]. Life is a precious gift from God." But when Bobby says his fate is up to God, Mrs. Gregg implores Bobby to "Think of your family. I lost a son in the war. I know what it is. I'd have wanted him back with no legs." When this statement gets no response from the boy, she goes on: "God does not ask that all the flowers in this garden be perfect. He has a special love for the ones. . ." and Robert finishes her final statement by saying, "Ones are crippled."[37] Mrs. McEvoy directs Bobby's attention to his leg, pulling away the covers of the bed against Bobby's wishes to reveal his gangrenous limb. The scene ends with Bobby resigned to his fate. He begins sobbing in the published screenplay; he faints in the film. In both, Mrs. Gregg touches the young man's face.

The viewer could easily ascribe the touch to matronly, loving care for even the lowest of the community. On the other hand, each statement from Mrs. Gregg about the proper solution for Bobby's leg deprives him of his own agency, converting him into human capital for her (son's) continuing use. God declares life precious; therefore, Bobby has no right to say he would rather be dead than lose a limb. If God's grace does not compel, think then of the parents who would be crushed at the loss of a child. Finally, Mrs. Gregg appeals to the only agency granted by the emerging neoliberal order: the opportunity to make oneself into enterprising-yet-controlled human capital. At Graniteville, everyone has a role and the same opportunity to succeed. There is even a special love for those who labor in the face of disability. Indeed, minutes later Bobby is shown, some weeks after his surgery, pushing a broom at the mill, working in spite of his lost limb.

Readers and viewers should note that Bobby McEvoy never provides verbal consent to the amputation. His leg's removal may be necessary for him to live, but he never assents to any operation. Mrs. McEvoy simply declares to the doctor after the conclusion of her bedside visit that he may fetch his assistant and proceed; after all, she knows her son can still put the boy to work at the mill.[38] Given these details, and Mrs. Gregg's comments later in the film to James Gregg about her husband's view that Graniteville is a "garden of industry," Mrs. Gregg seeing to Robert's amputation is part of tending a garden whose flowers are deprived of their own will. Her husband hated idleness, yet from his deathbed he hovered on the precipice of permanent idleness. And here Mrs. Gregg ostensibly prevents Graniteville from losing two workers to that permanent idleness in a short span. She works to ensure the garden remains fruitful. After all, from its early stages to the present, capitalism has relied on the existence of a fixed labor market, that is, people who are unable to make a living feasibly in any other manner. In the case of many mill towns, and specifically in Graniteville, this reliance requires chronic activity and industry among even the children of the workers, whatever their physical condition.

Even in her last appearance in *The Gardener's Son*, Mrs. Gregg is unable to see the contradiction caused by her desire both to treat her husband's workers and their children with dignity and tend to her husband's garden of industry. Near the screenplay's end, Martha McEvoy, Bobby's younger sister and the middle child, visits Mrs. Gregg, who assumes the purpose of Martha's visit is to plead with her to intervene and spare Bobby's life. Martha declares that she is there on her own accord, and that she "know[s] what people said about James," an allusion to James's sexual exploitation of girls working in the mill, which Martha had experienced firsthand: earlier in screenplay James attempted to entice Martha to sex in exchange for a gold coin. However, Mrs. Gregg immediately declares that she "always intended well toward [Bobby]. I am a christian woman. But he has put to perdition all the hopes of this family." Part of those hopes, she explains, were "A community of people working together, joined in a common enterprise. But my husband . . . My family's bond to this community was of the spirit, not of the flesh."[39] After Mrs. Gregg goes on to express dismay at the "ingratitude" of the workers at Graniteville, Martha tells Mrs. Gregg that her son "never done nothing to me" and expresses regret for James's death because someone from her family needed to do so.[40] This leads to a change in Mrs. Gregg's demeanor, who invites Martha to stay for tea. The stage directions from the screenplay state that Mrs. Gregg "*looks at* [Martha] *as if seeing one of these people for the first time.*"[41] The reference to "these people" is significant in the direction insofar as it suggests that Mrs. Gregg is now looking at Martha with the same condescension as did her late son. In dropping her pretensions that her family is in any way community-building, Mrs. Gregg embodies suddenly the central mystery of *The Gardener's Son*, admitting indirectly to Martha her confusion about Bobby's motives. "I look at you and I try to see some sign. Try to see something in your face," she squints. "These things must have beginnings somewhere. Be put in motion at some point. . . . But when I look at you I see nothing. I can see nothing in you to do with death and murder."[42]

As the conversation progresses, Martha mentions that if she had been asked to testify in her brother's defense and asked about it, she would have had to talk about the time James offered her the gold coin. "It didnt mean nothin," Martha says, and assures Mrs. Gregg that "Bobby could not have knowed nothin about it. You know I wouldnt of told him hotheaded as he was."[43] Snapping at the implication, Mrs. Gregg interprets Martha's comment as a threat and concludes aloud, "My son was right about you people."[44]

Taken together, these three episodes that prominently feature Mrs.

Gregg—Bobby's amputation, her conversation with James Gregg in the cemetery, and Martha's visit near the time of her brother's execution—show that she is more than comfortable with the public narrative that she is preserving her husband's legacy *and* shares her son's belief that Graniteville both owes its success to and provides opportunity for poor farmers who make up a new working class *only* when those people that she is intending to help exhibit a gratitude that fits her view of herself as a virtuous woman and (most importantly) actually have no agency. The young boy whom Mrs. Gregg buried long before the events of the narrative take place was unable to give consent or protest his burial and manner of his remembrance, much less even provide his own name. Bobby McEvoy does not verbally consent to his amputation and is deprived of agency through Mrs. Gregg's intervention. And Mrs. Gregg ends her conversation with Martha when the latter recounts her experiences with James Gregg that run counter to Mrs. Gregg's notion that the Greggs' bonds with the people of Graniteville "was of the spirit, not of the flesh." Despite this growing clarity for readers and viewers regarding the tensions of Granitville society, many of the participants in the narrative are incapable of seeing, much less processing, these contradictions, which can be extrapolated to American society writ large. This blindness in large part comes from the expectation among characters in the narrative (and readers, too) that there was some sort of specific reason that Bobby McEvoy shot and killed James Gregg. Many have accepted simple answers: Bobby was simply a "bad boy," says Mitchell; Bobby was avenging James's poor treatment of Martha; Bobby was retaliating for the poor treatment of workers, including his father; Bobby was upset at the loss of his mother. However, readers and characters alike capable of perceiving the nuances of social class and the contradictions of neoliberal capitalism in the 1970s might decide that an assertion of his own agency in direct opposition to an oppressive political economy was the reason Bobby McEvoy killed James Gregg.

Searching for a Moral

The published screenplay includes a bookending which is set several decades after the main events of the narrative. These bookending scenes do not appear in the film. In the opening scene, a figure known only as a young man, "Neatly dressed, well spoken. Under his manner a hint of truculence," is guided into the long-closed offices of the Graniteville mill by a "softspoken"

Old Timekeeper.[45] The latter reminisces on the past, describing the day he went to James Gregg's funeral and refuting a story passed among people at the mill that James Gregg had broken the young Bobby McEvoy's leg by running it over with his carriage. He rather confirms the story of McEvoy falling from the train car. After the young man spends some time rifling through boxes, the timekeeper says, "You wont find it here." "What wont I find?" the young man asks, but the timekeeper is not specific, saying only, "They're just boxes of records. There's some old pitcher albums in here somewheres. Mill used to keep . . . . They aint the thing. Old papers or pitchers. You copy something down dont mean you have it. You just have the record. Times past are fugitives. They caint be kept in no box."[46] Stage directions explain a montage of historic photographs overlaid with the opening credits, which transport the viewer back to the times during which the narrative takes place. As the story unfolds, readers come to understand that the timekeeper at the beginning assumed the young man is looking for the reasons Bobby McEvoy murdered James Gregg. The timekeeper's insistence that the past cannot simply be filed away is certainly a comment on how stories are passed down, and it could be read as a direct comment on historiography: a narrative about the past is but a representation, a "record," rather than primary source of understanding.

This young man returns to his search for meaning only in the closing scene of the screenplay, in which he visits an aged Martha McEvoy at the state hospital in Columbia. Stage directions note that when this young man approaches the elderly Martha, asleep in a chair, he sits on the bed holding flowers he has brought for her and looks at his feet. This is a "*Shot reminiscent of Bobby in his cell before execution*,"[47] providing, through overlay, a flashback to events that were so long ago for Martha but occurred just moments prior for readers. When Martha does rouse and begin conversation with this man, who introduces himself as William Chaffee, she comments on his affluent appearance. When Chaffee mentions that he had just come from Graniteville that morning, Martha begins to reminisce about her time growing up there and the people that she knew, noting that while she has many memories of her late mother, her little sister did not. When Chaffee asks if Martha's little sister remembers Bobby, Martha falls silent. She quickly realizes and Chaffee admits that he is a grandson of the Greggs, likely named for his grandfather.[48] He came to visit because, to him, the Greggs are only names in the family history. The incident between Bobby McEvoy and James Gregg, according to Chaffee, "was like something in a book. It didnt seem like real people." He tells Martha the purpose of his visit: "I just wanted to talk to you. You're the only one who knows what happened."[49] Because these events seem like something from a novel, Chaffee is searching for a moral to his family's story.

Martha's reply in the closing pages of *The Gardener's Son* are remarkable, standing in contrast as they do with her previous scene with Mrs. Gregg, who dominates the conversation. Unlike his grandmother, whom Chaffee describes as "eccentric" and "peculiar," the grandson is happy to let Martha talk.[50] It may come from a selfish desire to know more about his own family, but Chaffee is content for Martha to tell her own story. After Chaffee's explanation that she is the only one who knows what happened, Martha quickly denies that she knows much of anything. She says right away, "I dont even know where he's buried at," and moment later "I dont know why Bobby done what he done."[51] But as she tells her story, Bobby's "why" becomes apparent: her stories all revolve around the loss of agency. Martha tells Chaffee about how Mrs. Gregg could be nice to the children of the mill town, but she kept her father, the gardener, at work tending to the cemetery. She explains that there "used to be a stone up there it just said 'the little boy' and she would have flowers on it all the time."[52] In other words, a living child was deprived of attention for the benefit of a dead one, and at the direction of a capitalist. As she recounts these details, Martha ponders whether God has names for people, because are not all people the same in the eyes of God? Martha explains that her father always wanted to save money and return to the family farmstead at Pickens but was unable to do so after he paid his son's legal bills. "Daddy just never did come out of it," she says.[53] She explains that she was glad her mother was dead when Bobby died so that she did not have to endure that loss. Martha describes how her mother, about a year before her death, took her up to Pickens. On the visit, she briefly united with her family's horse, Captain, whom she greets with a tearful embrace in the street. Then the screenplay ends with a monologue from Martha, who says after looking down at the portrait of Bobby from the morning of his execution that she just a moment ago removed from a purse: "Sometimes I wish I'd not even kept it. That lawyer said that the image of God was blotted out of his face. That's what he said about Bobby. I ort not even to of kept it. Sometimes I can almost talk to him. I caint see him no more. In my mind. I just see this old pitcher."[54]

As a daughter in the household, Martha has not even the agency to oppose her family's decision to have left Pickens and the farming life. Once this decision is set in motion, she has no agency to escape the bleak reality of life in a factory town. Other forces worked to deprive Martha and all the youth of Graniteville of agency as well. In each one of Martha's memories, shared at the conclusion of the screenplay, a deprivation of agency connected to earning a living at Graniteville is laid bare. In light of Mrs. Gregg's earlier behavior, readers know that Mrs. Gregg demanded gratitude; therefore, her generosity deprived agency of the children of the town, including "the little boy" who could not protest when she interred him at the Graniteville cemetery. Martha's father's financial ruin after Bobby's trial deprives him of agency to ever achieve what William Gregg had when he started the mill: the ability to put funds rather than his hands to work. Working at Graniteville meant the family had to leave behind the horse Captain, whom Martha loved so dearly. And lastly, Graniteville and a judicial system that supported it caused the erasure of Bobby McEvoy. The words of the lawyer to Martha, that "the image of God was blotted out of his face," is eerily inverse to Mrs. Gregg's comment to Martha that she could not see the beginnings of evil deeds in her face. Bobby's loss of agency in the remedy for his broken, diseased leg and requirement for work in the mill leads him to conclude that he faces an abject loss of dignity and agency if he is to survive. This likely leads to Bobby's confrontation with James Gregg. But whether or not this compels Bobby to kill James is less clear, and is perhaps not as relevant. It is not the murder that makes Martha unable to see him; it is instead "this old pitcher," one through which he cedes his agency and ownership of himself so that the family he is leaving behind might have a little money from his misfortune to continue surviving in a socioeconomic system they cannot escape.

A Parable for Troubling Times

On the aftermath of the historical murder of James Gregg and the execution of Bobby McEvoy, Terrill writes,

> There was a clear message in the events that followed the murder. Paternalism had stark limits. The southern white elite had great power, at least within the South. When threatened, that elite could and would use its power forcefully and effectively. Finally, those events bluntly demonstrated the impotence of whites who worked and lived in cotton mills and mill villages and who were caught in the wake of the forces loosed by the industrial revolution.[55]

Terrill's comments eloquently sum up the plight of the McEvoys and the other workers at Graniteville in the wake of James Gregg's murder at the hands of Bobby. Poor, rural southerners working at Graniteville and other mill towns in the Southeast traded autonomy and the ability to dictate their own schedules and leisure activity for the housing and financial security that mill employment promised, and in that they surrendered a good deal of political power, both individually and collectively. Many such rural poor, as the fictional Bobby McEvoy, were not prepared for their loss of agency, the shock of industrialism, or the conversion to human capital in a system that valued them as so much machinery. *The Gardener's Son* shows readers how the *laissez-faire* liberalism of the American nineteenth century had helped produce the neoliberalism that would have been increasingly familiar to the late twentieth century viewer of the McEvoy-Gregg tale. This new economics was one that despite the laborer's hard work nonetheless deprives the worker of leisure, identity, and eventually agency at the same time as it converts him into human capital who must compete or die.

Cormac McCarthy's first screenplay thus shows American society that the costs demanded by neoliberalism—the loss of individual agency, the conversion to human capital—have not decreased but flourished by the time of the film's release, an era beset as it was with energy crises, economic recessions, declines in entitlement programs, and increases in privatization across sectors. Accepting or being forced into the neoliberal myth means forfeiting both collective action and community in the service of a competitive, winner-take-all arena, unless one already has the capital to *buy* one's way out of this forced competition. Because it was conceived and published in an era where neoliberalism had become dominant, *The Gardener's Son* remains worthy of our attention today. Since the film's production, workers' rights are at their weakest in more than a century and the injunction that subjects pursue only individual self-interest and private solutions to public problems is even more radically emphasized today, eating away at the social fabric.

It is perhaps ironic, then, that the Nobel Memorial Prize in Economic Sciences was awarded to none other than neoliberal economist Milton Friedman in 1976—the same year that *The Gardener's Son* first aired on PBS. Years before this award, Friedman claimed, in an article published in the *New York Times,* that for a business even to think of itself as having a "social conscience" is tantamount to socialism.[56] Rather, a person running a business for owners (read: shareholders) according to Friedman must "conduct the business in accordance with [owners'] desires, which generally will be to make as much money as possible while conforming to the basic rules of the society, both those embodied in law and those embodied in ethical custom."[57]

If that person running a business feels some manner of social responsibility, Friedman argues, they are certainly allowed to pursue them because "the corporate executive is a person in his own right," and may "feel impelled by these responsibilities to devote part of his income to causes he regards as worthy."[58] However, to exercise "social responsibility" in his capacity as a corporate executive, by increasing wages or not increasing prices during times of high inflation, means the executive "act[s] in some way that is not in the interest of his employers" and ultimately "reduce[s] returns to stockholders."[59] The awarding of the Nobel Prize to Friedman, coming two years after Friedrich Hayek won the same award, gave validation to such neoliberal ideas, which continued to gain traction in the US during and after the 1970s; Friedman went on to serve as an economic adviser to Ronald Reagan during the latter's 1980 presidential campaign and continued his counsel throughout Reagan's presidency.

With *The Gardener's Son*, McCarthy shows an American audience in the 1970s that Friedman's ideas were simply an extension of the Greggs' model—only carried out to macroeconomic ends. While the elder Gregg either had a very generous view of "ethical custom" or acted upon individual "social responsibility" to help ensure the mill's early success, the younger Gregg has a much narrower view of his obligations in a market economy and what society requires of him. He even villainizes workers broadly as idle drifters. The younger Gregg's actions in particular helped create a society in which workers, then and now, feel stuck: they must participate in the system created by those with capital that requires sacrificing agency, just as Bobby McEvoy and the enterprising photographer must. What was the alternative for workers in the 1870s? And what is the alternative for workers today? In *The Gardener's Son,* McCarthy presents a parable that shows the dire consequences of emphasizing individual profit at the expense of community and the common good. Without understanding that all constituents of a society are responsible to community, its members eventually become valued as means only, as capital useful only to the extent that they can be traded for more or better capital.

Notes

1. Cormac McCarthy, *The Gardener's Son* (ca. 1976; repr. New York: Ecco, 1996), 81; and Cormac McCarthy, *The Gardener's Son*, directed by Richard Pearce (1976; Arlington, Va., Public Broadcasting System). The film is out of print but available widely online: see Esoteric Archive, accessed 1 July 2024, https://youtu.be/-ubaXHo-SSI.

2. See Dianne C. Luce, "Cormac McCarthy's First Screenplay" in *Perspectives on Cormac McCarthy*, eds. Edwin T. Arnold and Dianne C. Luce (Jackson: Mississippi UP, 1999), 71–96; Dianne C. Luce, "The Archives and the Tennessee Years, II: *Child of God, The Gardener's Son,* and *Suttree*" in *Cormac McCarthy in Context*, ed. Steven Frye (Cambridge: Cambridge UP, 2020), 281–87; and Stacey Peebles, *Cormac McCarthy and Performance: Page, Stage, Screen* (Austin: Univ. of Texas Press, 2017).

3. Richard Pearce, "Foreword" in McCarthy, *The Gardener's Son*, vii.

4. Luce, "First Screenplay," 73.

5. Broadus Mitchell, *William Gregg: Factory Master of the Old South* (1928; repr. New York: Octagon Books, 1966), 327–28.

6. Ibid.

7. Cormac McCarthy, *Child of God* (1973; repr. New York: Vintage, 1993), 194.

8. Peebles, *McCarthy and Performance*, 24.

9. Ibid., 25.

10. Jonathan Elmore and Rick Elmore have been tugging at this thread, which they see as a crucial theme running throughout McCarthy's work. See "'You reckon there are just some places the good lord didn't intend folks to live in?': The Absences of Community in McCarthy's *Child of God*," *The Cormac McCarthy Journal* 17, no. 2 (Fall 2019): 134–47; "'You Can Stay Here with Your Papa and Die or You Can Go with Me': The Ethical Imperative of *The Road*," *The Cormac McCarthy Journal* 16, no. 2 (Fall 2018): 133–48; and "Life, Unity, and Suffering: The Moral of Cormac McCarthy's *Suttree*," *The Cormac McCarthy Journal* 19, no. 2 (Fall 2021): 138–56.

11. McCarthy, *Gardener's Son,* xi; McCarthy and Pearce (dir.), *Gardener's Son.*

12. J. Douglas Canfield, "Oedipal Complexities in Cormac McCarthy's *The Stonemason* and *The Gardener's Son*," *The Cormac McCarthy Journal* 2, no. 1 (Spring 2002): 12–22.

13. McCarthy, *Gardener's Son*, xii.

14. Ibid., 18.

15. Ibid.

16. Mitchell, *William Gregg*, 3–4.

17. Ibid., 4.

18. Ibid., 8–9.

19. McCarthy, *Gardener's Son,* 18.

20. Mitchell, *William Gregg,* 34, 48, 275.

21. Ibid., 47.

22. Karl Marx, *Capital: Volume I*, trans. Ben Fowkes (1867; repr. New York: Penguin, 1990), 255.

23. McCarthy, *Gardener's Son,* 22. Emphasis original.

24. This scene does appear in the shooting script cited by Luce, "The First Screenplay," 77.

25. McCarthy and Pearce (dir.), *Gardener's Son.*

26. Ibid.

27. Ibid.

28. Tom E. Terrill, "Murder in Graniteville," in *Toward a New South?: Studies in Post-Civil War Southern Communities*, eds. Orville Vernon Burton and Robert C. McMath Jr. (Westport: Greenwood Press, 1982), 199.

29. It is worth noting that in the quoted portions of the stockholder's eulogy published in the screenplay, but omitted from the film, the stockholder states that William Gregg "was himself was born in *indigent* circumstances" (McCarthy, *Gardener's Son*, 19, emphasis added). James Gregg

uses *indigent* to describe people he believes unwilling to work and unworthy of aid. It is possible that in the revisions that produced the shooting script for *The Gardener's Son* the eulogist's description of the elder Gregg as indigent-born was cut for time, or perhaps was cut to soften the incongruity between the neoliberal myth and the perspectives of those who benefit from it the most, such as the Greggs themselves. The knowledge of this contradiction between iterations of the work warrants emphasis on this word choice.

30. Luce, "First Screenplay," 77–78.

31. McCarthy, *Gardener's Son*, 8.

32. Ibid.

33. Mitchell, *William Gregg*, 78, 83–85.

34. Ibid., 76.

35. McCarthy, *Gardener's Son*, 9, 11.

36. Ibid., 13.

37. Ibid., 14. In the film version of this conversation, the two sentences in Mrs. Gregg's first statement are transposed. In the second, she implores Robert to "Think of your *family*." And lastly, she says "*And I think* he has a special love for the ones *that*. . . ."

38. Ibid., 16.

39. Ibid., 73.

40. Ibid., 74.

41. Ibid., 75.

42. Ibid., 76. In the film, Mrs. Gregg's words are "nothing in you of death, murder."

43. Ibid., 77.

44. Ibid., 78.

45. Ibid., xi, 1–3.

46. Ibid., 3.

47. Ibid., 90.

48. See Mitchell, *William Gregg*, 258. Mitchell acknowledges William Gregg's daughter, whom he refers to only as "Mrs. Chaffee," at the very end of the text and in various places in his notes. She appears to have been a primary source for his research.

49. McCarthy, *Gardener's Son*, 93.

50. Ibid., 94.

51. Ibid., 93–94.

52. Ibid.

53. Ibid., 95.

54. Ibid., 96.

55. Terrill, "Murder in Graniteville," 214–15.

56. Milton Friedman, "A Friedman doctrine—The Social Responsibility of Business Is to Increase Its Profits," *The New York Times*, 13 September 1970, pg. SM17, accessed 1 July 2024, https://www.nytimes.com/1970/09/13/archives/a-friedman-doctrine-the-social-responsibility-of-business-is-to.html.

57. Ibid.

58. Ibid.

59. Ibid.

2

"HE WANTED TO BUY YOU"

Value and Abjection in *The Road*, *All the Pretty Horses*, and *The Crossing*

Julian Caradec

It would be a reduction to posit that the later part of Cormac McCarthy's bibliography, starting during the Reagan years and onwards, falls completely under the capture of a neoliberal ethos. We can, however, observe neoliberalism's influence seeping into the narratives and shaping the relationships, fates, and outlooks of McCarthy's late novels and their characters. One of the main differences between liberalism and neoliberalism, as articulated by Michel Foucault, was the latter's insistence on taking control not merely of economic systems, markets, and means of production, but of its subjects' lives, right down to their imaginations and connections to the world around them.[1] It is an ethos which aims to establish itself as the natural and ultimate state of human civilization, as suggested by neoliberal thinker Francis Fukuyama's infamous notion of *The End of History*.[2] In other words, the mere fact of pervasive economic exchange is not the defining characteristic of neoliberalism; it is rather the inability to escape the paradigm of not only the economic exchange but competition in all aspects of life that characterizes the neoliberal moment. As Jason Read puts it, "neoliberalism is not just a manner of governing states or economies, but is intimately tied to the government of the individual."[3] This intimacy is observable in McCarthy's later novels where the trajectories of the characters are often guided by more-or-less visible market logics which permeate characters' interactions with the world around them and with each other. With the above in mind, this chapter will focus on three works—*All the Pretty Horses* (1992), *The Crossing* (1994), and *The Road* (2006)—to demonstrate McCarthy's broad interest in transactions, value, and exchange in the neoliberal economy and how such a transactional ideology has permeated relations between all humans and animals, which have all become consumer goods.[4]

In their study of neoliberalism in *No Country for Old Men* (2005), a version of which is included in this volume, Rick and Jonathan Elmore make the following observation:

> Neoliberalism frames all human interactions as economic choices, choices about how to use one's limited resources to achieve one's desired ends. Significantly this formulation interprets all social life through the singular lens of cost to benefit, as every individual decision becomes an attempt to garner the maximum return on one's "investments" while managing the risk of loss.[5]

The market logic described above is embedded within each of the novels treated below insofar as character actions which do not conform to this logic—that is to say, a logic of self-interest—are often acknowledged as unusual or even nonsensical by the novels' fellow characters or narrator. *All the Pretty Horses* uses the theme of the personal responsibility of the individual toward himself and others both through cases—Lacey Rawlins and John Grady Cole's begrudging responsibility toward the young Jimmy Blevins—and in explicit monologues (e.g., the monologue of Duena Alfonsa on fate and responsibility). *The Crossing* likewise tallies all the actions its protagonists take through a paper trail—receipts, proofs of purchase, *facturas*—weaving the narrative together at the same time as it addresses repeatedly the economic sense of each action taken, whether or not actions fit the neoliberal framework. Finally, *The Road* presents an economy of cannibalism against which the father evaluates his own morality and his capacity to resist his and his child's status as economic subjects in a system he abhors.

Each of these novels is concerned with developing notions of value and exchange while at the same time seeking to establish wards against a totalizing economic ethos. Figures of innocence—such as children and animals—serve to define the outer limits of market logic; their inclusion within it is routinely suggested as immoral and unspeakable. However, in the case of *The Road*, which I will examine first, it is the suffering of the child itself, suspended on the brink between innocence and the crushing market and consumerist logic of the cannibal economy, who reveals the terrifying truth of the economic and social value of the child. Indeed, one of the most chilling undercurrents in the novel is how it reveals the obfuscated status of children as banal economic subjects expected, within neoliberal reason, to produce value.

An early illustration of this dynamic can be found in *The Orchard Keeper* (1965). Although written before the official onset of the neoliberal era, McCarthy's first novel displays inchoate themes of the innocence of children and animals in the face of market logic. When the young John Wesley Rattner finds a wounded hawk, he initially tends to it and feeds it. After its death, John Wesley brings the dead hawk to the courthouse to collect a hawk bounty amounting to a dollar. After the collection, he walks around downtown and contemplates the shops' attractions while fiddling with his reward: "He patted the folded dollar again and started up Gay Street. When he got to the Strand he stopped and studied the pictures advertising the Saturday serial and fingered the quarter."[6] Freshly compensated, by virtue of the animal's death, John Wesley gains a new consumerist perspective on his surroundings. Still, it is important to note that the boy did not kill the hawk immediately but "fed him meat and grasshoppers for three days."[7] As such, the bounty was not John Wesley's first desire and this relationship to the animal will foreshadow his change of mind at the very end of the novel when he returns to the courthouse after the violent events of the narrative to trade the dead hawk back. As John Wesley whispers to himself after he learns that his hawk, along with any other kills brought in, are cremated:

> Burn em? He said. They burn em?
>
> I believe so, she said.
>
> He looked about him vaguely, back to her, still not leaning on or touching the counter. And thow people in jail and beat up on em.
>
> What? She said leaning forward.
>
> And old men in the crazy house.[8]

As a result, John Wesley returns the dollar and declares: "I cain't take no dollar. I made a mistake, he wadn't for sale." By leaving the dollar without receiving anything in return, the boy disturbs the transactional system and withdraws from its purview.

The Road and the Value of the Suffering Child

Building upon this ethos, and moving from McCarthy's first novel to his "last" (ignoring here the 2022 novels) the neoliberalism explored in *The Road* begins with an examination of the genre of post-apocalyptic fiction itself. If science-fiction novels are fertile literary grounds to deploy new thought experiments, new political visions, the post-apocalyptic genre can be seen as fundamentally reactionary—a mode which explores social dynamics that emulate the harshest social Darwinist tendencies of late capitalism. People fight to control dwindling supplies of fuel, food, or water and the losers of that fight are left to die in the wasteland. The genre—and McCarthy's novel—thus postulate the fact that humans will tear each other apart for survival after the apocalypse. The ubiquity of the genre in film and pulp literature in recent years illustrates the notion attributed to Slavoj Žižek and Fredric Jameson, and explored in Mark Fisher's *Capitalist Realism*, that "it is easier to imagine the end of the world than it is to imagine the end of capitalism."[9] In other words, the post-apocalypse does not offer a far-fetched alternative future, demanding an imaginative leap from its audience. It is, rather, a genre which assumes the world it represents to be the only logical or possible future for our society. Even so, the genre is compelling because it asks the human consumer the remarkably simple question: "what would you be prepared to do in order to survive?" Despite the literary recognition it achieved, *The Road* essentially asks this same tired question—the same as any B-movie in the genre. The answer to this question is, of course, couched within the assumption of an "every man for himself" posture that is reminiscent of "Capital's drive towards atomistic individualization."[10] In his seminal book *A Brief History of Neoliberalism*, David Harvey explains how "Neoliberal concern for the individual trumps any social democratic concern for equality, democracy, and social solidarities."[11] It should be apparent by now that the terms "neoliberalism" and "post-apocalypse" could be effortlessly swapped when it comes to social relations. Save for the father and his child, all human relations in *The Road* are transactional, based on gain and loss. The gangs and cults of the novel are alliances in an economic market, the currency of which is human meat.

In the post-apocalypse imagined by McCarthy, the cursors of human morality have drastically shifted into the abject insofar as the last inhabitants of a world in its death throes have resorted to organized cannibalism to survive. The initial premise of the novel presents a terrifying paradox, how to raise and educate a child in a dead world? What place does parental transmission have in a world without either future or basic moral tenets? The suffering of the child in *The Road* serves as an ontological revelator for many social and political dynamics in the post-apocalypse. Indeed, the education of a living child in a dead world constitutes an unsolvable dialectic which challenges the delineations of civilization, humanity, and parenthood. Throughout the narrative, the child will be in turn an object of potential consumption by cannibals, the son of a father ready to kill him rather than seeing him eaten by cannibals and, finally, the moral conscience of the wealthy class as he will beg his father for a fairer allocation of resources when the two come across a trove of food in a fallout shelter. By unwittingly assuming these roles, the figure of the suffering child is used to give new meanings and definitions to several social roles at the end of the world. In that sense, *The Road* is a sacrificial narrative, and it is only through his suffering that the child allows these revelations to emerge.

Several analyses across disciplines have pointed out that the discourse surrounding the death and suffering of children has known a number of shifts throughout the years. Viviana A. Zelizer, for example, demonstrates that the death of a child has not always been confronted with the same manners of grieving, and that child mourning has evolved alongside the development of capitalism:

> Until the eighteenth century in England and in Europe, the death of an infant or a young child was a minor event, met with a mixture of indifference and resignation. As Montaigne remarked, "I have lost two or three children in infancy, not without regret, but without great sorrow."[12]

In the United States, the sacralization of child life and the structural social changes that ensued only emerged after massive movements against child labor gained traction in the early twentieth century. The central thesis of Zelizer's book is that the end of child labor meant that the value of a child shifted from an economic one to a "sentimental" one. "The conflict over the propriety of child labor between 1870 and 1930 in the US involved a profound cultural disagreement over the economic and sentimental value of young children," Zelizer continues. "While opponents of child labor legislation hailed the economic usefulness of children, advocates of child labor legislation campaigned for their uselessness. For reformers, true parental love could only exist if the child was defined exclusively as an object of sentiment and not as an agent of production."[13]

The term "uselessness" needs to be clarified: the shift described here does not mean that children have lost their value when they cease to work, but merely that their value category has shifted. If the sentimental value of a child is economically unquantifiable, it is still strongly defined and socially constructed. Most importantly, a child is *expected* to produce that unquantifiable "use value": "In strict economic terms, children today are worthless to their parents. They are also expensive. The total cost of raising a child—combining both direct maintenance costs and indirect opportunity costs—was estimated in 1980 to average between $100,000 and $140,000. In return for such expenses a child is expected to provide love, smiles, and emotional satisfaction, but no money or labor."[14]

Theoretically, in our times, children are no longer used to yield economic value; in many nations they are prevented by law from both working outside the home and certainly from being sold or exchanged. However, as *The Road* shows, this "prohibition" is only true when the contemporary social contracts are intact. Indeed, McCarthy's novel illuminates the fact that the supposed "pricelessness" of children can be revealed to be an abject fabrication as soon as the social order is disturbed. When the child is being leered at by a salivating cannibal, for example, one of the aspects of the reader's emerging horror is the realization that children have always had an exchange value, that it is possible and even commonplace to turn their pain into a quantifiable profit. As a result, the re-emergence of the *price* of children does not mean that the notion had disappeared in a golden age of humanism and morality, but merely that it is made visible again in times of crisis, returning to haunt a failing social order (as recent events have illustrated, whether Jeffrey Epstein's child trafficking ring or migrant children in detention on the Mexican-American border used as political bargaining chips).

Moreover, in *The Road*, the specter of being eaten alive hangs over the narrative as a fate worse than death. However, considering the larger canon of McCarthy's *oeuvre*, cannibalism should not be understood as the far-fetched avatar of post-apocalyptic fiction since fundamental human taboos occupy a prominent position in McCarthy's novels—necrophilia in *Child of God*, rape and infanticide in *Blood Meridian*, and incest in *Outer Dark*. Rather, in *The Road*, cannibalism is, in a first analysis, employed as the mark of the other. It is the single practice which allows the father to repeat to his son that they are the "good guys." As Andrew Estes explains, "In McCarthy's fiction cannibalism serves as a marker of depravity; anthropophagy becomes the symbol and example of evil."[15] However, I would approach the human/inhuman distinction operated by cannibalism in another manner. Following Zelizer's situation of the shift in the "value" of children from economic to sentimental, I would argue that the specter of child-eating in *The Road* signifies a brutal reversal of this shift and the contemporary return to the economic value of the child.

To understand this shift, we must first observe the fact that, in the world surrounding the father and his child, labor can only take the form of hunting. The earth is irretrievably dead, its ecosystem is annihilated, and any form of agrarian work is hopeless. "Burnt forests for miles along the slopes and snow sooner than he would have thought," McCarthy writes. "No tracks in the road, nothing living anywhere. The fireblackened boulders like the shapes of bears on the starkly wooded slopes."[16] Such a sterile earth can only support scavengers. As a result, the economy of *The Road* weighs everything and everyone against their value as consumer goods. This idea is made particularly obvious in a passage of the novel when the father and his son witness the passing of a caravan of marauders:

> The phalanx following carried spears or lances tasseled with ribbons, the long blades hammered out of trucksprings in some crude forge up-country. The boy lay with his face in his arms, terrified. They passed two hundred feet away, the ground shuddering lightly. Tramping. Behind them came wagons drawn by slaves in harness and piled with goods of war and after that the women, perhaps a dozen in number, some of them pregnant, and lastly a supplementary consort of catamites illclothed against the cold and fitted in dogcollars and yoked each to each. All passed on. They lay listening.[17]

All manners of consumption are illustrated in this passage. If we compare the pregnant women with the "catamites" we understand that if the former may have a reproductive value, or even "agricultural" value as producers of "food," beyond their immediate value as sex slaves, the latter do not. A catamite is a young boy whose purpose is to be sexually consumed by older men. By employing this specific word, the text does not offer any mitigation as to these young persons' roles. The mention of "some crude forge up-country" is also significant, indicating that the only form of industry that has survived in the post-apocalypse is one geared only toward violence. The same goes for the slaves, who are not used as earth-toilers but as beasts of burden, drudging the spoils of pillage. The animating fear of the father is the horror of seeing his child consumed in such a manner. That is why he teaches his son to commit suicide and constantly assesses his own ability to kill his son should the need arise.

Beyond the immediate taboo of child-eating, the return to a state of things where the value of children is made visible is also part of the nature of abjection in *The Road*. This is the meaning behind the mother's last words before she takes her life: "Sooner or later they will catch us and they will kill us. They will rape me. They'll rape him. They are going to rape us and kill us and eat us and you wont face it."[18] Beyond the horrific prospects described, we can read in such lines the fear of being *consumed* writ large, of being considered as consumption goods. In Western literature cannibalism has been used as the fundamental mark of the other, the savage or alien. The cannibals of Herman Melville's work (e.g., *Moby-Dick, Typee*) are "a discursive product of the Western gaze": they serve to establish the frontier between Western civilization and barbarism.[19] However, in *The Road*, cannibals are the uniquely American dregs of Western civilization and are often described as displaying signifiers of Americana. In this respect, the encounter with the straggling cannibal is quite significant:

> He wore a beard that had been cut square across the bottom with shears and he had a tattoo of a bird on his neck done by someone with an illformed notion of their appearance. He was lean, wiry, rachitic. Dressed in a pair of filthy blue coveralls and a black billcap with the logo of some vanished enterprise embroidered across the front of it.[20]

Leaning on a white-working class aesthetic (coveralls, billcap, bird tattoo, company embroidery), McCarthy emphasizes the point that Western pretentions to exceptionalism drawn across the lines of taboo practices (and lines of class and race, to be less parabolic) are sure to crumble after the failing of the social order. Cannibalism no longer delineates the outer wilderness but reveals an inherent American savagery. However, the father is a protagonist who narrates himself and his son *as* protagonists ("the good guys"). Therefore, he must uphold the ontological bifurcation operated by "cannibalism" for this narrative to subsist. Or, as Pollock puts it,

> instead of reinforcing divisions between civilized and savage, normative and deviant, here and there, cannibalism today is typically invoked as a counter-hegemonic trope. One version presents capitalism and colonial-

> ism as the real cannibals. . . . Today "we" are the cannibals, both macro and micro-cosmically, rather than "they"; but this "we" is understood to bear within it the division that formerly constituted the other.[21]

Once again, these observations point out the mechanisms of the central ethos in McCarthy's *oeuvre*: peeling away a civilization's self-narrated veneer to reveal its soiled underbelly. American child-eaters defile the symbolic value of children while effectively erasing the frontier between civilization and wilderness.

The politics of post-apocalyptic fiction are often staunchly reactionary in that social interactions within their world are typically a mere exaggeration of a Hobbesian worldview of all-against-all wherein survivors kill to sustain their own lives. In *The Road*, as in the genre at large, accumulation of goods and wealth grows equal to accumulation of power, solidarity is non-existent, and attempts at community are often only defined by their capacity to withstand or enact violence upon others. In this respect, McCarthy's novel illustrates another function of the suffering child by punctually making him a cursor of morality regarding the allocation of resources.

I have mentioned how the economy of cannibalism puts the notion of *consumption* to the fore of the novel. However, I would like to focus here on a particular passage of the novel that extrapolates the concept of modern humanitarianism into the post-apocalypse. In *The Road*, food is wealth and wealth is scarce, especially for the father and the son who have made the choice to cut themselves off from human meat, the wasteland's foremost resource. At the mid-point of the novel, the pair stumble upon an undiscovered fallout shelter filled with canned goods. They hole up for a few days in the shelter before leaving it, taking as much food as they can carry with them. Of course, this accumulated wealth soon influences their relations with the people they meet and brings ethical questions to the fore, usually raised by the child. In the shelter, the child seems to be the only one concerned with the implications of both gratitude and charity when he asks his puzzled father to thank the absent owners for the goods that allow them to survive:

> Do you think we should thank the people?
> The people?
> The people who gave us all this.
> Well. Yes, I guess we could do that.[22]

Seeing his father confused, the child specifies "the people who gave us all this," suggesting he has a grasp on the inter-relational dimension of the "gift" in question—not to mention sharing—that his father does not. His use of the verb "give" for the situation they are in translates his instinctual belief in the self-evidence of gratitude and charity.

Later, as they are pushing their shopping cart full of canned goods along the road, the father and his son encounter another survivor:

> Late in the day following as they rounded a bend in the road the boy stopped and put his hand on the carriage. Papa, he whispered. The man looked up. A small figure distant on the road, bent and shuffling. He stood leaning on the handle of the grocery cart. Well, he said. Who's this?[23]

McCarthy's language here emphasizes the new relations of power have been created by the cart chock full of food. The father ponders the silhouette while "leaning on the handle of the grocery cart," quite literally considering the scene from the vantage point of his wealth. Even the son seems fearful for their food as he puts "his hand on the carriage." The description of the vagrant emphasizes his stench and raggedness: "He had a filthy towel tied under his jaw as if he suffered from toothache and *even by their new world standards* he smelled terrible."[24] The standards in question serve to establish a class distinction between the protagonists (with a full grocery cart) and the vagrant (lacking possessions and "smelling terrible"). This preliminary exposition makes the critical point that wealth does not exist in a vacuum and must, sooner or later, confront its influence in social relations: in this case, what happens when the *haves* encounter the *have nots*. The first thing to happen in the interaction is the suspicion by the man that the father and son acquired their wealth through treachery.

> I dont have anything, he said. You can look if you want.
> We're not robbers.
> He leaned one ear forward. What? he called.
> I said we're not robbers.
> What are you?
> They'd no way to answer the question.[25]

The implication of the exchange is that so much food could only have been accumulated through theft or coercion. Indeed, the unspoken part of the vagrant's last sentence is probably "what are you if you are not robbers?" The characters' inability to answer raises multiple questions: is there an answer as to whether or not they stole this food? If it was a gift, as the child said, what moral justification can there be for them to avoid sharing what they found?

Under pressure from his son, the father accepts to spare a can of food with the man and immediately proceeds to set limits to further acts of charity:

> What about a spoon?
> He's not getting a spoon.
> The boy turned and looked at him.
> I know what the question is, the man said. The answer is no.
> What's the question?
> Can we keep him. We cant.[26]

It is clear throughout this passage that the father would not have spared any food were it not for his child. His act of charity is an act of goodwill to maintain social peace between parties and not a self-evident humanistic action. Sparing a tin can is a way to maintain the "good guys" narrative at a relatively low cost and avoid social unrest on the part of the son.

I would thus like to argue that the child, at this precise moment, embodies the social impetus behind capitalist humanitarianism. Through his pleas, the father performs an act of minimal charity that will only be temporary and grossly insufficient but will act as a safety valve against an excess of guilt and resentment on the father's behalf, thus preventing the social pressure brought on by his son wherein the child could start questioning the "good guys" narrative and his father's authority. In other words, the father spares a tin can in order to avoid having to spare a dozen with everyone they meet. This fits the description of modern philanthropy, a model critiqued as early as Marx's and Engels's *The Communist Manifesto* and later by Oscar Wilde in "The Soul of Man Under Socialism." When the child convinces the father to give the man more food, the father does not hesitate to specify "I dont think he should have anything" revealing his perspective toward humanitarianism. It is not something he wants to do, or even feels compelled to do, but something he does to keep the child content.[27] When the child has convinced him to stay the night with the vagrant and even cook for him, the father replies:

> All right, he said. But then tomorrow we go on.
> The boy didnt answer.
> That's the best deal you're going to get.
> Okay.
> Okay means okay. It doesnt mean we negotiate another deal tomorrow.
> What's negotiate?
> It means talk about it some more and come up with some other deal.
> There is no other deal. This is it.[28]

This exchange confirms that the only purpose of the charitable act is to prevent further charitable acts and the entire passage reproduces the dynamics of humanitarianism at a miniature scale: a negligible gesture on the part of the ruling class to forestall potential dissent among its subjects. This is the meaning behind the sentence "There is no other deal"; the father explicitly states the purpose of his meager contribution. The fact that the gesture is initiated through the child's protest illuminates another point, illustrated by Lee Edelman's argument that the "Child remains the perpetual horizon of every acknowledged politics."[29] Indeed, it befalls the child of *The Road* to incarnate and voice the guilty conscience of accumulated wealth.

Transaction as Lingua Franca in *All the Pretty Horses* and *The Crossing*

Contrary to *The Road*, the first two novels of McCarthy's Border Trilogy spend their opening pages in search of their reason to move southward. *All the Pretty Horses* uses an American bildungsroman motif to move its characters across the border: the search for good, honest work. This original impetus is one of the reasons why the narrative of the first book is often considered much more streamlined and less disjointed than its sequel. It is, after all, a story initially built on a quest for self-interest and personal growth, familiar literary grounds. The original motivations of John Grady Cole and Lacey Rawlins dictate how they interact with the people they meet as well as their environment. Indeed, one of the repeated motifs of the novel is the use of transaction as a transnational *lingua franca* by the characters—one that while often misused, out of place, or misunderstood is repeatedly commented upon and pondered throughout the novel by its increasingly "economized" neoliberal subjects.

An early interaction between the boys and a Mexican caravan will serve as a first illustration of this phenomenon:

> They tried to buy water from the caravans but they had no coin among them small enough with which to do so. When Rawlins offered a man fifty centavos for the half pennysworth of water it would take to fill their canteens the man would have no part of it.[30]

Although it will appear clearer to the characters later on in the novel that not everything has a price in the country they traverse, and that barter and hospitality are still in effect, it is meaningful that the narrative voice itself chooses a monetary value "a half pennysworth" to define the amount of water needed. The refusal of the man to partake in a monetary exchange for water comes as a polite rebuttal to the transactional nature of the interaction, to the logic of self-interest as he could very well have extorted them for the smallest coin they had. The passage also suggests the two young boys as unwitting avatars of US imperialism insofar as the currency used by McCarthy to describe an amount of water on foreign soil is the American penny. Thus, the narration upholds the US dollar as the international reserve currency as established by the Bretton-Woods agreement signed a few years before the events in the novel.

Once in prison, the two protagonists find themselves among a closed society regimented almost exclusively by transactions:

> The fourth day was Sunday and they bought clothes with Blevins's money and they bought a bar of soap and took showers and they bought a can of tomato soup and heated it in the can over a candlestub. . . .[31]

During his confrontation with the influential prisoner Perez, John Grady tries to argue his way out of paying protection money to him only to be reminded, brutally, that one cannot simply wish away one's condition as an economic subject:

> Some people don't have a price.
> That is true.
> What about those people?
> Those people die.[32]

If Perez's line is first and foremost a veiled threat, it is also a warning against the hubris of the economic subject who may consider disputing his status as a neoliberal subject. In other words, even in a Mexican prison those who remove themselves from the economy serve no purpose to it and are bound to be purged. From Perez's point of view, nothing is allowed to exist outside the market lest it should become a threat to it. Perez's reduction of all relations to economic transactions is pushed even further when he mocks the concept of tainted money:

> Americans have this problem always I believe. They talk about tainted money. But money doesnt have this special quality. And the Mexican would never think to make things special or to put them in a special place where money is not used. Why do this? If money is good money is good.

> He doesnt have bad money. He doesnt have this problem. This abnormal thought.[33]

A few parallels can be gleaned from this passage. As financial instruments became more complex in capitalism's route toward its ultimate neoliberal form, Marx's notion of "commodity fetishism"—the belief that goods and commodities possess an inherent economic and relational value—came to be applied to money itself; the idea that the neutral entity "money" could be qualified as *good* or *tainted* is the result of such fetishism. This form of money fetishism is what Perez points out in this passage is a typically American artifact. Furthermore, the terms *dirty* or *tainted* money conjure a lexical field attached to drug-running and its heyday in the 1980s when American hegemony expanded by drawing specific moral lines around economic exchange. Arms sale and drug-running became criminal fixtures in film and television a decade after Richard Nixon launched his war on drugs; and under Ronald Reagan, America furthered its imperialist role as the moral arbiter of which kind of money and exchange were legitimate and which were tainted (even as the nation was busy compromising its own rhetoric publicly in the Iran-Contra scandal).

At the same time, Perez mocks the use of money "where money is not used," alluding to capital holding or speculation, complex and abstract practices which seem alien to the hyper-concentrated prison context where all economic exchanges are immediate and "zero-sum." As such, he deems it "abnormal" to attribute an exceptional quality to money, to establish a system of morality on money. Herman E. Daily explored this notion, writing that,

> Money fetishism is a particular case of what Alfred North Whitehead called "the fallacy of misplaced concreteness," which consists in reasoning at one level of abstraction but applying the conclusions of that reasoning to a different level of abstraction. . . . Marx, and Aristotle before him, pointed out that the danger of *money fetishism* arises as a society progressively shifts its focus from *use value* to *exchange value*, under the pressure of increasingly complex division of labor and exchange.[34]

In this sense, the journey of John Grady and Rawlins, spurred on by the search for good, honest work, is at several points confronted by the abstraction of their economic understanding of the world.

Another such confrontation happens when they come upon a group of men asking them to buy the young Blevins: "The man in the vest studied John Grady and he looked across the clearing at Blevins. Then he asked John Grady if he wished to sell the boy."[35] In the same way the father in *The Road* was confronted with an abject dimension of the economy wherein both he and his child were commodities in a cannibal world, here John Grady is presented by the matter-of-fact prospect of slavery as a simple economic exchange. Here again, John Grady attempts to imprint a morality system on the interaction in order to preserve himself from cold economic reality: "They did not look evil but it was no comfort to him."[36] Indeed the abject nature of the offer resides in the fact that he cannot resolve it in a moral abstraction, by perceiving the slavers as evil. They are simply attempting to engage in a transaction motivated by basic self-interested motivations, as it is with all transactions. As with *The Road*, there is an impetus, following this traumatic interaction, to protect the youngest from the reality of the economic system. We can see this attempt to protect youth when John Grady admonishes Rawlins after he reveals to Blevins what just occurred: "He wanted to buy you. . . . What did you go and tell him that for? said John Grady. There wasnt no call to do that."[37] Contact with the harshest finalities of a capitalist economic system spurs on a need in McCarthy's characters to protect the weakest among them, to keep them outside of transactional discourse.

From this moment on, until Blevins's death, the pair will wrestle with their responsibility toward him. When the young man is arrested for the theft of his own horse, Cole and Rawlins will contentiously argue whether they should rescue him, Rawlins believing they owe Blevins nothing. His point of view is one of a strictly rational economic subject. He has no relation to Blevins, kinship bond or otherwise, which would justify risking life and limb for him. To return to the Elmores' observations: "the neoliberal anthropology of competition extends economic relations to every aspect of individual action and reduces all choice and decision-making to the common denominator of risk management."[38] Thus should readers understand that the novel puts into play two different sorts of responsibility: A responsibility toward others, disinterested and selfless, emanating from a social contract; and a neoliberal definition of responsibility which only concerns itself with the choices and risks taken by an economic subject.

This second aspect emerges most saliently in *The Crossing* when, upon his return to the United States after losing his brother, the penniless and hungry Billy Parham attempts to enlist in the US Army. Here, McCarthy shifts his protagonist's trajectory from the promise of the open country, as in *All the Pretty Horses*, to the narrow treadmill of a prospect as a military grunt, trading one's freedom for bread: the initial process comes with the promise of a meal voucher that Billy, in that moment, sorely needs. These transactions outline the shape of neoliberal reason insofar as the exchange between Billy and the government is his life and limb for a meal voucher and one of the only forms of employment available to him. From a narrow economic viewpoint, which would take into its purview an exchange between two decontextualized entities, Billy is indeed making this decision of his own free will, as the Elmores explain, under neoliberal logic: "Individuals are free to do whatever they want but are necessarily responsible for each and every choice. This is . . . the heart of the 'biopolitics' of neoliberalism, no longer governing through explicit control of peoples' actions but through the manipulation of the horizon of possible."[39]

Of course, Billy's attempt is absolutely forced by hunger and the utter reduction of his "horizon of possible." The young and free bildungsromaneer reckons with the brutal truth of his position as the subject of a state deploying its military might into a war that will midwife its status as a modern imperialist superpower—in ways that will disempower the Mexican peasants who had more than once saved his and his brother's lives no less. The exchange of Billy's body for basic sustenance, metonymized by the meal voucher, is the state enforcing its sovereignty upon its subjects' bodies. At this moment, Billy experiences Achille Mbembe's concept of "necropolitics" wherein "the ultimate expression of sovereignty resides, to a large degree, in the power and the capacity to dictate who may live and who must die. Hence, to kill or to allow to live constitute the limits of sovereignty, its fundamental attributes. To exercise sovereignty is to exercise control over mortality and to define life as the deployment and manifestation of power."[40] By offering to be Billy's provider through a supposedly free and voluntary transaction, the state aims to extend its sovereignty upon his body and become the arbiter of his life and death.

Throughout *All the Pretty Horses* and *The Crossing*, transactions and exchanges are recorded through a series of receipts, proofs of purchase, *papeles*, and *facturas*. A thematic emphasis is placed on such a paper trail maintaining a truthful record of commerce and of events. Proofs of purchase for horses, identity papers, and death certificates are mentioned and required throughout the narrative to establish ownership and responsibility. This is especially true when Billy returns to the United States where relations are even more transactional. When the server in a diner offers him breakfast upon his return, it comes with the caveat—"Don't tell nobody where you got it"—suggesting that should the free meal become public knowledge, the destitute would swarm the place, throwing a wrench in the normal course of commerce.[41] However, the army recruiter is very quick to suggest Billy should forge his mother's signature on the form: "I guess you want me to sign my dead mama's name on that piece of paper," to which the recruiter responds "I didnt say that."[42] He did not need to "say that," of course; as an extension of the sovereign, the recruiter's power over Billy is self-evident.

Here, the representative of the US government demonstrates how the supposed propriety of notarial truth can be completely dismissed when it comes to matters of American hegemony. American sovereignty extends, that is, to Billy's body and to his family history, both of which are potentially used, shaped, and warped at will even as the illusion of propriety and the legality of the process crumbles. Of course, as it turns out, the only commodity Billy Parham has left to sell—his own body—is spoiled goods for the military as a preliminary medical exam reveals a heart murmur which bars him from enlisting. Upon hearing the diagnosis, Billy eructs: "If I'm going to die anyway why not use me?" fully acting his willingness to become the subject of the sovereign entity and its "work of death," as Mbembe put it.[43] The rules of commerce dictate that his possible death would be wasted if it did not produce any economic value, did not contribute to the gross domestic product.

Even so, the two border novels seem to posit certain entities as exempt from the realm of commerce and transaction, or at least they suggest that their inclusion within it would represent an abjection. This is certainly the case for Blevins: the specter of his enslavement tests the outer limits of the transactional system and delineates the borders of morality around it. However, the novels also use animals in a comparable way. Both suggest at different points that they represent atavistic spirits of pre-capitalist society who must be brought within the fold of capitalism. The first example of this resides in the description of the practice of horse-breaking:

> By midmorning eight of the horses stood tied and the other eight were wilder than deer, scattering along the fence and bunching and running in a rising sea of dust as the day warmed, coming to reckon slowly with the remorselessness of this rendering of their fluid and collective selves into that condition of separate and helpless paralysis which seemed to be among them like a creeping plague . . . all communion among them broken.[44]

The passage describes the breaking of the "fluid" collective in its natural state in order to make its individual components fit for purpose. The description of the practice is quite explicit regarding its methods and is in line with

David Harvey's observation that "The neoliberal state is necessarily hostile to all forms of social solidarity that put restraints on capital accumulation."[45] The long and detailed descriptions of horse-breaking in the novel are indeed very much in line with Harvey's description of the neoliberal ethos of social atomization wherein a united and integrated group is to be broken up into obedient monads. Modern managerial methods, union busting, and the mythmaking of individual success are all avatars of this long-observed trend. By the time Cole's and Rawlins's task is done, "The wild and frantic band of mustangs that had circled the potrero that morning like marbles swirled in a jar could hardly be said to exist."[46] From the vantage point of this extract we understand that the "wild" state of untamed animals defines their unfitness for human purpose and, by extension, their inability to produce value—elements of the American garden under the gaze of the machine, to borrow from Leo Marx.[47]

As we already saw in *The Orchard Keeper*, then, McCarthy's novels often establish animals as belonging to the outer perimeter of the transactional system and observe what occurs when they are brought into it or close to its border. This is also the case of the wolf in *The Crossing.* Billy Parham's trek during the haunting first chapter of the novel is punctuated by interactions with people trying to make sense of the wild animal the young man has in tow. One such early interaction opens with befuddlement—"Well Billy this might sound like a ignorant question but what in the hell are you doin with that thing?"[48]—but soon drifts into talk of commerce:

> What would you take for her cash money? he said.
> She aint for sale.
> What would you take if she was?
> I wouldnt. Cause she aint.[49]

No further explanation is given by the older rancher as to what he would or could do with a wolf. The interaction seems almost automatic, as if the strange situation must be decrypted through an exchange value which again serves here as a hermeneutic tool, a *lingua franca,* and another example of commodity fetishism. Even an animal which can be of no productive use must be brought—if only discursively—into the meaning-making system of the market. Things and beings must be deciphered through their price point and, as such, the man's offer seems like a reflex. Time and again throughout his journey, the people Billy encounters will similarly attempt to make sense of the wolf in terms of transaction and possession. Soon after the exchange with the rancher, McCarthy offers the following description: "The wolf was wearing a harnessleather dogcollar with a brass plate that had the rancher's name and [Rural Free Delivery] number and Cloverdale [New Mexico] stamped into it."[50] Here, the wolf is symbolically branded and identified as property. The subject of her ownership and commodification returns later when she is "seized as contraband."[51] The initial impetus for Billy's cross-border trek is never formulated in terms of gain and risk, as a result it becomes impossible to communicate except in those terms. The closer the novel gets to the conclusion of its first chapter, the more the wolf is commodified, seized, exchanged until becoming a paying attraction, therefore producing value. After her killing, Billy trades her remains for his rifle and the narration makes a final comment on the value of the wolf's body: "[The rifle] was worth a dozen mutilated wolfhides."[52] Upon her death, the transformation of the wolf into a commodity is complete and she is successfully and forcefully incorporated into the transactional system. On this point, Paul Auster's notion that "In life, a man and his body are synonymous; in death, there is the man and there is his body" is worth repeating. As Auster adds, "We say, 'this is the body of X,' as if this body, which had once been the man himself, not something that represented him or belonged to him, but the very man called X, were suddenly of no importance."[53] This separation is observable in McCarthy's discursive transformation of the *wolf* into *wolfhide*. Adopting the language of transaction, the narrative then describes Billy's effort to rescue the body of the wolf from becoming an object of transaction, to bury it and mourn it rather than seeing it used as a value-producing commodity.

Toward the end of the novel, Billy comes upon some road agents. During the violent encounter, one of the agents stabs Billy's horse out of anger and frustration. The senselessness of the act is noted both by the narrative voice—"Before anyone would have thought of such a thing occurring he plunged his knife into the horse's chest"[54]—and the other road agents: "The leader told him to get his horse. He said that he did not need his knife and that he had killed a good horse for no reason."[55] The explicitly senseless aspect of the act is clarified by the term "a good horse" meaning a horse that could produce use or exchange value. Here again, it is the value attributed to an object or a subject that dictates the meaning of actions taken. This theme is advanced later when Billy is unsure whether the horse will live and encounters the taciturn "gypsy." Eventually, the gypsy "asked Billy if he wanted to sell the horse and Billy knew for the first time that the horse would live."[56] What was not discussed up until this point is revealed through a potential transaction. Since the gypsy senses the horse will live, the animal recovers its status as a commodity and can be spoken about once again. The *lingua franca* of transaction returns to structure and even allow speech. As with many other instances throughout the two novels, only what can be exchanged can be measured, valued, or comprehended. Or, as Harvey put it, neoliberalism "holds that the social good will be maximized by maximizing the reach and frequency of market transactions, and it seeks to bring all human action into the domain of the market."[57]

One aftereffect of the Faulknerian literary tradition within which McCarthy's *oeuvre* is inscribed is its "behaviorist" roots and rigorous adherence to external focalization—avoiding the urge to explore characters' interiors. The result of such an aesthetic, though is that alternate systems of meaning are needed to replace the reader's access to characters' psychology, motivations, and interior. As we have seen, the second half of McCarthy's bibliography often takes advantage of value, transaction, and market logic—that is, neoliberal discourse itself—as one such system of meaning. In other words, replacing any internal focalization—or the first-person narrator who translates a character's sense of the world—is the chronic emphasis of the monetary, use value, or social value of *things*. This process, in itself, can be read as a revelator of the commodity fetishism ingrained in the global imagination of the modern neoliberal subject. Such an aesthetic results in the delineation of a market domain with both its own language and borders that can threaten to confront whoever crosses them with a ghastly truth about the system to which they are subject—commodification, slavery, or cannibalism. In the end, characters' actions can only be understood within the domain of the market because the nature of neoliberalism dictates that it become the totality of the human experience.

Notes

1. Michel Foucault, *The Birth of Biopolitics: Lectures at the Collège de France, 1978–79*, trans. Graham Burchell (New York: Palgrave-MacMillan, 2008).

2. Francis Fukuyama, *The End of History and the Last Man* (1996; repr. New York: Free Press, 2006).

3. Jason Read, "A Genealogy of Homo-Economicus: Neoliberalism and the Production of Subjectivity," *Foucault Studies* 6 (2009): 25–36.

4. See Cormac McCarthy, *All the Pretty Horses* (1992; repr. New York: Vintage, 1993); *The Crossing* (1994; repr. New York: Vintage, 1995); and *The Road* (New York: Vintage, 2006).

5. Jonathan Elmore and Rick Elmore, "Human Become Coin: Neoliberalism, Anthropology,

and Human Possibilities in *No Country for Old Men*," *The Cormac McCarthy Journal* 14, no. 2 (2016): 168–85.

6. See Cormac McCarthy, *The Orchard Keeper* (1965; repr. New York: Vintage, 1993), 78–80.

7. Ibid., 77.

8. Ibid., 233.

9. Mark Fisher, *Capitalist Realism: Is There No Alternative?* (2008; repr. Hampshire, U.K.: Zero Books, 2014), 2.

10. Ibid., 37.

11. David Harvey, *A Brief History of Neoliberalism* (Oxford: Oxford UP, 2007), 176.

12. Viviana A. Zelizer, *Pricing the Priceless Child: The Changing Social Value of Children* (Princeton: Princeton UP, 1994), 24.

13. Ibid., 72.

14. Ibid., 3.

15. Andrew Estes, "Cannibalism and other Transgressions of the Human in *The Road*," *European Journal of American Studies* 12, no. 3 (2017): parag. 19, accessed 1 July 2024, https://journals.openedition.org/ejas/12368.

16. McCarthy, *The Road*, 29–30.

17. Ibid., 91–92.

18. Ibid., 56.

19. Greg Pollock, "The Cannibal-Animal Complex in Melville, Marx, and Beyond," *Humanimalia* 2, no. 1 (2010): 9–31, accessed 1 July 2024, https://humanimalia.org/article/view/10091.

20. McCarthy, *The Road*, 63.

21. Pollock, "The Cannibal-Animal Complex," 10.

22. McCarthy, *The Road*, 145.

23. Ibid., 161.

24. Ibid., emphasis added.

25. Ibid., 162.

26. Ibid., 163.

27. Ibid., 165.

28. Ibid.

29. Lee Edelman, *No Future: Queer Theory and the Death Drive* (Durham: Duke UP, 2004), 3.

30. McCarthy, *Pretty Horses*, 66.

31. Ibid., 183.

32. Ibid., 193.

33. Ibid., 195.

34. Herman E. Daly, *Beyond Growth: The Economics of Sustainable Development* (Boston: Beacon Press, 1996), 38.

35. McCarthy, *Pretty Horses*, 76.

36. Ibid.

37. Ibid., 77.

38. Jonathan and Rick Elmore, "Human Become Coin," 170.

39. Ibid., 172.

40. J. A. Mbembe and Libby Meintjes, "Necropolitics," *Public Culture* 15, no. 1 (2003): 11–40.

41. McCarthy, *The Crossing*, 335.

42. Ibid., 336.

43. Mbembe and Meintjes, "Necropolitics," 341.

44. McCarthy, *Pretty Horses*, 104–5.

45. Harvey, *Brief History*, 75.

46. McCarthy, *Pretty Horses*, 107.

47. See Leo Marx, *The Machine in the Garden: Technology and the Pastoral Ideal in America* (New York: Oxford UP, 1964).

48. McCarthy, *The Crossing*, 66.

49. Ibid., 70.

50. Ibid., 72.

51. Ibid., 99.

52. Ibid., 124.

53. Paul Auster, *The Invention of Solitude* (1982; repr. London: Penguin, 1988), 12.

54. McCarthy, *The Crossing*, 396.

55. Ibid., 397.

56. Ibid., 402.

57. Harvey, *Brief History*, 3.

3
HUNGER
Cormac McCarthy, Land Use, and Ethical Consumption in the Face of Biodisaster

Lydia R. Cooper

In an undated letter to Guy Davenport, Cormac McCarthy mentions that he met Davenport's friend "Steven Gould" at a meeting with other MacArthur Fellows.[1] Stephen Jay Gould, one of the MacArthur Fellows class of 1981, was, in McCarthy's opinion, "An interesting man but a thoroughgoing materialist. An explainer, in short."[2] McCarthy's dismissive characterization of Gould as a "thoroughgoing materialist" raises an interesting question: What would evolutionary biology look like *not* in the hands of "an explainer"? And couldn't McCarthy be likewise charged? For rich as they are with scientific detail—from exhaustively researched gunshot wounds to notes on the "organic" production of gunpowder to whale song systems—McCarthy's novels have often been classed as literary naturalism, not just because of their attention to the natural world in all its material manifestations but also because they present a grim assessment of human nature as a function of biological instincts characterized by aggression and predation.[3] Even so, as much his literary style is indebted to the aesthetic and thematic traditions of American naturalism, McCarthy's corpus—shot through as it is with a sense of mystery and an apprehension of meaning—cannot be explained simply through scientific knowledge of the material world.[4]

The dominant forces in McCarthy's fiction are, of course, obdurately opposed to any sense of the world as mysterious, as essentially "other"; these forces represent a type of scientific knowledge, mechanical expertise, and philosophy of work that seeks to classify and organize in order to dominate, use, and control human and nonhuman others. The interdependence of sovereign species, of beings utterly different yet utterly essential in their freedom and flourishing, is anathema. For instance, Judge Holden, that brutal avatar of *Blood Meridian, or the Evening Redness in the West* (1985), calls the "freedom of birds . . . an insult" to him.[5] Holden's philosophy looms large over McCarthy's corpus, offering a justification for the consequences of human enterprises that have devastated human and animal populations, ecosystems, and the biosphere. Yet against the attention-grabbing rhetorical flourishes of the Judge in *Blood Meridian*, or Anton Chigurh in *No Country for Old Men* (2005), McCarthy also presents characters who seek and express a different sort of relationship with the natural world, one that is non-materialist. These characters—exemplified by John Wesley Rattner in *The Orchard Keeper* (1965), Billy Parham and John Grady Cole in the Border Trilogy, the man and boy in *The Road* (2006), and Bobby and Alicia Western in his latest duology, *The Passenger* and *Stella Maris* (2022)—understand humans as one species among many in a living, interdependent natural world. Unlike Holden or Chigurh, these characters express a different sort of relationship to other creatures—human and non—and to the living world itself. In a particularly illuminating line from McCarthy's unpublished screenplay *Whales and Men*, protagonist John Western says of humanity, "I believe that we are arks of the covenant and our true nature is not rage or deceit or terror or logic or craft or even sorrow. It is longing."[6] This longing characterizes the characters noted immediately above as people who yearn for healthy and bioregionally sustainable communities; express gratitude toward ancestors, the divine, or the universe generally; or quite simply express awe, a sense of wonder that defies the capacity of human language to codify.

Taken as a whole, McCarthy's fiction dramatizes how post-industrial societies, and the US specifically, have turned science and engineering into the mechanization of war (*The Orchard Keeper* and *Blood Meridian*); engaged in exploitation and decimation of natural and nonrenewable resources resulting in species extinctions, aridification, and the collapse of the social (*Blood Me-*

ridian, *The Crossing* [1994] and *Cities of the Plain* [1998]); and mass produced cheaply-made goods that both create epidemics of trash and metaphorically have "trashed" both ecosystems (*The Road* and *The Counselor* [2013]) and economic communities in the developed world (*The Passenger*). With all of this in mind, this essay will focus on these latter two points: exploitative land use resulting in species extinctions and aridification, and consumer culture resulting in "trashed" ecosystems. More specifically, this chapter will focus its analysis on the Border Trilogy, *The Counselor* and *The Road*, and *The Passenger* and *Stella Maris* to trace this through-line in McCarthy's corpus, focusing attention on how this theme has developed and flourished in his later works especially.

What this analysis reveals is that against the sometimes overwhelming violence toward and destruction of other living species in McCarthy's fiction, glimpses of characters who demonstrate a capacity to imagine and live out healthier and more sustainable lifestyles persist as counterpoints to the violence of McCarthy's "thoroughgoing materialists." It is true that these individuals and communities are largely imaginary, glimpsed but never given sustained description in McCarthy's works; one thinks of the possibly real, possibly non-cannibalistic family the boy meets at the end of *The Road*, for example. The ability of people to be and do better, in other words, remains just an idea, a hope. Still, this hope does recur, expressing a desperate yearning for better ways of living, a longing for a map of a world becoming rather than ending. McCarthy's fiction, in other words, draws attention to the radical nature of hope through literally and literarily hungering for alternatives to human aggression and predation.

Land Use and Matrices of Being in *The Crossing* and *Cities of the Plain*

The Border Trilogy as a whole pays exquisite attention to land use and its geopolitical, economic, and moral implications. I want to first turn my attention to this theme in *The Crossing* and *Cities of the Plain*, the least studied of the Trilogy's novels. *The Crossing* opens with a scene that establishes land use as its focus, with a young Billy Parham mapping his father's lands for his little brother, Boyd. His father's goal is to settle the "new country" to which they have recently arrived. When the Parham family first moves to New

Mexico, "You could ride clear to Mexico and not strike a crossfence."[7] But as the boys' father fences property for his grazing cattle, Billy learns to map the landscape, identifying property by claims of human ownership, both private and public. When he sets a trap for wolves to clear the land of a predator species and protect the newly introduced cattle, the narrator describes Billy "holding the trap at eyelevel" as if "truing some older, some subtler instrument. Astrolabe or sextant. Like a man bent at fixing himself in the world."[8] Billy is here "fixing" himself to a physical space, to a pattern and practice of land use, and to an entire way of being in the world—a method of living that brings with it certain ramifications for other species in that world.

Billy's ranching family's use of the land, however, is swiftly juxtaposed with another type of land use: that of the Mexican gray wolf. When a she-wolf is arrested by one of Billy's father's traps, Billy decides to release her into Mexico, a decision that will reverberate throughout his life. The she-wolf represents boundaryless land use. Rather than reading the world as a flattened map demarcated by boundary lines, the wolf transgresses human mappings in her inhabitation of a world she reads as a "matrix."[9] The wolf, for example, "crossed the international boundary line" between Arizona and Sonora into the San Luis mountains; later, when she dies, Billy holds the wolf's body and imagines her "running in the mountains, running in the starlight where the grass was wet and the sun's coming as yet had not undone the rich matrix of creatures passed in the night before her. Deer and hare and dove and groundvole all richly empaneled on the air for her delight, all nations of the possible world ordained by God of which she was one among and not separate from."[10] The wolf's world is three-dimensional, a matrix made of scents and species above and below and around her. The language of use value (that the wolf's being is interdependently connected to use of other species) is paired here with language of pleasure: prey species are "empaneled . . . for her delight." Earlier, Billy has imagined wolves "running in the whiteness of that high world as perfect to their use as if their counsel had been sought in the devising of it."[11] The wolf's perspective of the world, imaginatively revealed, challenges the American ranchers' ethos, suggesting that Billy's father's world is inimical to the wolf's.

In "Predator Politics," Mary Louisa Capelli studies anti-coyote rhetoric, the cascade effects of human predation on coyotes in North America, and how Barbara Kingsolver and Edward Abbey's fiction "articulate a biocentric worldview rooted in a politics of interconnectivity, which admonishes us that keystone predators not only contribute to the biodiversity of our environment, but are integral species in the maintenance of sustainable ecosystems."[12] Because coyote populations have deleterious short term effects on human populations—encroaching into farms, ranches, and suburbs and killing livestock and pets—significant anti-coyote rhetoric characterizes much of the discussion of human-coyote interactions, rather than creative language imagining more sustainable human communities that encroach less on coyote territory. McCarthy's treatment of the Mexican gray wolf in *The Crossing* functions similarly to Kingsolver's and Abbey's, not surprisingly given McCarthy's relationship with Ed Abbey and their conversations on the question of gray wolves and their possible reintroduction into Arizona and New Mexico.[13]

In addition to describing the interconnected "matrix" of life from the perspective of a predator species that perceives the world in terms of its proximities and possibilities rather than changing or erasing its geographic features and its many interconnected species, McCarthy also dramatizes exploitative land use and its aridification of the southwest in *Cities of the Plain.* In that novel, John Grady discusses with "old man Johnson" the tenuous future of Mac's ranch, and of ranching itself, in the western Texas and eastern New Mexican basin experiencing ongoing drought. Johnson explains that even the recent good rains will not be enough to rehydrate the Tularosa basin; in the end, "folks . . . might be glad to let the army have it."[14] The Tularosa basin in the Chihuahua mountain range east of the Rio Grande is where various streams flow in, but not out, creating what was at one point lush grasslands populated by the nomadic Apache nation until about 1850, when the region was claimed by US troops. After American settlement, non-indigenous cattle over-grazed the grassland it until dried out; ranchers drilled into the aquifer for more water and eventually emptied that too, over-salinating the region as a result. Given the subsequent devaluation of this property, the US Army purchased part of the basin and created what is now the White Sands Missile Range. This is the wider context in which Billy leaves Mac's ranch after John Grady's death by the Trilogy's end. The narrator explains that Billy quits ranching altogether when drought strikes Texas, after which point he works as an extra in a film in El Paso; when money dries up there, he travels west through Arizona.[15] The significance of Billy's departure, then, is explained by his shift from working at the ranch to nomadic labor across a bioregion, suggesting that Billy's life describes the Trilogy's answer to the ecological disaster wrought by empires in the American southwest and in Mexico. Indeed, throughout the entire Border Trilogy, McCarthy's prose persistently draws attention to the need for proper land use as part of an ethical commitment to communal wellbeing that considers nonhuman as well as human life, that understands being in terms of three-dimensional matrices rather than flat maps.

Trash and Hunger in *The Counselor* and *The Road*

Along such lines, two of McCarthy's more recent texts, *The Counselor* and *The Road*, examine the consequences of consumer capitalism and hope for a more sustainable future. As I have argued elsewhere, McCarthy's screenplay The Counselor is one of his most direct meditations on the human costs of not merely late capitalism but neoliberalism as a rationality.[16] In *The Counselor*, a lawyer from Texas, the narrative's eponymous lead, enters into a business deal with a drug dealer named Reiner and his partner Malkina. After the deal goes wrong, the counselor finds himself on the losing end of a vicious international game that ends with Reiner and the counselor's fiancée—along with many others—dead and a swaggering Malkina absconding to Hong Kong. Not surprisingly, capitalist excess is represented primarily through the obvious visual metaphors of predation—as in Malkina's hunting cats—and trash. Jacob Agner calls The Counselor a "trashy spectacle," and claims that the narrative's emphases on garbage form the film's visual argument about the excesses of late capitalism.[17] In addition to the sewage truck and the garbage trucks featured at key plot points, one of the final images in the screenplay is a landfill outside Juárez filled with "nameless trash"; as a garbage truck empties yet more trash into the landfill, the dead body of the protagonist's love interest "appears briefly and then disappears," swallowed into the morass of consumed goods.[18] The counselor's search for profit has literally trashed his love.

While thin metaphorically, *The Counselor*'s arguments are extensions of *The Road*'s examination of the problematic ethics of consumption in a neoliberal capitalist milieu. Even more explicitly than *The Crossing*, *The Road* turns the language of maps and matrices into metaphors for ethics and resource consumption. Using his "tattered oilcompany roadmap," the father "stud[ies] the twisted matrix of routes in red and black with his finger at the junction of where he thought they might be."[19] His obsession with finding himself on a now defunct map of roads and transportation routes is a metaphorical search for a way of locating himself in a functional grid of human society, also now obsolete. In response to his father's obsession with the map, the boy says, "We could go back. . . . It's not so far. It's not too late."[20] The ironic overlay of this dialogue, of course, is that the father is playing out those words mentally as he imagines a previous time and place, his family, and his ancestral home.

The son, by contrast, is obsessing over a boy he believes the pair have abandoned to violence on the road. "It's not too late" to save others and create a new form of human society, argues the son. But no oilcompany map can locate his imagined world, and it is the tension between the father's two-dimensional mapping of the world and the son's hunger for a richer matrix of interdependent life that drive the book's confrontation with the costs of consumer capitalism in this post-apocalyptic imagining of a world ended either by nuclear war or fossil fuel-driven climate collapse.

In a study for the National Library of Medicine, Alexander Leaf describes the effects of nuclear winter on food webs and human communities. "The early death of millions of humans and animals following a major nuclear war would not sufficiently compensate for the reduced available food supplies," Leaf writes.[21] *The Road*, as many scholars have noted, accurately depicts a possible scenario for a post-nuclear winter, with some exceptions. The most glaring moment of artistic license McCarthy seems to have taken with otherwise consistent research is the survival of human communities, however reduced, when there appear to be no other animals, even small burrowing animals such as voles, and no insects. Likely models suggest instead that arthropods and small vertebrates especially would survive nuclear winter better than human populations would. In an analysis of the depiction of species extinction in *The Road*, Sean Hermanson notes that, biologically speaking, "the bedrock of the food chain is surprisingly difficult to kill off."[22] Hermanson suggests that glimpses of regenerating vegetative life in *The Road* should therefore be taken seriously, though he doesn't address the remarkable fact of human survival in a world where fungi struggle to persist. How is it that the man and boy wander a world without a single cicada yet manage to run into several other humans? In *The Road*, in other words, all food is artifact or remnant (a can of soda, a tin of peaches), save human flesh. This is not sound science, based on predictive models of nuclear winter. Why, then, does McCarthy reduce the world that will survive to humans and the laws of consumption, to questions of cannibalism or feeding off the finite remnants of lost food webs?

The forced amplification of starvation drives the novel's focus on hunger, consumption, and cannibalism. The words "hunger" and "hungry" appear twenty-two times in the novel. Readers are introduced to the father and his son, their world reduced to ash and blacktop, and are given a summary of their quest in this way: "They ate sparingly and they were hungry all the time."[23] But hungry or not, the pair resist cannibalism. Even more than refraining from eating other people, the boy shows a remarkable resilience to the sensation of hunger and an overriding ethical principle. When they find a cache of food, for example, the boy prays to the absent people to thank them for their food: "We know you saved it for yourself and if you were here we wouldn't eat it no matter how hungry we were."[24] As I have elsewhere argued, the boy's ethic is not a testament to his inherent goodness, or anything quite so simple.[25] Rather, McCarthy's novel tests the limits and possibilities of human altruism against the reality of human tendencies toward consumption, exploitation, and aggression.

Indeed, several scholars have paid sustained attention to the critique of capitalism coded into the novel. Jordan Dominy argues that *The Road*'s representations of human comestibles stand for the world that came before the apocalypse: all the signposts from earlier life are present—billboards, advertisements, brand names—so that "The communication that endures is the plea to purchase a product."[26] Brian Donnelly's note on the novel calls the appearance of Coca-Cola a representation of a "self-consuming society."[27] The connection between late capitalism and the flashier metaphors of the novel—roving cannibalistic bloodcults—is not difficult to decipher.

Consumer capitalism is an economic system modeled on perpetual growth. Since the early 1970s, economists such as E. F. Schumacher have offered critiques of growth models, warning that perpetual growth violates what we know about the nature of ecosystems which require species diversification and balance.[28] With recent accelerating climatological crises driving more intense conversation about such models, a degrowth movement in economics has begun claiming more attention. Degrowth is an economic concept that "signifies radical political and economic reorganization" emphasizing dramatically reduced resource and energy consumption.[29] The root of the movement is a call to move away from intentions to find some sort of stability between axes of consumption and growth, where economic growth based on increased consumption continues to rise but is offset by "green" or new technologies. Instead, degrowth recognizes the impossibility of such a balancing act and calls for economies that shrink productively, where consumption is limited and where economic wellbeing is balanced with ecological wellbeing. Whether such a system, which seems to violate the rules of neoliberal capitalism itself, is possible, novels like *The Road* remind us of the moral imperative of imagination. We may struggle to imagine a degrowth-modeled society so contrary to our own, but to fail in that imaginative quest is to find ourselves inevitably in a world we do not recognize anyway. As the jefe says in *The Counselor*, "There will be other worlds. Of course. But they are the worlds of other men and your understanding of them was never more than an illusion anyway."[30] *The Road*, then, is a non-scientific literary study of the end of the road for humanity, the end of the line for consumer economics, and the possibilities of human and nonhuman "matrices" of being wherein complex ecosystems of resource sharing, hunger, and precarity all hang in the balance.

Fossil Fuels, Nuclear Warfare, Surveillance States, and the Penitential Pilgrim

Finally, I want to turn to the first of McCarthy's 2022 duology, *The Passenger* and *Stella Maris*.[31] In *The Passenger*, McCarthy reiterates earlier coded critiques of US consumer capitalism, particularly the fusion of capitalism with scientific discovery, resulting in global ecological collapse and mechanized warfare capable of global annihilation. Here, protagonist Bobby Western becomes a somewhat hapless nexus for each of these distinct aspects of US global hegemony. By the end of the novel, however, Bobby, driven away from all trappings of modern society, lives off-grid in Ibiza like some penitent for the postmodern age. In Bobby, then, the threads of many themes throughout McCarthy's corpus tangle and merge: he is implicated in the corporate fusion of fossil fuel extraction and the military-industrial complex that burgeoned in the latter decades of the twentieth century; his father's physics research, and potentially his sister's mathematics research, links scientific discovery to weapons of mass destruction; and, ultimately, his own narrative flight from these converging sources embodies the responsive, sustainable lifestyle McCarthy pictures as the antidote to late capitalist lifeways.[32]

The main narrative of *The Passenger* picks up as Bobby performs a salvage dive to investigate a downed private plane. His salvage company has been hired by wire transfer, masking the identity of whoever instigated the dive. On the dive, Bobby and his crewmate Oiler find an intact plane, yet three things are missing: a passenger, the plane's "black box," and the pilot's "Jepp" case (a Jeppeson attaché case that would contain flight records including, one assumes, the passenger manifest).[33] Following Bobby's and Oiler's discovery, two federal agents arrive at Bobby's apartment and ask him about the missing passenger. Bobby asks his boss Lou who hired them; Lou informs Bobby that their company is hired out by a shell corporation and are they not permitted to ask too many questions, "because that's Taylor's policy. Halliburton policy, for that matter."[34] In other words, Taylor, the salvage company Bobby works for, is a subsidiary of Halliburton, a major energy company with roots in the Oklahoma oil boom. Specializing in fossil fuels, Halliburton later expanded and became a global operator; it entered American public discourse when former Secretary of Defense Dick Cheney, then CEO of Halliburton and later America's Vice President, hired the company to supply mercenaries to support American soldiers in and around Iraq following Operation Desert Storm in 1991.[35] McCarthy's glancing reference to Halliburton being the parent company for Bobby's salvage job becomes significant as Bobby descends into paranoia—or, conversely, as he becomes increasingly aware of actual government surveillance, depending on the reader's interpretation.

After the salvage dive, Bobby decides to investigate the missing passenger and rents a skiff from Pass Christian, Louisiana, to search out traces of a man with an inflatable raft on an otherwise deserted island. Bobby does not find the man, so he talks Oiler into going back to the dive site on their own; they find no new evidence, and, shortly after, Bobby's friend and (perhaps) clairvoyant Debbie Fields has a portentous nightmare. In the next scene, Oiler is dead. Believing that the government is behind the missing passenger and that the flight may be linked to his father's research, Bobby returns to Wartburg, Tennessee, to look for any evidence remaining from the break-in at his former home two years previously when his father's research was stolen. There, he meets up with a researcher named Asher who may be writing a biography of the Western siblings' father, or may be investigating their father's research into S-Matrix theory. In this scene, the threads begin to weave together. On the one hand, Asher is attempting to ascertain how "dangerous" the Westerns' father's research was. Yet Bobby takes a sanguine approach to the military applications of his father's research. Questioned at one point if he carries some angst over his father's role in the creation of the atom bomb, Bobby responds that he does not "have a problem with my father" because the "bomb was always coming."[36] That is to say, for Bobby, the weaponization of the scientific breakthroughs of the twentieth century was inevitable; his father was hardly a factor.

In typical McCarthy fashion, the argument made on the surface is troubled by a subtle crosscurrent. In this instance, that crosscurrent is indicated through a seemingly pointless anecdote with which Asher opens their dialogue. Asher asks about a physicist and colleague of Western's father, "Rotblat." Joseph Rotblat was a Polish Jewish physicist who was able to obtain papers to flee Nazi-occupied Europe to the US, where he worked on the Manhattan Project. But Rotblat's family was unable to escape Warsaw, ending up in Belzec. In the novel, Asher asks, pointedly, "I just wondered if your father ever said anything about him. I guess even more specifically about his wife. Why she went to the gas chambers while he stayed home."[37] Bobby has no good answer for this question of what to think of a man who saved his own life while his family lost theirs, and at the cost of his selling his scientific acumen to build a world-destroying bomb.

While he does not follow through on this question, Asher's remark here seems to reflect Sheriff Ed Tom Bell's meditation on his Second World War experience in *No Country for Old Men*. In a scene near the novel's end, Bell reminisces about a maneuver where he managed to survive a German attack that killed the rest of his platoon. It is a similar situation: Bell's choice to remain and die with his men, much like Rotblat's choice to remain behind in Nazi-occupied Poland, would likely have accomplished nothing. And yet surviving when others do not carries an unfathomable burden. "I didnt know you could steal your own life," Bell says.[38] Complicity comes at a cost. If Rotblat is held to account, even in such a subtle way, then Bobby's own dismissal of his father's role, of his own familial heritage, seems too easy a burden to shrug off, at least in McCarthy's moral universe.

Although Bobby attempts to abnegate his own culpability for his father's research in this scene, there is a suggestion that he is more troubled by this role than he indicates. Toward the end of the novel, he visits Helen, a woman in the psychiatric institute Stella Maris who had befriended Bobby's sister, Alicia. Helen, who knows of Alicia's own opinion on their father's research, asks Bobby if his father had been "off his rocker" to "make bombs to blow everybody up." Bobby replies, "I guess that's a reasonable question."[39] Of course, Bobby's justification of his father's research—that the bomb was inevitable and that if he had not designed it, someone else would have—aligns with dominant American discourse justifying the deployment of the bombs. However, the novel can be read as an extended narrative of a man swept up in the larger political current of a situation to which he contributed but for which he attempts to bear no responsibility, much like Llewelyn Moss in *No Country*.

After Bobby's desultory investigation into the missing passenger, federal agents ransack his apartment, question him, and even lose (or confiscate?) his cat. The IRS puts a lien on his accounts and seizes his car.[40] More to the point, Oiler dies in suspicious circumstances, and, one by one, every man on his salvage crew dies. Alarmed, Bobby meets up with a lawyer named Kline who listens to Bobby's paranoid-sounding suspicions and agrees that "the government" is likely spying on him—that they believe he knows something he ought not know. And while Bobby believes himself innocent, the new (in 1980) threat of surveillance technology as a means of disciplining populations suggests that he will nevertheless be subjected to the attention of an authority he has not, to this point, even challenged. When he tells Kline that it feels like he is already under arrest, without trial or conviction, Kline says, "The truth is that everyone is under arrest. Or soon will be."[41] Bobby calls that viewpoint "paranoia," but Kline suggests that modern American society is characterized by such "madness."[42] Underscoring the connection between paranoia, surveillance technology, and the nation-state, Kline later launches into a long conspiracy narrative about the John F. Kennedy assassination. He does not specify a theory about the assassination, but rather focuses on the many witnesses who changed their testimonies and the pressure exerted on national news organizations by state agents to alter their reporting on the assassination by evoking the threat of nuclear war with Russia. Kline tells Bobby that Bobby's intelligence and experience make him believe that he is "exempt . . . from other considerations," but that regardless of whether he knows the "secret" or not, no US citizen is exempt from the carceral military-industrial state. Bobby, like any American, "can go to jail" at any time now, Kline says, and because of that risk he helps Western find a way to go "off-grid."[43]

In the end, Bobby loses more than just his citizenship; he tells Kline he "doesn't even know what a country is."[44] When Bobby travels to Ibiza, without passport or other documents of citizenship, without an ability to hold a legal job, he has a conversation with his barkeeper-friend João, who relates the story of a compatriot who died "in a state of belief," that is, in a state of belief "in himself as a man in a land under arms for a cause that was just for a people he loved."[45] His point is that here, at last, Bobby has lost such belief. Bobby has at last surrendered all claims to nationality, even his own name;

when a letter arrives for him, João reads the name on the letter and says, "No es suyo?" Bobby responds, "No."[46] Devoid of national identity, personal identity, or citizenship, and living in a "placeless" space, Bobby imagines his father's "latterday petroglyphs and the people upon the road naked and howling."[47] Having contemplated the end result of his father's physics research—Hiroshima—he desists from reading the mathematics of Grothendieck and Riemann, and blows out the light of an oil lamp. The pre-industrial technology noted here—the oil lamp—at the conclusion of a novel and a career gives reference to Bobby's abdication of industrialization, as well as his repudiation of the research that led to the nuclear age. Like Billy Parham at the end of *Cities of the Plain*, Bobby has divested himself of the talismans of citizenship; he has also quit his roles in, respectively, physics research co-opted by the state for war; racing cars, with its resonant symbolism[48] of conspicuous consumption; and as an employee of a Halliburton subsidiary.

Although Bobby is recently arrived at this newfound agnosticism about the moral implications of the contemporary nation-state, Alicia's novel, *Stella Maris*, indicates that she had long since lost such a "state of belief." As she tells her therapist, Dr. Cohen, only "a nation can make war—in the modern sense—and I don't like nations. I believe in running away."[49] Alicia's solution—running away—seems like a rather trite, and perhaps privileged, fantasy. However, her imagined "running away" entails moving to Romania, where her maternal ancestors hail from, where she would burn "everything" including her "passport" and clothes.[50] Her abdication of citizenship would render her like the nonhuman animals of the forest there; she sees herself as not a species apart from others, but of them, such that "when the last fire was ashes [the animals] would come and carry me away and I would be their eucharist."[51] Alicia's vision for what a good life—and good death—would look like inverts the neoliberal consumption model that has dominated McCarthy's corpus, from those who hunted bison to extinction in *Blood Meridian* to John Grady Cole's tear-filled killing of a deer in *All the Pretty Horses*. In Alicia's vision, it is the human who is food and the animals who consume; that she calls this vision a "eucharist" gives a salvific metaphorical weight to the offering of her body to sustain nonhuman animals.

Even more, Alicia's description of a "good death" reflects a larger resonance in her storyline that ripples back to McCarthy's earlier meditation on the need for the non-capitalist, non-racist communitarian life, described in *Suttree*. In *The Passenger*, Alicia's strange companion, the Thalidomide Kid, warns her about the "*day of the locus*."[52] As Michael Lynn Crews noted,

McCarthy was influenced by Nathanial West's 1939 novel, *The Day of the Locust*, while drafting *Suttree*.[53] West's novel depicts the false allure of opportunity in Hollywood during the interwar years, concluding with an uprising from the betrayed working class that sets the city afire. In *Suttree*, published right as neoliberal ideology was moving beyond academic theorizing and producing a coherent set of on-the-ground socioeconomic policies in the West, McCarthy imagines a more theological solution, with a Gnostic dream-vision of the poor and racially minoritized citizens of Knoxville setting it metaphorically alight.[54] In *The Passenger*, the Kid, who habitually gets aphorisms wrong and uses malapropisms, warns Alicia about the "day of the locus" instead of *locust*, making something of a pun out of West's novel and the Kid's own earlier reference to "stylus" and "graphs."[55] Yet the point the Kid makes is essentially born of the same hallucinatory dream-vision: the world as it exists will be ruptured by the violence wrought by late capitalism.

It is important to note that Alicia's sentiment that she "does not like nations" is less an economic or political assertion than a philosophical one; she projects the end of the world to be nuclear war, which she compares to a bankruptcy: "The longer you're able to put it off the worse it's going to be. . . . I agree with Plato that only the dead have seen an end to war. And people dont fight with rocks when they have guns."[56] Formulating an assertion that the twentieth century's innovations have led to greater capacities for violence that outstrip the benefits of transportation-based convenience and readily available goods, Alicia's argument here looms large over McCarthy's anti-industrial corpus. It is no surprise, then, that Alicia's imagined "good" death inverts the hunter mythos that haunts McCarthy's early western novels. Alicia, using the idiom of the sacrament, describes a non-anthropocentric worldview in which humans, too, are part of food webs. Accepting her non-anthropocentric role in this living world, she says, "would be my life. And I would be happy."[57]

Conclusion

Is all of this to say that McCarthy's fictional worlds offer hope for healthier ways of interacting with our environments? In short, yes—but only in the most qualified of forms, such as in the form of a murdered she-wolf, or of small, sustainable human communities in a post-apocalyptic wasteland. But the principle of recognizing neoliberalism or what Mark Fisher called "capitalist realism"[58] for the destructive dream that it is, recognizing the absurdity of Judge Holden's claim that the "freedom of birds is an insult," matters.[59] It is only within the machine-like trudge of bourgeois politics that the current economic and ecological devastation is sustained. If it is possible to be otherwise, to live otherwise, at some point, the ethical imagination, once sparked, will not be tamped down. It is here that I think McCarthy's sense of hunger is most relevant.

Although McCarthy's characterization of Gould as a "thoroughgoing materialist" may or may not have been fair, it is at the very least telling that he resists a world explained only by material reality. In *The Moral Economy* (2016), Sam Bowles, economist and director of the Behavioral Sciences Program at the Santa Fe Institute, argues that the myth of unregulated markets is akin to the myth of the *Homo economicus*—the assertion that at base people are "entirely self-interested and amoral."[60] Neither, in short, is entirely accurate. Some people, Bowles says, are indeed motivated by ethical considerations rather than and even in opposition to self-interest; all markets are regulated through processes of selective regulation and deregulation. Given these two factors, it is hardly a stretch to suggest that some markets should be restricted in order to sustain the political equality foundational to democratic culture, as argued by Debra Satz in *Why Some Things Should Not be For Sale*.[61] The hope of a world characterized by ethical agency; market regulations that seek to redress climate disaster through restricting fossil fuel consumption; and encouraging bioregional sustainability in trade, food webs, population growth, and housing seems increasingly fleeting, increasingly naive, and perhaps too optimistic. But what alternative do we have? The quotation from *Whales and Men* that I offered earlier concludes: "I know that we are lost but I no longer believe that we are doomed. That which we are lost to still exists and if there is a way out then there is a way back."[62] Unlike Gould, McCarthy is no "explainer." His fiction explains little about how we got here, or how to get out of this mess. But the questions McCarthy poses matter. Without map or matrix to guide us, we must commit ourselves nonetheless to search for answers to these questions, to build healthy and sustainable communities within vibrant, complex biotic homes, and to work as though all of this were possible to achieve.

Notes

1. This letter is included in Davenport's papers, but without an envelope, so it does not have a date stamp on it; however, the letter is sent from an address in Knoxville and was likely written in 1981 but not later than 1982.

2. See the Guy Davenport Papers, box 133, correspondence, The Harry Ransom Center at the University of Texas at Austin.

3. See, for example James R. Giles, "Teaching the Contemporary Naturalism of Cormac McCarthy's *Outer Dark*," *The American Literary Naturalism Newsletter* 1, no. 1 (2006): 2–7; Alan Gibbs, "'Things Happen to You They Happen': Cormac McCarthy, Morality, and Neo Naturalism," *The Cormac McCarthy Journal* 18, no. 1 (2020): 56–77; Eric Carl Link, "McCarthy and Literary Naturalism," in *The Cambridge Companion to Cormac McCarthy*, ed. Steven Frye (Cambridge: Cambridge UP, 2013): 149–61; Bill Hardwig, "Cormac McCarthy's *The Road* and 'a World to Come,'" *Studies in American Naturalism* 8, no. 1 (2013): 38–51; Michael Tavel Clarke, "The New Naturalism: Cormac McCarthy, Frank Norris, and the Question of Postmodernism," *Studies in American Naturalism* 9, no. 1 (2014): 52–78; and Steven Frye, *Unguessed Kinships: Naturalism and the Geography of Hope in Cormac McCarthy* (Tuscaloosa: Univ. of Alabama Press, 2023), all of whom have placed McCarthy in this tradition, broadly conceived.

4. This is not to say that American naturalism is closed to the possibility of the numinous or transcendent; indeed, a particular strain of naturalism pays exquisite attention to just such tensions in human experience, tensions between instinct, violence, aggression, and yearning for transcendence expressed through art, music, and religious faith. Steven Frye in fact makes this argument persuasively and comprehensively, with McCarthy as an exemplar, in his most recent book on McCarthy, *Unguessed Kinships*.

5. Cormac McCarthy, *Blood Meridian, or the Evening Redness in the West* (1985; repr. New York: Vintage, 1992), 208.

6. Cormac McCarthy, *Whales and Men*, The Cormac McCarthy Collection in The Wittliff Collections, n.d., 91.97.5, Alkek Library, Texas State University-San Marcos, 130.

7. Cormac McCarthy, *The Crossing* (1994; repr. New York: Vintage, 1995), 3.

8. Ibid., 22.

9. Ibid., 126.

10. Ibid., 24, 127.

11. Ibid., 31.

12. Mary Louisa Capelli, "Predator Politics: Coyote Wrenching in Edward Abbey's *Desert Solitaire* and Barbara Kingsolver's *Prodigal Summer*," *SAGE Open* 7, no. 1 (2017): 1–9, accessed 1 July 2024, https://doi.org/10.1177/2158244016679210.

13. See Richard B. Woodward, "Cormac McCarthy's Venomous Fiction," *The New York Times*, 19 April 1992, sect. 6, p. 28, accessed 1 July 2024, www.nytimes.com/1992/04/19/magazine/cormac-mccarthy-s-venomous-fiction.html.

14. Cormac McCarthy, *Cities of the Plain* (1998; repr. New York: Vintage, 1999), 62.

15. Ibid., 265.

16. Lydia R. Cooper, "Diamonds, drugs, and the digital age: Global capitalism in Cormac McCarthy's *The Counselor*," *Critique: Studies in Contemporary Fiction* 59, no. 4: 445–58.

17. Jacob Agner, "Salvaging *The Counselor*: Watching Cormac McCarthy and Ridley Scott's Really Trashy Movie," *The Cormac McCarthy Journal* 14, no. 2 (2016): 204–26.

18. Cormac McCarthy, *The Counselor: A Screenplay* (New York: Vintage, 2013), 174.

19. Cormac McCarthy, *The Road* (New York: Knopf, 2006), 36, 73.

20. Ibid., 73.

21. Alexander Leaf, "Food and Nutrition in the Aftermath of Nuclear War," *The Medical Impli-*

cations of Nuclear War, Institute of Medicine, Steering Committee for the Symposium on Medical Implications of Nuclear War, eds. F. Solomon and R.Q. Marston. National Academies Press, 1986, accessed 1 July 2024, https://www.ncbi.nlm.nih.gov/books/NBK219173/.

22. Sean Hermanson, "The End of *The Road*," *European Journal of American Studies* 12, no. 2 (2017): art. 7, accessed 1 July 2024, https://journals.openedition.org/ejas/12057.

23. McCarthy, *The Road*, 27.

24. Ibid., 123.

25. Lydia R. Cooper, "Cormac McCarthy's *The Road* as Apocalyptic Grail Narrative," *Studies in the Novel* 43, no. 2 (Summer 2011): 218–36.

26. Jordan J. Dominy, "Cannibalism, Consumerism, and Profanation: Cormac McCarthy's *The Road* and the End of Capitalism," *The Cormac McCarthy Journal* 13, no. 1 (2015): 143–58.

27. Brian Donnelly, "'Coke Is It!': Placing Coca-Cola in McCarthy's *The Road*," *Explicator* 68, no. 1 (2010): 70–73.

28. E. F. Schumacher, *Small Is Beautiful: Economics as if People Mattered* (1973; repr. New York: Harper Perennial, 2010).

29. Giorgos Kallis, Vasilis Kostakis, and Steffen Lange, "Research on Degrowth," *Annual Review of Environment and Resources* 43, no. 1 (2018): 291–316.

30. McCarthy, *The Counselor*, 150–51.

31. Cormac McCarthy, *The Passenger* and *Stella Maris* (New York: Knopf, 2022).

32. Not incidentally, insofar as Bobby Western becomes a stand in for the quintessential citizen/inheritor of the troubled legacy of American agency, he also functions as a (literal) metonym for the McCarthy's western landscapes, themselves geographic shorthand for the violent inheritance of westward expansion during the era of Manifest Destiny.

33. McCarthy, *The Passenger*, 46–47.

34. Ibid., 58.

35. Barry Yeoman, "Soldiers of Good Fortune," *Mother Jones* 28, no. 3 (2003): 38–43, accessed 1 July 2024, https://www.motherjones.com/politics/2003/05/soldiers-good-fortune/.

36. McCarthy, *The Passenger*, 285–86.

37. Ibid., 145.

38. Cormac McCarthy, *No Country for Old Men* (New York: Knopf, 2005), 278.

39. McCarthy, *The Passenger*, 260.

40. Ibid., 252–53.

41. Ibid., 284.

42. Ibid., 285.

43. Ibid., 344.

44. Ibid., 308.

45. Ibid., 379–80.

46. Ibid., 381.

47. Ibid., 383.

48. I have written extensively on this subject as well. See Lydia R. Cooper, *Cormac McCarthy: A Complexity Theory of Literature* (Manchester: Manchester UP, 2021), 33–68.

49. McCarthy, *Stella Maris*, 62.

50. Ibid., 190.

51. Ibid.

52. Ibid., 296.

53. Michael Lynn Crews, *Books Are Made Out of Books* (San Marcos: Univ. of Texas Press, 2017), 145–46.

54. For a fuller examination of this intertextual resonance, see Cooper, *Cormac McCarthy*, 207.

55. McCarthy, *The Passenger*, 296.

56. Ibid., 71.

57. McCarthy, *Stella Maris*, 190.

58. Mark Fisher, *Capitalist Realism: Is There No Alternative?* (2008; repr. Hampshire, U.K.: Zero Books, 2014).

59. McCarthy, *Blood Meridian*, 208.

60. Samuel Bowles, *The Moral Economy: Why Good Incentives are No Substitute for Good Citizens* (New Haven: Yale UP, 2016), 1.

61. Debra Satz, *Why Some Things Should Not Be For Sale: The Moral Limits of Markets* (Oxford: Oxford UP, 2010), 6.

62. McCarthy, *Whales and Men*, 130.

4

HUMAN BECOME COIN

Neoliberalism, Anthropology, and Human Possibilities in *No Country for Old Men*

Jonathan Elmore and Rick Elmore

Cormac McCarthy's novel *No Country for Old Men* begins with Sheriff Ed Tom Bell reminiscing about the only criminal he sent to the gas chamber. The man in question killed his fourteen-year-old girlfriend, and Bell's testimony was decisive in the guilty party's conviction and sentencing. During his conversations with Bell, the killer admits that "he had been plannin to kill somebody for about as long as he could remember. Said that if they turned him out he'd do it again. Said he knew he was goin to hell." In response to this candor, Bell confesses, "I thought I'd never seen a person like that and it got me to wonderin if maybe he was some new kind." This "new" kind of human does not appear irrational or unreasonable: "He was not hard to talk to. Called me Sheriff." He shows no regret; he expects no mercy or forgiveness. In fact, he is utterly clear that he will be held responsible for his actions: he knows he is "goin to hell." However, he is also incapable of acting differently, knowing he would kill again if given the chance. This combination of horror and reason gives Bell pause; after all, "what do you say to a man that by his own admission has no soul?"[1]

We see in this scene the overarching concern of *No Country for Old Men*, namely the emergence of a "new" type of human being, one frighteningly devoid of any recognizable humanity, yet one that remains rational, principled, and calculating. Bell, from the beginning, associates this new humanity with the character of Anton Chigurh, "a true and living prophet of destruction."[2] Moreover, Bell parallels this emergence of a new humanity with a "breakdown in mercantile ethics" that "reaches into every strata" of society.[3] It is, in fact, the large-scale change in political economy then underway that, Bell suspects, has brought about the emergence of this new kind of human. Set as it is at the beginning of the most robust period of neoliberal reform on a global scale[4] (1980), *No Country for Old Men* takes up the convergence of economics and human nature to suggest the emergence of a new kind of humanity arising from a shift in economic processes.[5] Key to this shift will be the conviction, embodied in the character of Chigurh, that a competitive market logic governs all human nature, social decision-making, and even reality itself. In what follows, we show how *No Country for Old Men* details the anthropology of neoliberalism both in the character of Chigurh and in its framing of the characters and narrative of the novel as a whole. In addition, we look at how the novel presents sites of resistance to this anthropology, particularly how it challenges neoliberalism's claim that current society is the necessary and natural outcome of our "competitive" human nature.

Homo Economicus

In "A Genealogy of Homo-Economicus: Neoliberalism and the Production of Subjectivity," Jason Read argues, following Michel Foucault, that neoliberalism is more than a political or economic program. Rather, it is an ideological transformation, "generated not from the state, or from the dominant class but from the quotidian experience of buying and selling commodities from the market, which is then extended across other social spaces."[6] The conviction that market logic and market forces determine all spheres of human life (social, political, economic, juridical) defines neoliberalism. As Foucault writes, "the starting point and general frame of reference for economic analysis [in neoliberalism] should be the way in which individuals allocate . . . scarce means to alternative ends."[7] Neoliberalism frames all human interactions as economic choices, choices about how to use one's limited resources to achieve one's desired ends. Significantly, this formulation interprets all social life through the singular lens of cost-to-benefit, as every individual decision becomes an attempt to garner the maximum return on one's "investments" while managing the risk of loss. Hence, under neoliberalism "everything for which human beings attempt to realize their ends, from marriage, to crime, to expenditures on children, can be understood 'economically' according to a particular calculation of cost for benefit."[8] There has been much written on neoliberalism's interpretation of all societal relations in terms of market forces[9]; however, Foucault's analysis uniquely focuses on neoliberalism's inherent anthropology. Based on this anthropology, the architects of neoliberalism assert that a market logic explains and governs all spheres of human life. Read argues that Foucault's analysis offers an exploration of this anthropology, an exploration of how neoliberalism creates certain forms of subjectivity that justify and enforce neoliberalism's economic claims about the world. In what follows, we explore the character and effect of this anthropology, paying particular attention to how it flattens all aspects of human life, social relations, ethical reasoning, and personal responsibility to the common denominator of market forces—and how this flattening naturalizes neoliberalism's assertions about human nature and the world.

This anthropology begins from the assertion that humans are fundamentally competitive creatures. Where classical liberalism defines humans and human society by exchange, neoliberalism sees humans and their social interactions as governed by competition: "In neo-liberalism—and it does not hide this; it proclaims it—there is also a theory of *Homo œconomicus*, but he is not at all a partner of exchange. *Homo œconomicus* is an entrepreneur, an entrepreneur of himself."[10] Shifting from an anthropology of exchange to one of competition creates a notion of the human in which a competitive logic of self-investment governs all actions and choices. In a world in which humans do not merely exchange with one another for mutual advantage but compete at all times, all activities become part of this logic of competition. The Nobel Prize winning economist Gary Becker terms this logic of self-investment "human capital" in the sense that individual existence is itself a form of investment, an entrepreneurship of the self. Embracing an anthropology of competition, in fact, reframes all consumptive practices as productive practices.[11]

Under the logic of human capital, consumption is the primary process by which individuals improve or diminish their value. Every choice about clothing, food, cosmetics, dieting, exercise, body augmentation, entertainment, and even seemingly conspicuous consumption becomes a moment of self-investment and, consequently, a site of economic concern.[12] From this perspective, there is no neutral action, no decision that escapes the logic of social competition, no choice that is not explainable by its cost or benefit. This marks the profound difference between the logic of exchange and that of competition. In exchange, what brings people together is a common need, but not every interaction aims at the satisfaction of needs. The logic of exchange allows for a whole spectrum of non-economic relations and interactions. But the logic of competition and human capital does away with the non-economic; in a world governed by competition, any decision not leading to a competitive advantage, any economically "neutral" decision, would be an unnecessary cost, a failure to manage one's investments as efficiently as possible. In short, the neoliberal anthropology of competition extends economic relations to every aspect of individual action and reduces all choice and decision-making to the common denominator of risk management.

In a world in which competition and human nature are synonymous and market calculations are the basis for all social decision-making, "risk" becomes the fundamental logic which explains human choices. This logic holds for both positive and negative choices; as fundamentally competitive, self-interested creatures, humans will always choose what they believe to be in their interest, what they believe will garner them the most reward for the least cost. One of the results of this logic is that neoliberalism plays on the classical liberal notion that capitalism is "synonymous with rationality," an economic extension of the assumed rationality of the liberal subject.[13] However, this implicit extension of the rational nature of the human subject to all social formation shows neoliberalism's reliance on anthropology to ground its economic and social claims. As Read puts it, in neoliberalism "it is not the structure of the economy that is extended across society but the subject of economic thinking, its implicit anthropology."[14] The anthropologically grounded logic of risk management, of greatest benefit for the least cost, explains not only individual actions but those of social groups and of society as a whole. From a neoliberal perspective, social realities like government, education, crime, healthcare, and child-rearing are all made though a logic of cost and benefit, risk and return. This reliance on "risk" as the vehicle of social decision-making entails that if one wants to "positively" influence social activities under neoliberalism, one does so through "market incentives or deterrents," disincentivizing negative social behaviors and incentivizing positive behaviors.[15] It is for this reason that many critics of neoliberalism argue that although neoliberalism focuses on privatization, this should not be confused with a reduction in institutionalized social control.[16] On the contrary, neoliberalism does not advocate for less governing or less control; rather, it argues for the transfer of government functions to private institutions, a logic that actually *increases* social control insofar as the regulation of market forces is extended over all social activities. Hence, on the basis of its anthropology, neoliberalism interprets society solely in economic terms, an interpretation that not only increases social control but radically reframes our understanding of morality and ethics.

The result of an anthropology that assumes humans to be competitive agents whose actions are determined entirely by a logic of cost-benefit is that individuals become totally responsible for all of their actions. Because each individual makes rational investments in themselves and the world, when those investments lead to losses or negative results individuals alone are responsible for their "bad" investments.[17] This is the price paid for the seeming toleration of non-normative behaviors, like crime: individuals are free to do whatever they want but are necessarily responsible for each and every choice. This is, for Read, the heart of the "biopolitics" of neoliberalism, no longer governing through explicit control of peoples' actions but through the manipulation of the horizon of possible choices and the "isolating and dispersing" of individuals into their own private "companies of one."[18] Here the normative and oppressive aspects of neoliberalism's flat anthropology come to the fore.

The reduction of all social activities to the logic of competitive advantage and the positing of competition as the heart of human nature results in the flattening of all social realities to the common denominator of investment and risk. In neoliberalism "states, corporations, and individuals are all governed by the same logic, that of interest and competition."[19] This flat anthropology condenses all social activities, relations, responsibilities, and forces into the single category of individual investment. From this perspective, not only is every social activity explainable, but all social inequalities and all "oppressions" become simply the result of poor investments by individual agents, a logic that naturalizes social inequalities as natural, inevitable, and justified. In a society where we are all "companies of one," some companies (that is some individuals) must necessarily be eliminated by the competition of the market. In neoliberalism, people "bear the *entire* burden of their investment."[20] Interestingly, this logic of absolute responsibility conceptually eliminates the possibility of control or oppression by an authority since, if one happens to be in an oppressive situation, this must be the result of one's "poor" investments or choices. This is the logic by which one can make, for example, the indigent responsible for their poverty or the "deviant" responsible for the social, political, legal, and economic challenges they experience. This naturalizing of social inequalities illuminates the tendency of neoliberalism to eliminate any site of resistance to its market logic, as there is nothing that escapes this reduction, no "outside" from this totalizing conception of the world.

The anthropological reduction at work in neoliberalism eliminates or co-opts resistance to its interpretation of the world. This reduction of resistance yokes the reduction of all social life to the common denominator of market logic. It provides not only an explanation for all social life but also naturalizes existing social structures: "as a political rationality, [neoliberalism] is without an outside. It does not encounter any tension with a competing logic of worker or citizen, with a different articulation of subjectivity."[21] Moreover, this reduction of resistance puts neoliberalism at odds not only with left-leaning forces for social and economic justice but also conservative and religiously inspired forces for whom the *laissez-faire* flattening of society to market forces marks a problematic moral relativism.[22] This is not to suggest that neoliberalism's devotion to market principles does not resemble in important ways a form of religiously inspired "market fundamentalism," rather it highlights the powerful way neoliberalism's interpretation of society reduces the space for resistance by incorporating resistance as itself a form of market calculation (the rational desire by the economically disadvantaged to achieve economic advantage). However, neoliberalism grounds this incorporation of resistance on its anthropological commitments to a human nature defined as competition and self-interest.

Grounded upon the anthropological reduction of humans to competitive market calculators, apologists for neoliberalism reduce choice, social interaction, crime, resistance, and the entire world to the rational economic calculation of risk and investment. On the basis of this reduction, the entire existing world becomes explainable and justifiable since, insofar as social formations are the result of the competitiveness and rational market nature of humans, such formations come to be the reflection of the natural and unavoidable processes of human nature. This rationalizing of the world in itself naturalizes and also blames individuals for social, economic, and political inequalities, which are read as the result of poor market decisions on the part of those who suffer those inequalities. Although neoliberalism takes a variety of forms and has developed in an uneven fashion in the United States, Great Britain, and the rest of the world, its interpretation of society takes root in its anthropological commitments, a fact that points to the value of Foucault's analysis insofar as it traces the ways in which neoliberalism marks the development of a new subjectivity, as much as a shift in production practices, monetary policy, and economic modeling. This connection between the shift in economics or "mercantile ethics" and human nature returns us to Cormac McCarthy's fiction.

Neoliberalism's New Humanity in *No Country For Old Men*

The question of human nature is a major theme across many of McCarthy's best-known texts. From the profound violence of *Blood Meridian, or the Evening Redness in the West* (1985) to the confusion of cultural and familial loss in the Border Trilogy, McCarthy returns again and again to how human nature shapes and is shaped by the gritty elements of American culture and history. At the heart of these ruminations is the pivotal role economics plays in shaping our humanity, a connection that is nowhere more explicitly developed than in *No Country for Old Men* and, particularly, the character of Anton Chigurh.[23]

Chigurh embodies the neoliberal subject: a creature defined and motivated by market logic, risk management, and the elimination of competition. The extent to which market forces define his identity develops throughout the novel, as he becomes increasingly cognizant that market forces govern not only his nature but also all humans and the nature of reality itself. In Chigurh's worldview, everything is the determinate outcome of individual choices—choices for which every individual is entirely responsible. Although Chigurh is often read as a "psychopath" who embodies moral and political nihilism, fatalism, or determinism, we argue that he is better understood as the ideal neoliberal subject, a *homo economicus* in the purest sense: a subject whose entire identity is reducible to market logic.[24] From this perspective, Chigurh is not the product of the failure of post-Fordist capitalism or the decay of moral virtues but is the realization of neoliberalism's flat anthropology and, consequently, the realization of the archetypal, modern capitalist subject.

Chigurh's market-driven competitiveness is on display in the scene at the filling station. This encounter opens with Chigurh reacting adversely to the proprietor's off-handed remark about the weather: "And what business is it of yours where I'm from friendo?" bristles Chigurh.[25] Seemingly concerned that the proprietor has identified where he is from, Chigurh extracts, in an adversarial manner, a series of personal facts from the shop owner: he goes to bed "around 9:30"; he "lived in Temple Texas for many years"; he came to Sheffield "about four years ago"; and he "married into" this business. He also implies menacingly that he might return after the shop closes. We are introduced to Chigurh as a threatening individual worried that anyone might have information about him. It is in this worry that we first glimpse the competitiveness of Chigurh's character. However, this fundamental competitiveness is on display throughout the novel: for example, when he kills Pedro's men in the desert or when he destroys a car in front of a pharmacy as a distraction in order to access medical supplies. For Chigurh, every action is a calculation of risk and benefit, a calculation of what must be done to achieve a desired result or avoid unnecessary risk. Moreover, this competitiveness is framed, from this scene on, in economic terms: cost and benefit.

Economic language and symbolism punctuate the encounter between Chigurh and the proprietor, from Chigurh asking about the price of the cashews he purchases to the proprietor trying to end their conversation with the excuse that he must close soon (i.e., end their economic exchange). Additionally, Chigurh emphasizes twice that the proprietor has "married into" his business, raising questions of property ownership and implying that the shop owner did not earn what he has, and the proprietor returns Chigurh's change "stacked . . . before him the way a dealer places chips" foreshadowing the game of chance about to be played out in the coin toss. Framed in terms of economic exchange, property ownership, and gambling, this scene suggests that, fundamentally, it is economics that governs these men and their relation.

Amplifying the economic overtones of this scene, the coin toss extends economic calculation to the life of the shopkeeper and to the nature of the world. Having asked the shop owner "what's the most you ever seen lost on a coin toss?" Chigurh flips and catches a quarter, instructing the shop owner to "Call it." The confused shop owner replies,

> For what?
> Just call it.
> Well I need to know what it is we're callin here.
> How would that change anything?

For Chigurh, everything collapses into the simple distinction between profit or loss, winning or losing. There is nothing that humans can do to change this inevitable logic, no knowledge that could fundamentally affect it, as every choice leads one inevitably to the present: "I didn't put nothing up," insists the proprietor. "Yes you did," snaps Chigurh. "You've been putting it up your whole life. You just didnt know it." This inevitability extends to the entire world as this coin has "been traveling twenty-two years to get here. And now it's here. and I'm here. And I've got my hand over it. And it's either heads or tails. And you have to say. Call it." The inevitability underscores the shopkeeper's absolute responsibility for the outcome of the coin flip: "You need to call it. . . . I cant call it for you. It wouldnt be fair. It wouldnt even be right. Just call it." For Chigurh, profit and loss are moral as well as natural principles, as it would be "wrong" to deny or tamper with the act of calling the toss. In fact, market logic is literally built into all things, for Chigurh, in that "anything can be an instrument [of this logic]. Small things. Things you wouldnt even notice." This interaction demonstrates the essential composition of the anthropology of neoliberalism explored above: the reduction of human nature to competition, the extension of economic market rationality to human nature, the naturalizing of this rationality into the fabric of the universe, and the shifting of all responsibility onto individuals.

These aspects of Chigurh's worldview and the depth of his commitment to a market-based anthropology are developed further in his interactions with Carson Wells.[26] Speaking with Wells just before executing him, Chigurh ruminates on himself:

> Getting hurt changed me, he said. Changed my perspective. I've moved on, in a way. Some things have fallen into place that were not there before. I thought they were but they werent. The best way I can put it is that I've sort of caught up with myself. That's not a bad thing. It was overdue.

Chigurh has reached a new point of self-realization. He has always been a *homo economicus* and is just now coming to understand fully what that means. He reflects on two previous encounters; in one he kills a stranger in a parking lot for saying something "that was hard to ignore." An hour later, he "let" a deputy arrest him because he wanted to see "if [he] could extricate [him]self by an act of will." Yet after looking back on these events, after his "overdue" self-realization, Chigurh understands his actions as "foolish" and "vain." From a neoliberal perspective both of these incidents were unnecessary risks or costs, as there was nothing tangible gained from these events. Chigurh's competitiveness is not only economically framed but fundamentally governed by a cost/benefit analysis. Consequently, when Wells attempts to buy his life with the offer of "fourteen grand," they both agree that it would be a "good payday." However, Chigurh rejects the offer because "it's just in the wrong currency." Wells assumes that, like himself, Chigurh is motivated by the acquisition of wealth. Yet Chigurh understands his own motivation as something more fundamental than money or "profit" in a purely monetary sense.

When Wells responds to Chigurh's reflections with, "Do you have any notion of how goddamned crazy you are," Chigurh replies with a question of his own, "If the rule you followed led you to this of what use was the rule?" Everything is reducible to a simple principle: "I'm talking about your life. In which now everything can be seen at once." Wells has made a series of bad economic choices, suggests Chigurh, a series of poor investments leading inevitably to his death. Yet the difference between them is far more fundamental than making different choices. Chigurh sees their different natures: "You think I'm like you. That it's just greed. But I'm not like you. I live a simple life. . . . You've been giving up things for years to get here. I dont think I even understand that." Wells has sacrificed to get ahead, given up "things" in exchange for wealth; Wells has lived as an exchange partner in a liberal economy. Chigurh sees the neoliberal structure of the current economy and understands that, in this context, Wells's "rule" of exchanging and sacrificing only for explicit monetary reward makes poor business sense. The latter's greed has led him to "give up" possible advantages, to overlook risks, and to allow inefficiencies in his choices. In this sense, Chigurh cannot help but ask how Wells let himself "get in this situation?" Chigurh, whose natural habitat is a neoliberal economy, would never give up any advantage, no matter the wealth involved because he understands that the current economy rewards effective competitors above all else. Competition and investment shape Chigurh's identity, not exchange and profit. For Chigurh, individuals compete effectively or give way to more efficient competitors.[27] Moreover, we also see here the principled nature of Chigurh's commitments to a market-based conception of human nature and the world.

As Wells's outburst quoted above suggests, questions of Chigurh's sanity arise repeatedly. In his interactions with Wells, though, Chigurh is far from irrational or crazy. Rather, he is, more than any other character in the novel, exceedingly rational, governed by an unwavering code of conduct. He is "completely reliable and completely honest," as he explains when returning the drug money near the novel's conclusion.[28] Chigurh's rationality hinges on his absolute commitment to the cultivation of a competitive edge and the elimination of potential threats, a commitment that exceeds all other concerns. Chigurh is the perfect neoliberal subject, a subject with "no enemies" because he does not "permit such a thing."[29] The "horror" of Chigurh's character emerges not from some dark, irrational, and unfathomable sociopathy but precisely from the cold, calculative rationality of the market. It is the reduction of human nature to market logic that defines Chigurh's monstrousness, which is to say, the anthropology of neoliberalism. Although Chigurh is the clearest embodiment of the anthropology of neoliberalism within the novel, this anthropology frames the entire novel.

We are first introduced to Llewelyn Moss, for example, as he hunts game, a scene that both foreshadows the hunting of Moss by Chigurh and Chigurh by Bell and echoes the anthropological history of humans as hunters: "The rocks there were etched with pictographs perhaps a thousand years old. The men who drew them hunters like himself. Of them there was no other trace."[30] Similar reflections on the development of human nature recur throughout the novel, most notably in Bell's concern that a change in "mercantile ethics" has led to not only a new kind of human, but to a new world, one in which he worries only a miracle can save us: "I wake up sometimes way in the night and I know as certain as death that there aint nothin short of the second comin of Christ that can slow this train."[31] The novel evokes the figure of the human as hunter, an allusion to a survival-of-the-fittest motif, and connects this figure to developments in economics and, ultimately, to a world doomed but for the intervention of God. In broad strokes, the novel represents human nature in terms of survival, economics, and destruction suggesting that something has gone terribly wrong with human life or that perhaps something was always wrong but is only now coming to pass. However, in more specific terms, the novel frames human life and human nature, not just the character of Chigurh, in competitive terms.

Having come upon the drug-deal-gone-wrong in the desert, Moss discovers the satchel of money: "His whole life was sitting there in front of him. Day after day from dawn till dusk until he was dead. All of it cooked down into forty pounds of paper in a satchel."[32] Here we see human life "cooked" down to its fundamental economic expression: all humans, under capitalism, spend their lives accumulating wealth—or at least trying to do so. Furthermore, this scene suggests that such economic expression is the totality of one's "whole life" captured in the money one possesses. Similarly, Bell, reflecting on his job, concludes: "It's money. . . . You have enough money you don't have to talk to people about cats in trees. Well. Maybe you do."[33] Money provides humans the opportunity to live a different life, one presumably free from tedium and the competitive forces of everyday life. Although, the quick caveat at the end of this thought suggests that perhaps money does not provide all the freedom it first appears. This notion of money as something that fundamentally shapes human life returns in Bell's conversation with Carla Jean, where, referring to Moss, he says, "Well, I guess in all honesty I would have to say that I never knew nor did I ever hear of anybody that money didnt change. I'd have to say he'd be the first."[34] Human life, in the neoliberal era, is reducible to its economic production, and money fundamentally shapes the character of humans. This is not merely a truism mouthed by characters within the novel, as economic exchange conditions not only the relationship between Bell, Moss, Chigurh, and Wells, but is even at work in Carla Jean and Llewelyn's marriage, as we discover that they met only because Carla Jean took a low-wage job at the local Walmart.

The themes of calculation, risk, and chance recur throughout the novel. On a narrative level, the actions of characters are frequently described in a step-by-step manner, mapping their actions in a systematic way. For example, when Moss returns home from the desert with the money:

> He got his flashlight from the glovebox and climbed out and took the machinepistol and the case from behind the seat and crawled up under the trailer. . . . He wedged the H&K up into a corner and pulled the insulation down over it and lay there thinking. Then he crawled back out with the case and dusted himself off and climbed the steps and went in."[35]

The methodical, systematic description and the repeated use of "and" emphasize the sequential nature of the actions. Similar sequential narration repeats throughout the novel and across characters, giving the characters' actions a sense of deliberate, rational calculation. The novel's narration codes all the characters' actions as rational choices, yet the emphasis on chance and luck suggests that their choices are determined by forces beyond their direct control. The narration mirrors the market logic of neoliberalism in which everything is understood both as the result of deliberate cost-benefit analysis and the risk and chance of the market. From this perspective, neoliberalism frames the action of the novel as whole. In fact, the main storyline between Moss and Chigurh demonstrates neoliberal self-interest, as Moss tries to protect the money he has discovered by chance. While the narration and storyline of the novel structures itself with the neoliberal anthropology embodied in Chigurh, it is precisely the failure of other characters, and particularly Moss, to act as pure neoliberal subjects that keeps the plot moving.

Although Moss's attempt to keep the money marks him as a neoliberal subject, his failure to pull off his escape is the result of his inability to follow a truly self-interested, competitive logic. His return to the desert with water for the man in the pickup truck, his unwillingness to kill Chigurh in the hotel, and his decision not to sacrifice the girl in the gunfight that ultimately ends his life all signal Moss's disruption of neoliberal logic. These decisions confound the logic of absolute competition, and, simultaneously, motivate the storyline of *No Country* insofar as one can hardly see how Moss would have failed to escape if he had not gone back to the desert or if he had killed Chigurh in the hotel. In addition, these "irrational" actions are Moss's most "human" choices in that his inability to forget the man in the desert, to kill Chigurh, or to sacrifice the girl are precisely acts of empathy, mercy, and courage.

Although *No Country* traces the shift from liberal to neoliberal subjectivity, it also suggests the instability of this shift. Chigurh's visit to Carla Jean, fulfilling his promise to Moss, highlights neoliberalism's totalizing market logic even as it suggests the fragility of neoliberal reason generally.[36] When Carla Jean finds Chigurh—and his sense of inevitability—waiting for her, she says:

> You've got no cause to hurt me.
> I know. But I gave my word.
> Your word?
> Yes. We're at the mercy of the dead here.

Even though Moss is dead, Chigurh's "word is not dead"; Moss made a choice that did not include saving his wife, and his choice inevitably leads to her death. Chigurh knows she is blameless: "None of this is your fault. . . . You didn't do anything. It was bad luck." Yet in a neoliberal economy, moral blame or fault are irrelevant; everyone is finally and absolutely responsible for their place in the economy. When Carla Jean exclaims, "I dont know what I ever done. . . . I truly dont" Chigurh replies, "probably you do . . . there's a reason for everything." Everything comes down to choices and investments individuals make.

At the end of Carla Jean's life, Chigurh offers another economic choice, his signature coin toss: "All right, he said. This is the best I can do." Having agreed that "none of this was [her] fault," Chigurh offers the coin toss as a "last chance." He holds it up for Carla Jean to see the "justice" of the coin and tosses it. After Carla Jean loses, Chigurh explains, "every moment of your life is a turning and every one a choosing. Somewhere you made a choice. All followed to this. The accounting is scrupulous." Neoliberalism, in other words, places absolute responsibility on individuals rather than structures, systems, or environments. As entrepreneurs of themselves, all subjects within a neoliberal economy are responsible for their choices throughout their entire lives; each investment leads to profit or loss. This logic is absolute, built into the very nature of humans, society, and the world.

Neoliberal logic extends to the totality of human existence. As Chigurh explains to Carla Jean, "The shape is drawn. No line can be erased. I had no belief in your ability to move a coin to your bidding. How could you? A person's path through the world seldom changes and even more seldom will it change abruptly. And the shape of your path was visible from the beginning." The passive voice is telling here; Chigurh describes Carla Jean's situation as everyone's situation. His explanation is anthropological and, consequently, totalizing and inevitable. The determinism of neoliberalism is absolute. All entrepreneurs make a series of economic choices, some resulting in profit and others in loss. The sum of these choices makes up a human life. All social interactions, all decisions, every individual, literally the totality of human existence, falls under the flat anthropology of profit or loss: heads or tails.

However, Carla Jean's responses outline a critique of Chigurh's neoliberalism and possibilities for resisting its totalizing, flat logic. Carla Jean denies the seamless transition between an individual's choice and her place in the economy. She does this by recognizing that Chigurh enforces the system of which he claims to be only a part: "You make it like it was the coin. But you're the one . . . the coin didnt have no say. It was just you." In this moment, Carla Jean rejects the notion that Chigurh's reasoning is not itself enforced by Chigurh. It is not the determinism of the coin toss but Chigurh who decides who is subject to the coin's determination. In this sense, Chigurh plays the role of the social and political institutions within neoliberalism which simultaneously administer market reason while claiming that their administration is just a reflection of nature.

With her final plea, Carla Jean gets Chigurh to voice his own role in the neoliberal economy within which he claims to be only an instrument: "She looked at him a final time. You dont have to, she said. You dont. You dont." He responds, "You're asking that I make myself vulnerable and that I can never do. I have only one way to live. It doesn't allow for special cases. . . . When I came into your life your life was over." The repeated first-person pronouns betray his agency in their exchange. As long as Chugurh is the ideal neoliberal subject, that subject retains its agency. Carla Jean's final words illustrate that while the neoliberal economy creates an environment within which new humans like Chigurh thrive, it is their actions which perpetuate and broaden the reach of neoliberalism.

Still, Carla Jean rightly articulates neoliberalism as a construction of humans rather than a reflection of their nature. As such, Chigurh becomes an enforcer of this construction, a fact evident in his conversation with Pedro: "Because I'm in charge of who is coming and who is not."[37] The identification of Chigurh as enforcing the supposedly "natural" and anthropological claims of neoliberalism challenges its naturalization precisely because a truly natural system requires no enforcement. Hence, enforcement marks precisely the "unnatural" and constructed elements of neoliberalism. Both in Moss's violations of neoliberal self-interest and in Carla Jean's identification of Chigurh as the enforcer of neoliberal reason, a countercurrent of resistance to neoliberalism emerges within the novel. The most profound suggestion of resistance comes in Bell's dreams at the end of the novel.

The novel closes with the idea that resistance to neoliberalism involves renegotiating our understanding of our shared social history. Bell concludes the novel thinking of his father and calls the natural direction of time into question: "*I've been older now than he ever was for almost twenty years so in a sense I'm looking back at a younger man.*" The past is behind him, but it is also younger than the present. Bell knows that he has not "*done* [his father] *justice*" and reflects back on his younger father in economic terms: "*He went on the road tradin horses. . . . He told me the first time or two he got skinned pretty good but he learned.*" His reflections on his father are of him as a partner in an economic exchange: as a liberal subject. In this way, Bell, who too has been skinned pretty good in his own life of horse trading, is looking back at a younger America, at both a marketplace and a community as they functioned before neoliberalism.[38]

Yet Bell's dreams of his long dead father suggest a dissonance in understanding the world through economic exchange. In the first dream, Bell and his father are "*in town somewheres*" and his father gives him some money and Bell loses it.[39] A failed economic exchange between father and son symbolically opens a space within the economic relationship between past and present that is not an inevitable transition. The failure of this exchange renders visible cracks in the totalizing narrative of neoliberalism's flat anthropology in which everything follows necessarily from the economic character of human nature. Casting the relation between past and present, figured in economic terms, as an unnatural and troubled transition, McCarthy, in the end, questions whether the present state of the world is actually the result of human nature.

Bell's second dream calls for a reconsideration of history, as the past is put in front of the present. Both men were "*back in older times*" and his father "*rode past*" him "*and kept goin.*" Bell's dream self, "*knew that he was goin on ahead and that he was fixin to make a fire. . . . I knew that whenever I got there he would be there. And then I woke up.*"[40] Bell's father and the past are ahead of him, ahead of the present. Bell's closing dream contrasts sharply Chigurh's certainty that we "are at the mercy of the dead."[41] The flat anthropology of neoliberalism depends upon the inevitability of human nature, the certainty that we are, and have always been, *homo economicus*, competitive creatures making rational choices. It is by naturalizing the past that neoliberalism asserts its totalizing narrative of competition and market logic in the present. If human nature has always been competitive, then the current neoliberal structure of society is nothing but the expression of that human nature. However, by placing the past before the present, out in front of us in the dark, the novel concludes by questioning our understanding of and relationship to our own cultural, social, and anthropological history, a questioning that strikes at the very heart of neoliberalism's claims to its own inevitability and legitimacy.

While our analysis and the novel itself both end with suggestions for resisting the totalizing logic of neoliberalism, the novel is *homo economicus*'s story. Consequently, it is the story of America since at least 1980. Yet the voice we hear the most is Sheriff Bell's, the novel's "old man" whose own "mercantile ethic" *precedes* neoliberalism. At the end of a career that has defined him, older than his own father, Bell bears witness to his generation's values and worldview coming to a seeming end. But Bell represents another kind of "old man" as well: *Homo sapiens*. In this way does the full meaning of the novel's title becomes clear. These old men—*Homo sapiens*, the liberal subject, and perhaps even truly "humane" humans—find themselves no longer the dominant species in their own country, the one they built. And while the novel depicts a nightmarish country no longer hospitable to this older kind of human, no longer hospitable to any non-economically understood notion of human nature, community, or relation, it is nevertheless this old man, Bell, who gets the last word on the new political economy: "And then I woke up."

Notes

1. Cormac McCarthy, *No Country for Old Men* (2005; repr. New York: Pan MacMillan, 2010), 4–5.

2. Ibid., 5.

3. Ibid., 304.

4. We are not the first commentators to connect this novel to its setting in late twentieth century American culture. Stephen Tatum, in "'Mercantile Ethics': No Country for Old Men and the Narcocorrido," *Cormac McCarthy: All the Pretty Horses, No Country for Old Men, The Road*, ed. Sara L. Spurgeon (New York: Continuum, 2011), 77–93, casts the novel as a kind of *corrido* or border ballad that "indexes both directly and indirectly the political, financial, moral or ethical, and even linguistic crisis emerging along the U.S.-Mexico border in the wake of the Vietnam War." Along similar lines, John Vanderheide, in "No Allegory for Casual Readers," *No Country for Old Men: From Novel to Film*, eds. Lynnea Chapman King, Rick Wallach, and James Welsh (Toronto: Scarecrow Press, 2009), 32–45, flatly states that all of McCarthy's novels consistently critique the capitalist mode of production. He goes on to argue that *No Country* "serves to illuminate the preconditions, consequences, and virtue" of renunciation of nihilism (and its capitalist "vehicle"), and that the stakes of such a renunciation are one's very humanity. Raymond Malewitz, in "'Anything can be an Instrument': Misuse Value and Rugged Consumerism in Cormac McCarthy's *No Country for Old Men*," *Contemporary Literature* 50, no. 4 (Winter 2009): 721–41, focuses on the use/misuse of commodities to argue that both Moss and Chigurh "present but cannot fully acknowledge a quintessentially American alternative to the alienating conditions of late capitalism: a new, rugged consumerism."

5. For a historical account of the rise of neoliberalism see Giovani Arrighi, *The Long Twentieth Century: Money, Power, and the Origins of Our Time* (London: Verso, 1994); David Harvey, *A Brief History of Neoliberalism* (Oxford: Oxford UP, 2005); Leo Panitch and Sam Gindin, *Making of Global Capitalism: The Political Economy of American Empire* (London: Verso, 2012); Wendy Brown, *Undoing the Demos: Neoliberalism's Stealth Revolution* (Princeton: Princeton, 2015); and Wolfgang Streeck, *Buying Time: The Delayed Crisis of Democratic Capitalism*, trans. Patrick Camiller and David Fernbach (New York: Verso, 2017).

6. Jason Read, "A Genealogy of Homo-Economicus: Neoliberalism and the Production of Subjectivity," *Foucault Studies* 6 (2009): 25–36.

7. Michel Foucault, *The Birth of Biopolitics: Lectures at the Collège de France, 1978–1979*, trans. Graham Burchell (New York: Palgrave Macmillan, 2008), 222.

8. Read, "A Genealogy," 28.

9. See, for example, Jamie Peck and Adam Tickell, "Conceptualizing Neoliberalism, Thinking Thatcherism," *Contesting Neoliberalism: Urban Frontiers*, ed. Helga Leitner, et al. (New York: Guilford, 2007), 26–50; Wendy Brown, "American Nightmare: Neoliberalism, Neoconservatism, and De-Democratization," *Political Theory* 34, no. 6 (2006): 690–714; Shannon Winnubst, "The Queer Thing about Neoliberal Pleasure: A Foucauldian Warning," *Foucault Studies* 14 (2012): 79–97; and

Andrew Dilts, *Punishment and Inclusion: Race, Membership, and the Limits of American Liberalism* (New York: Fordham UP, 2014).

10. Foucault, *The Birth of Biopolitics*, 226.

11. See Read, "A Genealogy," 28; Dilts, *Punishment and Inclusion*, 69; and Peck and Tickell, "Conceptualizing Neoliberalism," 28.

12. One interesting aspect of this logic, notes Read in "A Genealogy," 28, is that much of one's "human capital" seems difficult to improve, as, for example, one's genetics, body, class position, gender, and racial identity are in many ways given to one in advance in a way that makes them difficult to modify.

13. Read, "A Genealogy," 32.

14. Ibid.

15. Brown, "American Nightmare," 705.

16. Brown, "American Nightmare," 705; Peck and Tillich, "Conceptualizing Neoliberalism," 33.

17. Dilts, *Punishment and Inclusion*, 77.

18. Read, "A Genealogy," 34.

19. Ibid., 35.

20. Dilts, *Punishment and Inclusion*, 77.

21. Read, "A Genealogy," 35.

22. This is why commentators like Wendy Brown, "American Nightmare," 700, mark an important tension between neoliberalism and neoconservatism.

23. On the role of economics in *No Country*, see, for example, John Cant's *Cormac McCarthy and the Myth of American Exceptionalism* (London: Routledge, 2013); Patrick O'Connor's "Saving Sheriff Bell: Derrida, McCarthy and the Opening of Mercantile Ethics in *No Country for Old Men*," *The Cormac McCarthy Journal* 15, no. 2 (2017): 152–76; and Robert Wyllie's "'Principles that transcend money': Veterans Between Markets and Fate in *No Country for Old Men*," *The Cormac McCarthy Journal* 21, no. 1 (2023): 73–92.

24. For example, Linda Woodson, "'You are the Battleground': Materiality, Moral Responsibility, and Determinism in *No Country for Old Men*," *No Country for Old Men: From Novel to Film*, eds. Lynnea Chapman King, Rick Wallach, and James Welsh (Toronto: Scarecrow Press, 2009), 1–12, uses Fischer and Ravizza's definition of a psychopath, an individual of "'coldness and detachment'" to describe Chigurh. Instead, Lydia Cooper, in "'He's a psychopathic killer, but so what?': Folklore and Morality in Cormac McCarthy's *No Country for Old Men*," *Papers on Language and Literature* 45, no. 1 (Winter 2009), reads Chigurh as the embodiment of nihilism. Alternatively, Jay Ellis, "'Do you see?:' Levels of Ellipsis in *No Country for Old Men*" in Spurgeon, *Cormac McCarthy*, 94–116, contends that "Chigurh functions not only as an executioner, but also as a Socratic figure who, when he has time, engages in extended dialogue intended to help his victims see what they could not before see, that their past actions, in conjunction with chance events, have determined their fated end at his hands." See also "Micah Donohue's "'He's a Ghost. But He's Out There': Borderlands Science and the Gothic in *No Country for Old Men*," *Western American Literature* 55, no. 3 (2020): 261–87.

25. All quotations in this paper referencing the filling station scene can be found in McCarthy, *No Country*, 52–57.

26. All quotations in this paper referencing Chigurh's conversation with Carson Wells can be found in McCarthy, *No Country*, 173–75.

27. This stoicism about the realities of competition seems to apply equally to Chigurh himself; when he is faced with his own potential defeat by another competitor in the scene with Moss in the hotel, Chigurh seems to accept his potential death as just the way things go. See McCarthy, *No Country*, 112.

28. McCarthy, *No Country*, 252.

29. Ibid., 253.

30. Ibid., 11.

31. Ibid., 159.

32. Ibid., 18.

33. Ibid., 41.

34. Ibid., 128.

35. Ibid., 20.

36. All quotations in this paper referencing the conversation between Carla Jean and Chigurh can be found in McCarthy, *No Country*, 255–61.

37. Ibid., 251.

38. Ibid., 308.

39. Ibid., 309.

40. Ibid.

41. Ibid., 255.

5

"IN WHAT DIRECTION DID LOST MEN VEER?"

Late Capitalism and Utopia in Cormac McCarthy's *The Road*

Casey Jergenson

The critical conversation surrounding Cormac McCarthy's 2006 novel *The Road* is varied and diverse, reflecting the novel's complex interrogations of McCarthy's characteristic themes: the brutality of human nature, the crisis of meaning in the postmodern world, and the destructive trajectory of human history. This chapter offers a reading of *The Road*'s political content—a particularly divisive topic in the criticism referenced above. *The Road* lacks the overt political commentary found in many dystopian and post-apocalyptic novels, yet its preoccupation with the material and conceptual detritus of contemporary America compels readers to understand the world of the novel in historical and political terms. This chapter uses Walter Benjamin's idiosyncratic variant of historical materialism to make the case that the novel's simple narrative of survival and paternal love delivers a searing critique of late capitalism and consumer culture. *The Road* articulates this critique through its staging of dialectical relationships between past and present, survivor and material world, and self and other. Ultimately, however, the novel's politics move from critique to hope as *The Road* frames the praxis of the father and son as the unrealized utopian negation of the dominant rationalities of the pre- and post-apocalyptic worlds.

Apocalypse and Human Agency

The popularity of post-apocalyptic narratives today is not an incidental feature of our historic moment: it is reflective of a widespread sentiment in the post-9/11 western world that some sort of massive, world-altering cataclysm is possible, and perhaps even imminent. Collective anxieties stemming from climate change, the seemingly insurmountable power of multinational corporations, and the perennial threat of nuclear war inevitably seep into our cultural productions. Post-apocalyptic narratives can, in some iterations, compel readers to engage critically with the possibility of a cataclysmic future. They can serve cautionary functions by extrapolating contemporary economic practices and social relations into the future, allowing readers to view the dangerous contradictions defining the present order from a critical distance. They can also, however, orient these visions of the future toward redemptive horizons, finding in the disintegration of contemporary civilization the possibility to construct radical new alternatives.

The Road is an unusual participant in this critical project. It simply does not look like more obviously political works of dystopian and post-apocalyptic fiction by authors such as Margaret Atwood or Octavia Butler. It avoids attributing the apocalypse to human agency, its depictions of social relationality are limited in scope, and it does not offer much hope that civilization can be renewed. As such, *The Road* participates in a bleaker, more pessimistic strain of post-apocalyptic fiction: the survival narrative in which a white male protagonist must contend with the various depravities of human nature unleashed by the collapse of civilization. The superficial apoliticism of this narrative conceals a reactionary disposition insofar as it affirms that, as neoliberal discourse has always claimed, humans are brutes whose relentless pursuit of self-interest must be harnessed by the free market to serve the collective good. *The Road* certainly engages with some of the tropes of this reactionary narrative—the fascination with cannibalism, for instance—but it notably avoids that narrative's descent into nihilism. The father and, to a greater extent, the son, persist in acting decently. The novel, furthermore, avoids simply presenting the apocalypse and the depravity that ensues from it as the expression of an essentially violent human nature. It instead provides a framework for reading these phenomena as consequences of contingent historical processes and ideological formations.

One of the main objections to politicized readings of *The Road* is that the cause of the apocalyptic event is never specified. The two most popular theories are that the disaster is caused by either nuclear war or a meteor strike. Steven Frye explains what is at stake, here: "A nuclear holocaust would be the result of human evil, and the meteor or asteroid the outcome of natural evil."[1] A number of critics have pushed back against readings that assume that *The Road* depicts the aftermath of a nuclear holocaust. Dana Phillips writes that "the critical discussion of *The Road* has been skewed by an impression, possibly erroneous, that in it the end of the world is brought on, and not merely exacerbated by, human agency: specifically, by all-out nuclear warfare."[2] According to this view, the tendency to attribute the apocalypse to human agency may be a distortion of a narrative that is simply focused on other matters. Phillips delivers a close reading of the only scene in the novel that provides a description of the apocalyptic event, arguing that the passage's imagery seems more applicable to a meteor strike than to a nuclear detonation. This reading derives support from a 2007 *Rolling Stone* article that documents McCarthy's interest in meteor strikes.[3] John Cant, alternately, accepts the nuclear disaster hypothesis while noting that the novel's setting is not an entirely accurate description of nuclear winter. He attributes these inconsistencies to McCarthy's choice to privilege the novel's allegorical structure over its scientific accuracy, claiming that "the 'nuclear holocaust' is a metaphorical explanation for the state of the world that McCarthy creates as his wider metaphor for the condition of man in the realization of his cosmic insignificance."[4] Cant focuses on the event's formal role in the narrative, reading the novel as an expression of humanity's "cosmic insignificance" and taking the nuclear event as a plot point that simply facilitates the text's existential musings. Cant's analysis is an example of a popular reading of *The Road*, according to which McCarthy's wasteland functions, like T. S. Eliot's, as a representation of the crisis of meaning in the modern (or postmodern) world. Such a reading collapses the pre- and post-apocalyptic worlds of the novel—as well as the "real" world of the reader—into a unitary existential condition defined by instability and the slippage of signification.

Such readings tend to liken the father and son to many other McCarthy protagonists: Job-like figures locked in hopeless struggles against a harsh and implacable universe. In the Border Trilogy, it is possible to identify the antagonistic force opposing both John Grady Cole and Billy Parham as the advance of modernity and the technologies and ideologies associated with it. In *The Road*, however, only traces of these processes remain, and the novel does not offer an obvious reason for their passing, leaving open the possibility that the apocalypse had little or nothing to do with the destructive potential of modern civilization. Because of this, some critics offering politicized readings of the novel avoid making their readings contingent on a particular understanding of the apocalyptic event. David Huebert's ecocritical analysis of the novel argues, for instance, that

> in *The Road* McCarthy is more interested in how his characters respond to their journey of torments than what, precisely, causes the horrors they endure. Whether or not he intends to portray a post-climate-disaster world, in this novel McCarthy depicts the imminent and universal horror of a terrestrial climate irrevocably altered.[5]

Huebert suggests that even if the novel's apocalypse was not the result of human action, the novel still performs a socially critical function through its chilling representation of a world in which the climate has radically changed. Despite his effort to de-emphasize the role of the apocalyptic event in the text, Huebert later claims that "the profusion of cannibals populating the text suggests that the cause of the disaster was ecological cannibalism."[6] Huebert's ambivalence is symptomatic of the novel's complexity: he acknowledges that the catastrophe is not named before suggesting that the text's political function is not canceled or lessened by that omission, but he still ultimately posits a reading of the catastrophe as an ecological disaster caused by human action.

There certainly are reasons to attribute the apocalypse to human agency, particularly to the environmental toll of late-capitalist production and consumption. For instance, the father reflects early in the novel that there is "no fall but preceded by a declination," suggesting that the end of the world was the culmination of a process of social and environmental decline rather than the outcome of an inexplicable natural disaster.[7] Nonetheless, Huebert is correct that the novel's socially critical functions are not wholly predicated on the cause of the apocalypse, and parsing the novel's approach to social commentary in other passages provides insight into how to understand the apocalyptic event. As Fredric Jameson writes in *Archaeologies of the Future*, "the social totality is always unrepresentable, even for the most numerically limited groups of people; but it can sometimes be mapped and allow a small-scale model to be constructed on which the fundamental tendencies and the lines of flight can more clearly be read."[8] Compressing a "social totality" into a small-scale model through symbolism and synecdoche is precisely what *The Road* does, as it represents the material and ideological residues of late capitalism that linger after the apocalypse. These remnants force a dialectical revaluation of the relationship between past and present, insisting simultaneously on their difference and unity.

McCarthy's Archaeology of the Future

Walter Benjamin's variant of historical materialism, particularly as articulated in his "Theses on the Philosophy of History" and certain aphorisms in *The Arcades Project*, provides useful insight into McCarthy's representations of history. Indeed, Billy Parham and John Grady Cole in the Border Trilogy and the father in *The Road* are all fitting literary analogues for Benjamin's famous "angel of history," who gazes back into the past as the catastrophic storm of progress "irresistibly propels him into the future to which his back is turned."[9] *The Arcades Project*, Benjamin's sprawling, unfinished study of the Parisian Arcades, is a massive constellation of notes, images, and quotations that seeks to communicate a narrative of nineteenth century French capitalism—its rise and its subsequent transmutation into a new form that left the old structure, embodied by the Arcades, decrepit and obsolete. Central to Benjamin's analysis is his concern for the ontology of historical objects—artifacts from the past that speak to the transience of their historic moment. Susan Buck-Morss writes that "such outdated products of mass culture were to provide a Marxist-revolutionary, political education for Benjamin's own generation of historical subjects, currently the victims of mass culture's more recent soporific effects."[10] This "political education" enabled by the historical object consists of demystification. According to Graeme Gilloch, *The Arcades Project* "charts a natural history of the commodity . . . the inscrutable fetish and stupefying spectacle of the recent past is demystified and rendered legible."[11] The historical object, formerly fetishized as a commodity but now demystified and reduced to its sheer materiality, bears witness to the mutability of its epoch's material and ideological order. The demystified past demystifies the present; it compels the subject to historicize the present by reexamining its relation to the conditions that produced it. *The Road* presents readers with just such a subject—the father—who encounters the terrifying relationship between past and present in the charred artifacts of neoliberal America.

One of the aphorisms in *The Arcades Project* declares that "as Proust begins the story of his life with an awakening, so must every presentation of history begin with an awakening."[12] *The Road* follows this mandate quite literally; the novel begins with the father waking in the dark woods of the fallen world from a dream in which he and his son wandered in a primordial cave. In this dream, a grotesque reptilian creature lurks on the bank of a subterranean lake, and the father can see its bones and organs through its translucent skin before it turns and "lope[s] soundlessly into the dark."[13] Lydia Cooper describes this dream as "a nightmare vision of humankind's participation in its own destruction."[14] As a metaphor for a corrupt civilization in decline, the decaying creature endowed with brain and heart recedes willingly into darkness. This haunting passage is the first instantiation of the motif of awakening in the novel. It is an apt beginning to *The Road*, which several times describes the father awakening from dreams of a prosperous and idyllic past life to the nightmare of the present.

The Road's landscape is littered with the skeletal remains of pre-apocalyptic America, and these remains are often freighted with significance. The "tattered oilcompany roadmap" that the father and son use to navigate the wasteland is a useful example of this pattern in the text.[15] The map, notably, "had once been taped together but now it was just sorted into leaves and numbered with crayons in the corner for their assembly."[16] The father tells the boy at one point that the black lines on the map "used to belong to the states. What used to be called the states." "What happened to them?" the boy asks, and the father responds, "I don't know exactly."[17] The United States of late capitalism is mapped here by a corporation, a representative of the economic interests that shaped the material and ideological terrain of the vanished nation. The map's tattered condition reflects the condition of the constructs it represents, but the father and son still rely on it to navigate the post-apocalyptic world. Their relation to the material world is still mediated by the constructs of the past, cobbled roughly and precariously together. The attribution of the map to an "oilcompany" sharpens its symbolic function by introducing a direct reference to the fossil fuel industry. This is significant in the context of a novel that describes an ecologically blighted future. The novel never explicitly attributes the apocalypse to climate change, or any other disaster initiated by humans, but this does not render the event unknowable. The father's and son's interactions with material objects over the course of the novel produce something like an archaeological record of late-capitalist America, one that allows the subject to discern, in Benjaminian fashion, a repressed, subversive history.

The artifacts of late-capitalist America tend to remain anonymous. They are rarely associated with a brand name or identifying label. The roadmap's association with the fossil fuel industry has political resonance, but the adjective "oilcompany" remains vague, making it easier for readers to scan over it uncritically than would be the case with a pointed reference to extant corporations like BP or ExxonMobil. The father and son pass through "the ruins of a resort town," but the resorts and the town remain nameless.[18] They see billboards featuring "a pale palimpsest of advertisements for goods which no longer existed," but the novel does not provide a description of these goods or any mention of the corporations that produced them.[19] This absence may be explained when McCarthy writes of "The names of things slowly following those things into oblivion. Colors. The names of birds. Things to eat. Finally, the names of things one believed to be true. . . . The sacred idiom shorn of its referents and so of its reality."[20] The dearth of brand names in the text emphasizes the dissolution of the commodity form. Marx documented the process by which objects become fetishized commodities: the traces of the labor process are erased from the material object through the imposition of quasi-mystical monetary and cultural values. *The Road* describes what remains when a commodity is de-fetishized. The relics of consumer culture, once luminous repositories of monetary and cultural value whose names participated in the "sacred idiom" the father refers to, have relapsed into their material character as various configurations of matter, some of which are useful and some of which are not.

The can of Coca-Cola the man and the boy find in the grocery store is a striking exception to this trend:

> By the door were two softdrink machines that had been tilted over into the floor and opened with a prybar. Coins everywhere in the ash. [The father] sat and ran his hand around in the works of the gutted machines and in the second one it closed over a cold metal cylinder. He withdrew his hand slowly and sat looking at a Coca Cola.[21]

The man's first impression of the object relates to its materiality: it is a "cold metal cylinder." Only when he looks at it is he able to associate the material object with its brand name. This juxtaposition of the object's identities as material entity and as commodity underscores the distinctness of the two identities and the significance of the moment of transition in the object's history. As Benjamin writes, the "present determines where, in the object from the past, that object's fore-history and after-history diverge so as to circumscribe its nucleus."[22] The father experienced the moment in the past when the historical object ceased to be a commodity and became a mere material object, when the implosion of late capitalism evacuated its products of their monetary and cultural values, altering forever the texture of the material world. The coins scattered across the ashen floor are reminders of the decommodification of objects such as cans of Coca-Cola. The coins and the softdrink no longer exist in relation to each other as exchangeable signifiers of value, a point echoed later in the novel when the father finds a small round object in a field and cannot tell if it is a coin or a button. In this latter scene, after identifying the object as a coin, the father "looked about at the gray country and the gray sky and he dropped [it]," discarding an object that has become worthless in the context of the desolated world.[23] Brian Donnelly, in his analysis of the novel's grocery store scene, suggests that McCarthy chooses to label the Coca-Cola can because of the brand's cultural resonance, noting that "the expanding corporate machine that is Coca-Cola has worked to forge an ideology for its customers, one that promotes the product and its consumers as part of a global family of happy, peaceful, refreshed drinkers."[24] This association seems superficial and hollow in the context of the novel's present, which demonstrates that even if capitalist production was not directly responsible for the demise of that happy, familial world, it was incapable of ensuring its reproduction.

Many objects other than the Coca-Cola contribute to this element of the text's critical function. The father and son enter a drugstore where "The pharmacy was looted but the store itself was oddly intact. Expensive electronic equipment unmolested on the shelves. . . . Sundries. Notions. What are these?"[25] The father's question "What are these?" foregrounds the ontological instability of the material world in a historical period in which the relation of humans to that world has changed irrevocably. The contingency of the normal, of all that was taken for granted in the past, rises out of the effort to relate the electronic devices to a changed historical context in which they have no monetary or cultural value, or any utility in the effort to survive. The electronic devices are, furthermore, "expensive" luxury items, making them fitting artifacts of American consumerism. Susan Kollin offers a detailed analysis of the grocery cart in which the father and son carry their belongings, writing that "as a symbol of late-capitalist consumer culture . . . the cart is a reminder of the irrational exuberance that characterized the economy of contemporary America."[26] As is the case with the oil company map and the can of Coca-Cola, a tension arises from the grocery cart's insertion into the context of the post-apocalyptic wasteland. This is a tool that facilitated consumption in a world characterized by abundance, and it now holds the father's and son's paltry possessions as they try to survive in a world of scarcity. The image of the man and the boy dressed in ragged clothes and pushing their belongings down the road in the cart is also a stereotypical representation of urban homelessness, compressing in the cart symbolic evocations of the related phenomena of extreme excess and deprivation in contemporary American society.[27]

Readers of *The Road* are constantly confronted with the material remains of the neoliberal past, compelling them to sort through the Benjaminian "rags and refuse" of postmodernity where they lie in charred constellations of condemnation and hope, delivering an implicit indictment of the novel's prehistory and the reader's present. The novel's representations of social relationality demand a similar historicizing project. Jameson describes the radical social transition often represented in futuristic texts as a process in which "custom and law are swept away, a social chaos ensuing from which a new social order emerges only slowly and from new and unpredictable, hitherto marginal areas."[28] The image Jameson describes resonates to a degree with McCarthy's depiction of social collapse, but in *The Road*, the past continues to inflect the thought and behavior of the apocalypse's survivors. The father functions as a sort of conduit, struggling to construct a new system of values out of the symbolic fragments of the old structure while mediating their transmission to his son. Despite the father's rhetoric, he never succeeds in fully realizing his moral code. This is the task of the son, who receives the reconstituted altruistic traditions of the past and applies them through a form of praxis that opposes the instrumental rationality of the majority of the apocalypse's survivors.

Post-Apocalyptic Praxis

"In what direction did lost men veer?" the father wonders midway through the novel.[29] The apocalypse's disoriented survivors tend to veer in one of two directions: some toward cannibalism, and some toward community. The cannibals in *The Road* may be read as representatives of humanity's essential barbarism, the "taste for mindless violence" continually blighting McCarthy's storyworlds.[30] According to this reading, the cannibals demonstrate the alternative to the father's remobilization of the values of the past:

they submit to the meaninglessness of the post-apocalyptic condition and suspend the outmoded moralities that in this world prove to be liabilities and obstacles to survival, such that the world is quickly "populated by men who would eat your children in front of your eyes."[31] The value system passed from father to son is rooted in the distinction between the animalistic "bad guys" who engage in murder and cannibalism and the Promethean "good guys" who carry the fire and seem imbued with spiritual energy. The son, as the embodiment of love and goodness, appears to the father as a being "from some unimaginable future, glowing in that waste like a tabernacle,"[32] set in stark opposition to the one cannibal that the pair encounter up close: "The reptilian calculations in those cold and shifting eyes. The gray and rotting teeth. Claggy with human flesh."[33] The text supports a reading that frames the cannibals as embodiments of humanity's animal instincts and the son as the bearer and representative of the spiritual energy symbolized by the fire. Essentializing the characters in this way, however, by contrasting a brutal human nature with the spiritual principle embodied by the son, elides other resonances of their practices. Here, as elsewhere in the novel, it is worthwhile to consider how the landscape of *The Road* changes when it is understood as shaped by politics, by historical contingencies subject to human agency.

The cannibalism featured in the novel may be viewed not as a regression to some bestial state outside of ideology, but rather as a performance of ideology, a behavioral residue of late-capitalist consumer culture. Donnelly notes the connection between the pre- and post-apocalyptic forms of consumption described in *The Road*: "the supermarket epitomizes just the sort of self-consuming society McCarthy sends to its demise. . . . Cannibalism as a metaphor for consumption is realized in this novel."[34] The hierarchical structure of the cannibal groups is established through power and competition, the reification of the subject and the consumption of the weak by the strong. In a famous passage, the father and son stumble upon a group of humans imprisoned in the basement of a farmhouse, treated as livestock by captors who are slowly consuming them. In another passage, McCarthy describes a nomadic band organized according to strict hierarchical and patriarchal terms:

> An army in tennis shoes, tramping. . . . Behind them came wagons drawn by slaves in harness and piled with goods of war and after that the women, perhaps a dozen in number, some of them pregnant, and lastly a supplementary consort of catamites illclothed against the cold and fitted in dog-collars and yolked each to each.[35]

The extreme gender imbalances here are notable. The dearth of women—there are only about a dozen in an apparently large group of survivors—speaks to humanity's dwindling ability to reproduce itself. A few of the women are pregnant, but a later passage in which the father and son encounter "a charred human infant headless and gutted and blackening on the spit," leaves little doubt as to the fate of any children born to these women.[36] When the women die, they presumably share the fate of their offspring—to nourish those with power.

The image of the cannibal referenced previously describes an intersection of animal instinct and utilitarian, instrumental rationality. Particularly disturbing—and evocative of the nightmare creature of the novel's opening—is the reference to the "reptilian calculations" taking place in the cannibal's brain. Reasoning is presented as cold-blooded and inhuman in this passage, where it reduces humans to consumable objects and legitimizes cannibalism as an amoral means to an end. Clearly, these small pockets of human society are not capitalistic. There is no exchange, no paid labor, no commodity form, and so on. Manuel Broncano, in fact, emphasizes the atavism of these groups by describing them as a "return to the primitive hunter-gatherer epoch."[37] His later reference, however, to "the agony of a race that tries to survive on its own waste and whose offspring are not meant to perpetuate the species, but to serve as fodder for the men-turned-beasts, thus eventually completing its own annihilation," describes an unsustainable social order that has apparently come into existence because the social order that preceded it was, itself, unsustainable.[38]

The relationship between the cannibalistic present and the capitalistic past should be understood dialectically; the two historical moments and their corresponding social forms are structurally different yet joined by a shared set of ethics and assumptions, and, potentially, a relationship of historical causality. Understanding the cannibalism in the novel in this context reveals its continuity with economic structures predicated on the unfettered consumption of commodities that are too often produced by exploited, disempowered people. These structures have historically been shored up through ideological operations that posit competition, greed, and the pursuit of self-interest as fundamental—and, indeed, salutary—qualities of human nature. This correlation is particularly instructive in an era in which celebrations of capitalism are increasingly couched in the language of corporate responsibility. Slavoj Žižek criticizes this "new ethos of global responsibility" which seeks to represent capitalism "as the most efficient instrument of the common good . . . [while] *leaving these very capitalist relations intact*."[39] *The Road* projects the ethics of late capitalism into a post-apocalyptic context of hunger and scarcity remote from the legitimizing ideological operations of the past. It describes the brutal consequences of those ethics when carried to their logical extreme, revealing their incompatibility with the humanitarian ethos described by Žižek and referred to also in Donnelly's discussion of the Coca-Cola scene.

In one of the notes compiled in *The Arcades Project*, Benjamin briefly defines three "basic historical concepts: Catastrophe—to have missed the opportunity. Critical moment—the status quo threatens to be preserved. Progress—the first revolutionary measure taken."[40] The catastrophe Benjamin refers to here is not the moment when history is ruptured. Rather, it is the moment when the window of opportunity forced open by that rupture slams shut, when the dominant ideology is reinscribed and the status quo is reconstituted. *The Road* describes two catastrophes: the disruption of history and the way humanity responds to it, the dissolution of civilization and humanity's subsequent failure to replace the old order with more equitable and humane social forms. The naturalization of exploitation is a basic feature of the post-apocalyptic world and of the society that produced it. The past has not been cleanly swept away, and those elements of pre-apocalyptic social relations resurrected by survivors of the catastrophe contribute to the future's nightmarish character. Any substantive break from the antagonistic modes of relationality institutionalized before the apocalypse and seemingly legitimized by the material conditions ensuing from it is, indeed, revolutionary.

The father and son reject the reduction of the human subject to a consumable object. Christopher Pizzino argues that in the world of *The Road*, "There is still the possibility that life can be lived on other terms than those of murder and cannibalism, and that this life can come not from remembrance of the past but from an ethical commitment to futurity."[41] Key to this reading is the boy's growing insistence on expanding the father's ethics beyond their immediate familial contexts and into broader communal contexts. Both past and present have been thoroughly demystified for the father by the novel's beginning; he has learned of the universal "frailty of everything," but he seeks to forestall this process in his son through acts of ideological reconstruction. This process entails an imbrication of the spiritual and the socio-political as the father uses Christian terms and symbols to articulate a belief system defined by communal values. The father reflects early in the novel that "If [the boy] is not the word of God God never spoke," immediately associating the son with divinity.[42] This designation is elaborated throughout the text: the father insists to his son that the pair are "carrying the fire" and he describes the boy as a "Golden chalice, good to house a god."[43] He "evoke[s] the forms," adopting Christian images and applying them to a new spiritual being in whom he sees the wasteland's only instance of goodness and salvific potential: the son.[44] These textual moments should not be construed as an attempt by the father to maintain traditional religious faith, nor should they be viewed as an effort to construct a wholly new system of belief. History is a palimpsest of new orders constructed on the foundations of the old. The father selects fragments of the traditions of the past and remobilizes them, adapting them to the social and material realities of the post-apocalyptic world while maintaining the values of love and goodness that animated them.

Love and goodness cannot be practiced in isolation, and while the father is hesitant to interact with any other survivors, the boy understands that their value system obligates them to relate in a certain way to those they encounter. Late in the novel, the father asks the boy if he would like to hear a story, and the boy declines, saying "in the stories we're always helping people and we dont help people."[45] This moment, Cooper notes, "suggests that [the boy] sees the necessity of a functional correlation between fictional ideas and real-world praxis."[46] The ideals of the father impel the boy into the risky acts of kindness and generosity of which the father remains wary. Paul Knox discusses the centrality of community to the stories and lessons the father imparts to the son: "surviving the wasteland requires re-creating the communities that the apocalypse has erased—even if those communities will exist only in the imagination."[47] The novel focuses on the relationship between the boy and his father, but their orientation toward the rest of the world—their conviction that they are among the "good guys"—presupposes the existence of other good guys and situates community at the heart of their value system. "I don't know what we're doing," the boy says at one point in the novel, and the father responds, "There are people. There are people and we'll find them. You'll see."[48] When the boy raises doubts about the purpose of their journey, the father's only response, though he may not fully believe it himself, is that they need to find other good people and enter into community with them. This possibility gives meaning to their continued efforts to survive.

The boy's unyielding commitment to his values leads him to insist on sharing food with the few harmless survivors they encounter on the road. When the pair meets the old man Ely midway through the novel, the son meekly suggests "Maybe we could give him something to eat," and after Ely eats a can of fruit cocktail the boy asks, "Can we give him something else?" before insisting "We could cook something on the stove. He could eat with us."[49] The father acquiesces reluctantly, and Ely shares a meal with them, but as the two grow thinner and sicklier, the father's practicality clashes with the boy's altruism. "Just help him, Papa. Just help him," the boy pleads late in the novel when the father leaves the thief who stole their cart naked and alone on the road.[50] The thief stole the cart in response to desperate material circumstances, and the father's reaction is to punish him. The boy recognizes what the father chooses to ignore—"he was just hungry, Papa."[51] Though the father does not always succeed in performing his ideals to his son's satisfaction, he is responsible for instilling in the boy the values of goodness and communal sharing that he sees as being the only antidote to life in the fallen world. These values answer Thomas Schaub's question regarding "the status of the ethical, as well as the reason for being, in the absence of the social."[52] The ethics of the father and son are predicated on their enduring faith in the possibility of the social, in the potential for society to be, if not renewed, at least rejoined communally and on a microcosmic scale.

The Road and Messianic Time

As noted above, it is debatable to what extent the behavior of *The Road*'s characters is attributable to ideology, and to what extent it is rooted in ahistorical essences. Animalism converges and seems compatible with capitalist ethics in the figures of the cannibals, and the father's and son's value system has a spiritual valence that interacts with its gesture toward communal social forms. This mingling of social and theological possibilities in the figure of the son is articulated in Broncano's argument that the son represents "a religion without gods and without demons, based on the brotherhood and sisterhood of those who still claim themselves as human."[53] The theological language applied to the son cannot be dissociated from the socio-political implications of his values and practices. According to Cooper, the novel's application of grail imagery to the son designates him as "both grail and grail-bearer, vessel and antidote to the world's toxicity."[54] The son, as grail, is an object infused with spiritual energy—perhaps some sort of divinity, perhaps simply human compassion—and this property compels him to perform the role of grail-bearer, propagating goodness through salvific acts of communal sharing. The son's praxis is a profound disruption of the social relations that preceded the apocalypse and that found continuity in the cannibalism that ensued from it. Whether the fire is human love, divinity, or an imaginary construct, the values and practices associated with it throughout the novel are subversive.

These imbricated spiritual and socio-political possibilities imbue the novel's conclusion with a positive note rare in McCarthy's corpus, a faint utopian hope that exists in tension with the overwhelming bleakness surrounding it. The closing image of brook trout, for instance, with its nostalgia for a past "which could not be put back. Not be made right again" combines the beauty of McCarthy's prose with, seemingly, an acknowledgment that humanity's progress toward extinction may be irreversible.[55] To grapple with the bittersweet tone of the conclusion, it is useful to turn to Benjamin's theory of messianic time. Benjamin invokes the Messiah not as a hypothetical future savior, but rather as a historical potential. He writes in the final aphorism of the "Theses on the Philosophy of History" that "We know that the Jews were prohibited from investigating the future. . . . This does not imply, however, that for the Jews the future turned into homogeneous, empty time. For every second of time was the strait gate through which the Messiah might enter."[56] To live in messianic time is to live with an awareness of the future's radical indeterminacy, to see the future not as empty time, nor as a homogeneous perpetuation of the status quo—because every second brings with it the possibility of unimaginable change. Catastrophes, for Benjamin, are moments of opportunity, unforeseeable events that arrest the destructive trajectory of history and rupture the status quo, making visible the utopian potentials arrayed across the social and material worlds, such that the possibility for revolutionary change flashes in on the historical subject "with the sobriety of dawn."[57] Jameson writes that,

> The very idea of the messianic then brings the whole feeling of dashed hopes and impossibility along with it. . . . You would not evoke the messianic in a genuinely revolutionary period, a period in which changes can be sensed at work all around you. . . . This is the notion of the non-announced, the turning of a corner in which an altogether different present happens, which was not foreseen.[58]

Critics such as Allen Josephs have convincingly described the son as a Christ figure, as a redeemer imbued with divinity, but it is also useful to consider him as a messianic figure in the Benjaminian sense.[59] The son represents the historical potential for a just, equitable, and sustainable society, even if the conditions under which such a society could feasibly be established have passed, and even if that society—the "unimaginable future" the son seems to anticipate—cannot be wholly conceived or visualized. He is the bearer of a radical consciousness, born out of catastrophe, which is antithetical to the social conditions he is embedded in: a consciousness in which the self/other dialectic is resolved through an utter surrendering of self-interest, such that each becomes "the other's world entire."[60]

The origins of good and evil are recurring concerns in McCarthy's novels, in which instrumental rationality often defines the terms of humans' relationships with nature and with each other, their brutality seemingly in accord with the economic policies spurring society toward crisis. Naomi Klein writes that "neoliberalism's single most damaging legacy" is that "the realization of its bleak vision has isolated us enough from one another that it became possible to convince us that we are not just incapable of self-preservation but fundamentally *not worth saving*."[61] *The Road* offers an alternative to this "bleak vision," and as such, it should be understood as a hopeful novel. It affirms the capacity of humans to practice compassion, mutual aid, and communal sharing even in a historical context that seems uniquely inhospitable to such forms of social relationality. While the landscape of the novel is ecologically ravaged and depopulated of most forms of life, *The Road* remains oriented toward horizons of possibility, as the son and his new companions carry the fire into an undetermined future.

Notes

1. Steven Frye, *Understanding Cormac McCarthy* (Columbia: Univ. of South Carolina Press, 2009), 169.

2. Dana Phillips, "'He ought not have done it': McCarthy and Apocalypse," in *Cormac McCarthy: All the Pretty Horses, No Country for Old Men, The Road*, ed. Sara Spurgeon (New York: Continuum, 2011), 176.

3. David Kushner, "'If It Doesn't Concern Life and Death, It's Not Interesting': Cormac McCarthy's American Odyssey," *Rolling Stone*, 27 Dec. 2007: 6.

4. John Cant, *Cormac McCarthy and the Myth of American Exceptionalism* (New York: Routledge, 2008), 269.

5. David Huebert, "Eating and Mourning the Corpse of the World: Ecological Cannibalism and Elegiac Protomourning in Cormac McCarthy's *The Road*," *The Cormac McCarthy Journal* 15, no. 1 (2017): 66–87.

6. Ibid., 74.

7. Cormac McCarthy, *The Road* (New York: Vintage, 2006), 15.

8. Fredric Jameson, *Archaeologies of the Future: The Desire Called Utopia and Other Science Fictions* (New York: Verso, 2005), 14.

9. Walter Benjamin, "Theses on the Philosophy of History," *Illuminations: Essays and Reflections* (New York: Schocken, 1969), 257–58.

10. Susan Buck-Morss, *The Dialectics of Seeing: Walter Benjamin and the Arcades Project* (Cambridge: MIT Press, 1989), 4–5.

11. Graeme Gilloch, *Walter Benjamin: Critical Constellations* (Hoboken: Blackwell, 2002), 135.

12. Walter Benjamin, *The Arcades Project*, trans. Howard Eiland and Kevin McLaughlin (Cambridge: Harvard UP, 2002), 464.

13. McCarthy, *The Road*, 4.

14. Lydia Cooper, "Cormac McCarthy's *The Road* as Apocalyptic Grail Narrative," *Studies in the Novel* 43, no. 2 (2011): 218–36.

15. McCarthy, *The Road*, 42.

16. Ibid., 42.

17. Ibid., 42–43.

18. Ibid., 29.

19. Ibid., 128.

20. Ibid., 89.

21. Ibid., 23.

22. Benjamin, *Arcades Project*, 476.

23. McCarthy, *The Road*, 204.

24. Brian Donnelly, "'Coke Is It!': Placing Coca-Cola in Cormac McCarthy's *The Road*," *The Explicator* 68, no. 1 (2010): 70–73.

25. McCarthy, *The Road*, 183–84.

26. Susan Kollin, "'Baren, Silent, Godless': Ecodisaster and the Post-abundant Landscape in *The Road*," in *Cormac McCarthy: All the Pretty Horses, No Country for Old Men, The Road*, ed. Sara Spurgeon (New York: Continuum, 2011), 161.

27. Ibid., 168.

28. Jameson, *Archaeologies of the Future*, 90.

29. McCarthy, *The Road*, 116.

30. Cormac McCarthy, *Blood Meridian, or the Evening Redness in the West* (New York: Vintage, 1985), 3.

31. McCarthy, *The Road*, 181.

32. Ibid., 273.

33. Ibid., 75.

34. Donnelly, "Coke Is It!," 71.

35. McCarthy, *The Road*, 91–92.

36. Ibid., 198.

37. Manuel Broncano, "Grocery Shopping in the Commissary of Hell: *The Road*," in *Religion in Cormac McCarthy's Fiction: Apocryphal Borderlands* (New York: Routledge, 2014), 126.

38. Ibid., 126.

39. Slavoj Žižek, *First as Tragedy, Then as Farce* (London: Verso, 2009), 35.

40. Benjamin, *Arcades Project*, 474.

41. Christopher Pizzino, "Utopia at Last: Cormac McCarthy's *The Road* as Science Fiction," *Extrapolation* 51, no. 3 (2010): 358–75.

42. McCarthy, *The Road*, 5.

43. Ibid., 41, 75.

44. Ibid., 74.

45. Ibid., 268.

46. Cooper, "*The Road* as Apocalyptic Grail Narrative," 232.

47. Paul Knox, "'Okay Means Okay': Ideology and Survival in Cormac McCarthy's *The Road*," *The Explicator* 70, no. 2 (2012): 96–99.

48. McCarthy, *The Road*, 244.

49. Ibid., 163–65.

50. Ibid., 259.

51. Ibid.

52. Thomas Schaub, "Secular Scripture and Cormac McCarthy's *The Road*," *Renascence* 61, no. 3 (2009): 153–67.

53. Broncano, "Grocery Shopping in the Commissary of Hell," 139.

54. Cooper, "*The Road* as Apocalyptic Grail Narrative," 227.

55. McCarthy, *The Road*, 287.

56. Benjamin, "Theses on the Philosophy of History," 264.

57. Benjamin, *Arcades Project*, 474.

58. Fredric Jameson, *Valences of the Dialectic* (New York: Verso, 2009), 176–77.

59. Allen Josephs, "The Quest for God in *The Road*," in *The Cambridge Companion to Cormac McCarthy*, ed. Steven Frye (Cambridge: Cambridge UP, 2014), 133–47.

60. McCarthy, *The Road*, 6.

61. Naomi Klein, *This Changes Everything: Capitalism vs The Climate* (New York: Simon & Schuster, 2014), 62.

6

"PLEASE DONT TELL HOW THE STORY ENDS"

The Road and Neoliberalism

Christine Chollier

Many critics who comment upon *The Road* (2006) frame it as a post-apocalyptic novel, one that reads as a critique of modernity's disastrous effects.[1] Unlike earlier apocalyptic texts, for example those captured in Judeo-Christian scripture, contemporary post-apocalyptic works typically do not disclose utopian renewal scenarios but often question the very notion of utopian revelation. "The deconstruction of traditional apocalyptic logic . . . is taken up by the contemporary post-apocalyptic novel," Cristofaro argues.[2] Like other dystopian speculative fictions, McCarthy's novel anticipates a catastrophe which has already occurred in the fictive time, stressing the devastating consequences and side-effects of "the road taken."[3] So it is that what Peter Brooks calls the "anticipation of retrospection" in narrative emphasizes the value of what has been undone and possibly encourages conservation of what is to be preserved.[4] Post-apocalyptic texts thus raise contemporary questions about the relevance of "progress" to mankind: Is all that which is offered as progress necessarily beneficial to human beings? Drawing upon Jean-François Lyotard's metanarrative, Jacques Derrida's deconstruction, and

Michel Foucault's genealogy, Cristofaro asks this very question, suggesting that progress just is "the modern metanarrative *par excellence*, 'represent[ing] the main example of the secularization of apocalypse' and of its utopian telos."[5] Within this frame, readers of such fiction, including *The Road*, face the subsequent dilemma: Is post-apocalyptic fiction necessarily and implicitly conservative? Or can it highlight the contradictions of our postmodern epoch and raise useful anthropological questions? With McCarthy's novel as its primary focus, this chapter looks at the implications of such questions by reference to the work of philosopher Barbara Stiegler, who, alongside others, proposes renewed insights into the phenomenon of neoliberalism.[6]

In her 2019 study, Stiegler argued that the proximity between the terms "liberalism" and "neoliberalism" suggests a mere continuation from the former to the latter, with the prefix "neo" actually preventing us from understanding the new paradigm. She traces neoliberalism back to Walter Lippmann's book *The Good Society*,[7] and to the Walter Lippmann Conference (Paris 1938), which advocated the advent of a new stage in the development of capitalism: while liberalism was based on free trade and was exempt from any moral imperative other than profit-making, neoliberalism added a biological necessity by way of a translation, or a transcoding, of Darwin's theory of species adaptation to the environment into the struggle of individuals, or entities, within the social and economic fields.[8] This naturalist view of human life gave Stiegler her title—*"You've got to adapt"*—wherein the author explains earlier writers' moral imperative requiring uninitiated people to be trained for and persuaded into the necessity of socioeconomic changes, as though they were stubborn children.

Given *The Road*'s two major characters, a father and a child, the good guys "carrying the fire" and steering clear of the bad guys, I want to examine McCarthy's text not as the writer's conservative or progressive intention—*intentio auctoris*[9]—but as an allegorical story which, beyond the simple tale of intra-family relationships, tells us something about the contradictions, if not the contradictory injunctions, of our time. Leaving the nature of the catastrophe unspecified, *The Road* does not explicitly advocate a new ecological ethic, or, as David Holloway puts it, "another reformist agenda comfortably assimilated within the patterns of domination they oppose."[10] Instead, I argue that the allegorical dimension of exchanges within the brutally indifferent wasteland of the novel reflects the new socioeconomic paradigm which is often pushed to the top of the agenda after various catastrophes leave countries, societies, and economies devastated.[11]

Stiegler also insists that citizens' consent must be manufactured, as Lippmann famously put it, to achieve the new *telos*. Those in charge of manufacturing such consent are the leading "experts" who are "supposed to know" and to know how.[12] Even though such experts are usually invisible, their slow, patient, pedagogical or educational mission heavily relies on communication within a deliberate top-down approach.[13] This communication regime includes the mass market novel. Insofar as the father guides the child on the path to life in an increasingly lethal environment, I want to offer an allegorical reading of *The Road* as the locus of the contradictions a patriarch finds himself in charge of solving for his child's benefit. Amid those contradictions, readers can perceive flickering anthropological values asserting an extant, though declining, epigenetic cultural core resisting, while yielding to, the biological and economic imperative applied to human life.[14] Thus, McCarthy's ultimate trick might be posited as a language which reasserts—albeit feebly or pessimistically—what is denied the subject of neoliberalism.

"The cold illucid world," or Extinction

The wasteland described by McCarthy is not so much a newfound tabula rasa on which history can be written, or a place where everything—human animates, fauna, and flora—has died or gone extinct. It is no virgin land for pioneers to conquer but the result of conquest and exploitation. The pulverized wasteland and the directionless road rewrite the well-known American chronotopes of Manifest Destiny. The shopping cart carrying the characters' few belongings is a degraded buggy, which transforms *The Road* into "a 'reversed story' of the conquest of the American West," just as the novel's frozen train car signals the end of the expansionist myth.[15]

As everyday life is reduced to basic human needs such as food and shelter, metaphysical life is too stripped down to a basic question: not *who are we?* but *what are we*? "Will they know *what* we are?" the boy asks (emphasis added).[16] The question, which is now about roles, has replaced the former one about individual identity: "Who is it? . . . I don't know. Who is anybody?"[17] Somebody has become anybody, if not anything, in the ultimate commodified world. Indeed, the derivatives of the shift to *some*, *any*, and *no,* as well as the compounds of the word "thing," all contribute to defamiliarizing life and the surrounding environment itself. *Some*, implying an unspecified quantity, quality, or identity of the word it qualifies in an affirmative context, blurs the general outlines: "like pilgrims of some common order"; "They were some fifty miles west of where he'd thought."[18] *Any*, being a pronoun of indifference meaning "one or more, no matter which" in an affirmative context, also contributes to the dissolution of the physical world: "Looking for anything of color. Any movement. Any trace of standing smoke."[19] In a negative context, "any" will neutralize the existence of the slightest quantity otherwise provided: "What if that little boy doesnt have anybody to take care of him?"[20] And when all those derivatives are combined, the conflation implies utter emptiness or irretrievable loss of "a thing which could not be put back. Not be made right again": "No tracks in the road, nothing living anywhere."[21] Even memory has faded away, "He lay there a long time, lifting up the water to his mouth a palmful at a time. *Nothing* in his memory *anywhere* of *anything* so good" (emphasis added).[22] Through the use of indetermination, McCarthy's language seems to perform the extinction it narrates: "Finally the names of things one believed to be true. More fragile than he would have thought. How much was gone already? The sacred idiom shorn of its referents and so of its reality. Drawing down like something trying to preserve heat. In time to wink out forever."[23] This preoccupation with language extinction is recurrent in McCarthy's *oeuvre* and reappears in his final novel proper *The Passenger* (2022): "The legacy of the word is a fragile thing for all its power."[24]

Space is given the same erasure. For example, the father's roadmap is useless as the two wanderers never find themselves where they thought they were. Usual bearings have been blown up. A word like "neighborhood" has been emptied of reference to human life (surrounding neighbors) and it is now limited to some vague location in space:

> I'll be in the neighborhood. Okay?
> Where's the neighborhood?
> It just means I wont be far.[25]

Just as space is characterized by indeterminacy, with the sea being as disappointingly gray as the rest of the landscape when father and son reach it, time is described as diluted in the prevailing indistinction: "It could be November. It could be later."[26] Chronology is also made impossible: "The days sloughed past uncounted and uncalendared."[27] Time is measured in an unspecified number of days, nights, weeks, and years, and this lack of grammatical determination being recurrently conveyed by the plural form Ø-s. Day is "hardly a day at all," "such day as there was," "such few hours," meaning a "day" cannot be defined by comparison with anything else; it is self-determining.[28] At best, it is described somewhat negatively, as "hardly light," by "the grudging light that passed for day."[29] Time is no longer oriented by human action and will: "No lists of things to be done. The day providential to itself. The hour. There is no later. This is later."[30] The present and the future having been preempted by the past catastrophe, these notions do not make sense anymore. The father's past life has become a hazy "long ago" and there is no future either.[31] Like the earth, the mind is an ash-covered palimpsest.

To evoke extinction, McCarthy's language of disaster euphemizes the environment and life: odor is now a "rumor," with diction playing down intensity and blurring the lines between olfactory and auditory semantic fields. Cows are extinct and only their metonymical odor lingers on.[32] Metonymy transforms life and world into traces, fossils. Not only is the represented world destroyed, but the language used performs that destruction, as though submitted to the annihilation too. The parataxis, which consists in erasing links of coordination or subordination usually indicated by connecting words, has been interpreted by one critic as a way to put an end to the anthropocentric view of the world: "the paratactic style and structure all but erase the concepts of causality and hierarchy, stripping the world of anthropocentric epistemological categories and thus creating a space for the 'background' to take prominence."[33] What is striking, too, is the novel's extensive use of nominal clauses after perception verbs linked to the father's discovery and evaluation of his surroundings:

> He lay listening to the water drip in the woods. Bedrock, this. The cold and the silence. The ashes of the late world carried on the bleak and temporal winds to and fro in the void. Carried forth and scattered and carried forth again. Everything uncoupled from its shoring. Unsupported in the ashen air. . . .[34]

> They passed through the city at noon. . . . The city was mostly burned. No sign of life. Cars in the street caked with ash, everything covered with ash and dust.[35]

> . . . he could see almost to the rear of the box. Human bodies. Sprawled in every attitude. Dried and shrunken in their rotted clothes.[36]

The high number of past participles and regular adjectives testifies to the descriptive quality of the consequences of the disaster in those sentences. Nominal clauses being, by definition, devoid of predication and of verbs signifying state or process, they convey a completely frozen environment lying before, but totally unrelated from, the observer's eyes. Having blown up the world, the catastrophe has broken up connections, movements, order. Words lie in chaotic disorder, just as things do: "Bedrock, this"; "Well should he."[37] Syntax is broken, extinct. Sentences read like a jumble of words.

Thus, even logic itself seems to have faded away, just as McCarthy's syntax no longer carries markers of causality: "They were moving south. There'd be no surviving another winter here."[38] Causality is implicit and brings survivors and readers back to cause number one—the disaster and its collateral damages: "He kept constant watch behind him in the mirror. The only thing that moved in the streets was the blowing ash."[39] Life is completely determined by the result and consequences of this unspecified apocalyptic event which cannot even be named. Allusions made to this "cause" or to the time of this event are scattered into the text, as though it were buried, too. However, if the catastrophe has broken syntax and logic, the past, on the contrary, is the time when things could be causally related: "They walked through the diningroom *where* the firebrick in the hearth was *as* yellow *as* the day it was laid *because* his mother could not bear to see it blackened."[40] The narration of the visit to the house where the man grew up hardly conceals the kind of causal link that is to be found nowhere else in the account of the post-disaster drifting.

All of this—the dissipation of logic, the erasure of time, and the dismantling of meaning—are the effect of neoliberalism, which produces a certain "primitivism" McCarthy seems to suggest. The novel's catastrophe is characterized as having thrown man back into a time when use value mattered more than exchange value. In *The Road*, this applies to the qualitative value given to what used to be exchanged for money (quantitative value): "Chili, corn, stew, soup, spaghetti sauce. The richness of a vanished world."[41] What used to be *riches* (concrete) are here returned to their *richness* (abstract). But, of course, in the highly competitive predatory milieu exacerbated by the disaster, which might be understood as the epitome of capitalist competition, the late discovery of use value works to accentuate loss of riches, so that use value is just reminiscent of irrevocable loss. As for exchange, it has been annihilated by mass destruction and scarcity predation. The very symbolic instrument of exchange—money—has become a mere archaeological artifact, as the coins found here and there suggest: the Kruggerands from South Africa, the Spanish coin in the boat, and the sextant, which symbolizes the great discoveries of the late fifteenth century. Thus, each object has two sides, like a coin: one testifying to the rise of civilization; the other bearing witness to its decline. Finally, what remains, McCarthy suggests in *The Passenger*, is "survival value."[42]

The wasted physical world depicted in *The Road* has universally been interpreted as the blatant failure of economic *laissez-faire*, a "critique of the devastating consequences of consumer-driven global market-capitalist systems," says Cooper.[43] Roaming the earth are a father and his son trying to flee from cannibals who have already adapted to their environment, as required by a model assumingly derived from Darwin's natural selection. As As Cooper continues, "*The Road* depicts three types of people: those who consume each other . . . those who are consumed; and those who insist on an equitable parsing of what meager goods remain."[44] The terrifying combination of the biological and the technological is all that is left in a godforsaken world where the political branch is as invisible as Adam Smith's hand of the market, because the experts' imperatives have been internalized. Immersed in that hostile environment are the man and his son, who are summoned to adapt to new conditions in order to survive.

"The good guys . . . keep trying," or "You've got to adapt"

In most novels, characters are built through description of their physical attributes, perception, feelings, language, ethical values, and attitude. In *The Road*, as in most post-apocalyptic texts, physical description of isolated characters becomes irrelevant, especially if they are given a universal dimension. What they see, or fail to see, matters only insofar as perception is blocked by the ash dust cover and a non-descript brownish gray, a restricted color palette which prevents cognition and aesthetic pleasure.[45] As some critics have noted, what readers are left with are dialogues, memories, dreams, and feelings revolving on ethical preoccupations. The remaining characters' lives are determined primarily by survival, which becomes the sole purpose of saying, acting, doing, or enjoying. All legal, aesthetic, erotic, rhetorical, and ethical norms have collapsed under the pressure of survival alone, which reduces life to biological and technological norms.

The father and his son are obviously both the victims of the disaster and the agents of the new paradigm: the man, Cooper argues, is the product of industrialism and he is now the locus of adaptability and resilience. However, the father's effort to offer hopeful guidance to his son clashes with inevitable moments of despair attached to mental processes such as remembering and dreaming. Dreams and memories fulfill both the function of informative narrative flashbacks and that of increasing the tension between dispossession and control: "Rich dreams now which he was loathe to wake from. Things no longer known in the world."[46] These dreams operate via memory of euphoric moments that ultimately emphasize dysphoric[47] loss, such that, as David Holloway notes, they enact a sort of cruelty "in the relationship between narrator and protagonist, in the way that the narrative voice . . . violently withdraws the essential status of the wish object . . . while leaving the perception and the desire of the protagonist more or less intact."[48] Yet, this loss is not centered on the self but rather on universals: "he would begin to sob uncontrollably but it wasn't about death. He wasn't sure what it was about but he thought it was about *beauty* or about *goodness.*"[49] As Tsutserova put it, the man is endowed with "the consciousness of a non-existing something," and the realization of these non-existing transcendent ethical values results in the mother's suicide and the father's death.[50]

The Promethean fable of the good men "carrying the fire" in contrast with the cannibalistic bad guys is eventually internalized by the boy who "is always other-focused and forward-looking."[51] Therefore, it is tempting to conclude that the mother "represents a lost present, the father the brute instrumentalist survival of tradition and the past, and the child represents possibility and the future."[52] However, the man's death and the youth's undecidable future articulate the difficulty of ethics in a dog-eat-dog environment, the clash between intention and fact. As Cristofaro notes, the boy:

> anxiously keeps asking his father whether they are still the "good guys," since in order to survive the man is forced to perform morally questionable acts—from killing one of the "bad guys" to leaving another without clothes or shoes in the cold. The blurring of the distinction problematizes the simplistic sense-making structure of apocalyptic moral dualism and challenges the self-righteous policies this dualism legitimates, including the messianic innocence of post 9/11 politics.[53]

In such an environment, ethical imperatives cannot be aligned with biological dictates, which demand that individuals stop inhibiting the so-called natural flow of change. The characters' premonitory dreams also foreclose any possibility, as they announce each other's death.

The father's premonitory nightmare is paralleled by the son's: "He'd seen the boy in a dream laid out upon a coolingboard and woke in horror" is echoed by "I was crying. But you didn't wake up."[54] The boy's first premonitory dream in the novel is, primarily, a proleptic announcement of his father's death, and thus of his future isolation; secondly, it is a shift to the child's consciousness, which so far was overshadowed by the adult's. The reader is thus gradually prepared for the father's declining life and for the child's taking over. The switching of roles takes place a few pages after the aforementioned dream and involves a nightmare the son will not tell: "When your dreams are of some world that never was or of some world that never will be and you are happy again then you will have given up. Do you understand? And you cant give up. I wont let you," the father says.[55] It seems that the impossible combination between the anthropological and biological prescriptions urges the disconnection between dreams—utopia—and real life: "You've got to adapt." In the next pages, the characters come upon mummified figures charred and shrunken by fires, and it is the child who takes the lead, saying: "Why don't we just go on."[56] Here, "go on" certainly means "plod on" but in the context which has just been described the phrase also reads as a new leadership of sorts. The growing exposure of the child's self is first conspicuous in a dialogue where he is asked to speak his mind and where he finally brings his father to assert that they are the good guys and that they are carrying the fire. Further down, the young one's language borrows an idiom from the adult's: "long term goals."[57] If the phrase is just mimicry, it also resonates as parody of economic terminology. Is the torch still a metaphor of *both* the ethical principle and the economic one?

The final exchange of roles takes place when a question usually ascribed to the son is asked by the father, and the laconic answer attributed to the child: "What are we going to do Papa? he said. Well what are we, said the boy."[58] And indeed, it is the child who at that point takes care of the man just as the father has taken care of his son. The third-person singular pronoun tentatively shifts to the boy: "He'd wanted to try and make a tent out of the tarp but the man would not let him."[59] If the father's point of view is dimming in the final sequences, there is, however, no direct switch to the boy's consciousness, except to his premonitory dreams. The end of *The Road* relies on direct discourse—between the now orphaned boy and the cheek-scarred man who wrapped the father in a blanket—and on a mythological parable, which is a refusal to provide an end to history.[60] If, as Cristofaro suggests, "postmodern theory debunks the end as the privileged site of meaning" because an ending "makes everything fit . . . and it closes down time by conferring a spurious sense of inevitability on the sequence actually realized," then post-apocalyptic fiction turns down any closure, "defying chronology, linearity, continuity, foreshadowing, cause and effect and the sense of an ending itself."[61] Significantly, the father's soliloquy, "Please dont tell how the story ends,"[62] reads as a metafictional commentary on both the genre and the *telos*, since indeed "the end of the road has nothing to do with the road."[63]

Before dying, though, the father's encouraging words teach his son some basic ethical and linguistic principles. First, he explains that the fire they have been carrying is something internalized, something symbolic: "It's inside you. It was always there."[64] Secondly, he prospectively sets up imaginary communication between them, in order to bridge the gap opening by his impending death: "If I'm not here you can still talk to me. You can talk to me and I'll talk to you. . . . You have to make it like talk that you imagine. And you'll hear me. You have to practice."[65] After his father's death the child is left to live by himself. His first challenge is to face a "veteran" down the road, and he expresses his feeling of helplessness: "I don't know what to do."[66] Then the assessment of the man's goodness is carried out through the main criterion of whether the stranger eats people or carries the fire. Finally, he "tried to talk to God but the best thing was to talk to his father and he did talk to him and he didn't forget."[67] In other words, the child is able to speak about himself, to communicate with another, and to relate to the dead. His limited but newly acquired skills make it possible for him to evoke the three anthropic zones which have been described by linguistic anthropology as symbolically articulating mankind's specific experience: namely, the sphere of identity; the zone of proximity; and the realm of the distal, or absent, world, with the latter including the dead, ancestors, idols, heroes, gods, laws, principles, and sacred books—all that is found in dreams, madness, and religious or mystic visions.

The connection between the semiotic mediation and the symbolic one can be explained in anthropological terms.[68] In spite of the cold indifference of the de-anthropomorphized universe, the child's final role is to inhabit and couple, on the one hand, the semiotic sphere between the real world and the realm of representations, and, on the other hand, the three anthropic zones—described as dealing with oneself, with connections between oneself and the other, and with relationships between one's empiric milieu and the absent world. It might be tempting, then, to read the child's continuing life as promotion of mankind's eternal adaptation. However, like Patrick O'Connor, I venture that "it would be unwise to read the boy joining a family at the end of the novel as McCarthy's unambiguous affirmation of the family unit."[69] What matters at that point is McCarthy's argument that the cultural is part of man's epigenetic heritage while the biological imperative seemingly borrowed from the theory of evolution is being naturalized and thus removed from the analytic register.[70]

The Road shows how liberalism's *laissez-faire* and neoliberalism's biological paradigm are incompatible with the preservation of the natural and social environments. The threats and flaws of the unspecified global sphere in which characters are immersed reveal humans' failures to imagine an alternative "otherwise."[71] However, "*The Road* expresses a desire for the universal: that which transcends belonging and community offers more resilience to human values than any community."[72] The characters' reduced lives can be described as a combination of stasis and motion which contradicts the simplistic dualisms offered by the thinkers of neoliberalism.[73] Stiegler, for instance, outlines Lippmann's philosophy in terms of dualisms between mind versus body, cognition versus action, and purpose versus means, contrasting Lippmann's preference for the passive masses' education by experts with John Dewey's refusal to endorse the blaming of the public for stopping the flow of change.[74] Stasis, Stiegler argues about Dewey, does not deny the necessity of flow but makes it possible to examine and regulate change.[75] In *The Road* the two main characters can be described as isolated individuals having to adjust locally in the dark, the result of Lippmann's society atomized into a mere addition of individual desires and choices with no links between one another. Yet, they are also signed as agents methodically performing tasks which they endow with meaning. Starting a fire, cooking, setting up the tarp are detailed as age-old gestures which give significance to a life where nothing else makes sense. Thus, McCarthy's "naked individual," one might venture in Dewey's terms, articulates both the *telos* of neoliberalism and the complex interaction between organism and environment which is precisely denied by neoliberalism.[76]

"All these things he saw and did not see," or The Hermeneutic Paradigm Against Communication

When the father loses sight of the idea of possibility, the contradictions between ethical and material injunctions become blatantly incompatible.[77] His death results from the collapse of a pragmatic attitude accommodating survival imperatives with a realization of irretrievable loss, from a crunch between memories of the euphoric past and dysphoric feelings of loss within living conditions where only survival matters. The father's death, the open ending, and the son's continuing life actualize conflicting ideas of termination and purpose, which co-exist as opposites in the *telos*. The contradictions are not only confronted by the characters but they are also addressed to readers by McCarthy's performative use of language.

Throughout the text readers face defamiliarizing stylistic devices which actualize the disturbing meaning of the words themselves. In this world of dog-eat-dog and man-eat-man, literally, the thin borderline between animal flesh and human flesh is suggested long before the two main characters are faced with cannibals and have to struggle for self-preservation: "In an old batboard smokehouse they found a ham gambreled up in a high corner. It looked *like something fetched from a tomb*, so dried and drawn. He cut into it with his knife."[78] The term "tomb" in this instance suggests the possible meaning "human," the juxtaposition of which casts doubt on what exactly is going to be eaten without bringing the matter to a conclusion.

Polysemy in the novel offers many additional examples. Depending on the context, which is actualized differently by each reader, a sentence can take on several meanings in addition to the most plausible one provided by the linguistic context: "In the shallows beyond the breakwater an ancient corpse rising and falling among the driftwood. He wished he could hide it from the boy but the boy was right. What was there to hide?"[79] The occurrence "he could hide it" here seems to mean "What thing was left to be hidden? or What was that thing to be hidden?"; while "shallows" and "shore," being flat places, make it possible to infer "What was there to hide in / what was hiding in?," which incidentally likens the survivors' situation with that of the corpse. "What was there to be hiding from?" comes up as another interpretive possibility and exposes the characters' vulnerability. This variety of potential meanings signals an opening of paths which are overlooked in a rapid reading of the text but which transform the text into something other than a mere semantic string once they are built. In other words, contextual interpretation is what a human mind does when it works out complex semantic operations.

Not only are father and son faced with an apparently directionless and meaningless world, but readers are challenged to make sense of words which are not immediately transparent in their given context. In addition to the broken syntax and the loss of temporal and logical organization, sentences may appear stubbornly tautological, as in "the snow fell nor did it cease to fall," where the coordination "nor" does not introduce a second alternative or further information because "[not] cease to fall" seems to just repeat "fell."[80] The second, coordinated clause merely introduces a new shade of meaning: that of uninterrupted duration, which "fell" might have expressed already, but which is made more obvious despite the double negation. The diaphora thus apparently performs a meaningless repetition until the second occurrence of the word is dissimilated to the first one. In the following example, the verb "see" is both asserted and negated: "all these things he saw and did not see."[81] The statement expresses stark contradiction unless one dissimilates /perception/ to /intellect/, in which case the father cannot mentally construe the visible clues as possible interpretation. Thus, semantic dissimilation may be interpreted as readers' refusal of general equivalence.

McCarthy's writing also scavenges language for defamiliarizing Greek and Latin roots which contribute to the depiction of the stripped-down material and ethical wastelands. When the two traveling survivors go through a city just before revisiting the house where the father grew up, they come upon the mummified dead: "They were discalced to a man like pilgrims of some common order for all their shoes were long since stolen."[82] The phonetic proximity between "calcinate" and "dis-calce" creates prior confusion until doubt is lifted by the reference to shoes. Any number of dictionary entries for "discalcinate" remind us that the word means "unshod," "barefoot," coming from the past participle of calceare, or "to furnish with shoes," as "calceus" means "shoe." Given the importance of shoes to pilgrims, one is made to understand how these bodies were robbed of their footwear. What is also prefigured in this image of death is the characters' fate as shoes and food have previously been identified as what mattered most: "That [shoes] and food."[83]

Further down, the army of cannibals marching past and watched by the man and son from a hiding place is called a "phalanx," from a Greek word meaning "stick," which befits their pipes fitted with chain and used as bludgeons; "infantry corps," which suits their army-like organization; finally, the reference to antiquity is echoed by a description of the phalanx's slaves, used for drawing wagons, pregnant women, and catamites.[84] The mummified figures seen later are like "victims of some ghastly envacuuming" and the characters are passing them "in silence down that silent corridor through the drifting ash where they struggled forever in the road's cold coagulate."[85] The coagulated blood is transferred from the humans to the road because their blood has been drawn, as though by a vampire-like machine or monstrous creature whose process is called "envacuuming." The "cold illucid world" watched at dawn inherits the antonym of "lucid" used in its rare etymological sense referring to light, which the context "it was almost light enough to see" actualizes, while virtualizing the reference to consciousness usually applied to animates.[86] Either one virtualizes /consciousness/ because "il-lucid" is attributed to an inanimate, or one transfers /consciousness/ from "il-lucid" to "world." However, the intermittent co-existence of "lightlessness of inanimates" and "clearness of animates' thought" opens up possibilities which have to be elaborated by readers—such as the negativity of the world as animate. Thus, it is not so much the real which must preserve the words, or the words which must preserve the real, as the human species moving within this semiotic milieu and establishing constant interactions with it.

McCarthy's linguistic talents also include his ability to re-literalize metaphorical language. His valley of ashes has obviously none of the metaphorical value it took on in Fitzgerald's *The Great Gatsby*. When, in *The Road*, the skinny boy plays with the roll of the surf and undresses, the father observes "the razorous shoulder blades sawing under the pale skin."[87] The shoulder bones having inherited the form of blades in standard English, the next step is to turn them into razor edges, which is reinforced by "sawing." The cutting emaciation is all the more frightening as it goes to the essential core of the boy's body, his skeleton, which becomes dangerously thin, and the perception is placed in the universe of a loving father, who, in spite of all his efforts, could not prevent such thinning. Standing on the edge of the coast, the two characters are perilously poised on a razor's edge too. Literalization—the undoing of metaphor—might thus be interpreted as a refusal of "the dead equivalence of words with all other words," returning language "back into what looks like a system of relatively stable, self-sufficient signs."[88]

At the end of his book-length study of McCarthy, *The Late Modernism of Cormac McCarthy*, Holloway suggests that toward the conclusion of the Border Trilogy "optical democracy,"[89] defined as "a resistance of the simulacrum by way of the simulacrum itself," might be a "waning form" demanding "thinking again."[90] McCarthy's prose engages the two meanings of the word "ideology" that Holloway articulates as follows: "where the 'complex term' merely conceals contradiction, the utopian neutral term first renders contradiction visible and then cancels or annuls it in whatever figurative way."[91] If optical democracy as a dialectical design is still to be found in post-*Blood Meridian* works such as *The Road*, it reemerges as a political unconscious (per Fredric Jameson) or as a dimly conscious solution going against the communication model considering interaction between signifier and signified, as well as interaction between text and interpreter, as irrelevant in the commodity world extending equivalence to words. Clashing antonyms, semantic dissimilation, creative polysemy, defamiliarizing archaisms, and literalization ("de-metaphorization") do not only return the fictive world to its de-anthropomorphized and pre-neoliberal life; they also testify to a linguistic practice which does not communicate anything top-down, from sender to receiver, but which requires meaning to be built in by readers who are neither consumers nor consumed commodities.[92]

McCarthy's writing confronts us with brutal semiotic contradictions and situations. Far from the communication model, it addresses the rhetoric/hermeneutic paradigm which trusts readers with an inert text whose meaning must be built within the ethical limits of the constraints imposed by the linguistic context. Readers are cast in the role of wanderers plodding through the "neoliberal" narrative and are constantly invited to actualize neoliberalism's ethical constraints within the imposed linearity of the text. McCarthy's political unconscious lies in his ethically demanding prose, a prose which does not interpellate us as consumers, or as children, but which engages us as responsible interpreters. *The Road* does not teach us to accept the *telos*; it forces us to actualize the contradictions, and the possibilities, of our time.

Notes

1. Cormac McCarthy, *The Road* (London: Vintage, 2006).

2. Diletta de Cristofaro, *The Contemporary Post-Apocalyptic Novel: Critical Temporalities and the End Times* (2019; repr. London: Bloomsbury Academic, 2021), 14.

3. "The Road Not Taken" is a well-known poem by American poet Robert Frost, taking up and transforming the *topos* of the road as life, and describing the possibility, and difficulty, of choice. One might venture about McCarthy's novel that the road is the physical surface imposed on travelers whereas the route has to be decided upon and it is "the one [road] less traveled by."

4. Peter Brooks, *Reading for the Plot: Design and Intention in Narrative* (Cambridge: Harvard UP, 1984), 94.

5. Cristofaro, *Contemporary Post-Apocalyptic Novel*, 12.

6. Barbara Stiegler, *"Il faut s'adapter." Sur un nouvel impératif politique* (Paris: Gallimard, 2019). See also Serge Audier, who in *Néolibéralisme(s)* (Paris: Grasset, 2012) focuses his own exploration of neoliberalism on the nuances between various schools and models, arguing that Michel Foucault underestimated the differences between, for example, the German and the American models.

7. Walter Lippmann, *The Good Society* (1937; repr. New Brunswick & London: Transaction Publishers, 2005). The current French translation of *The Good Society* is, interestingly, entitled *La Cité libre* (1938; repr. Paris: Les Belles Lettres, 2011), with "cité" aligning the project with older

utopias such as Campanella's, thus erasing the socioeconomic ideology and the moral design ("good") for the benefit of more consensus-based values like "liberty."

8. *The Origin of Species* (Charles Darwin, 1859) was hailed as the opportunity for renewed treatment of moral, political, and religious issues. See also John Dewey, "The Influence of Darwinism on Philosophy" in *The Middle Works*, vol. 4, *1899–1924* (Carbondale: Southern Illinois UP, 1977), 15; Herbert Spencer, *Principles of Psychology* (London: Brown, Greens and Longmans, 1855), who raises the question of organisms' adaptability to their environment; and Graham Wallas, *Great Society: A Psychological Analysis* (New York: Macmillan, 1916), where Wallas argues that either humans have to adapt to their environment, or the environment must be fitted to human faculties. Eventually, the question came around to how to adapt ill-fitted or ill-fitting human beings to their environment, either through top-down education or through eugenics. For a discussion of the biological sources of the debate, see Stiegler, "*Il faut s'adapter*," chapter 3 and pgs. 39–41 and 132–33.

9. Umberto Eco, *The Limits of Interpretation* (Indiana UP, 1991). Adding an Althusserian turn of the screw, Jean-Jacques Lecercle wrote in *Interpretation as Pragmatics* (Basingstoke and London: Macmillan, 1999), 75, that "the reader is interpellated by the representation she constructs in the place of the author; the author is interpellated by the representation of the readers she fantasises."

10. David Holloway, *The Late Modernism of Cormac McCarthy* (Westport: Greenwood Press, 2002), 172–73. Similarly, McCarthy's writing from a de-anthropomorphized point-of-view is one more referential illusion, although a very interesting and productive one.

11. Philosophers such as Stiegler and Audier have noted that crises like the 1929 Stock Market Crash, the Depression, World War II, the 1974 oil shock, not to mention the "Great Recession" of 2008–2009, have offered conditions favorable to the new agenda. But the debate, which primarily emerged in the 1920s and the 1930s, forcibly pushed its political and economic agenda in the 1980s, with the Ronald Reagan presidency and Margaret Thatcher's leadership in the U.K.

12. Stiegler refers to Noam Chomsky & Edward Herman, *Manufacturing Consent: The Political Economy of the Mass Media* (1988; repr. New York: Pantheon Books, 2002), although the phrase "manufacture of consent" is Lippmann's.

13. The pedagogue in Greek is the slave leading ("agein") the child ("podos") to the teaching master. Pedagogy is thus the science of children's education. Education, with its prefix 'ex,' is expected to either take ("ducere") the children out of their primary state of ignorance or root out what is lying dormant in them; it refers to the pressure put on someone by someone else. Cristofaro, in *Contemporary Post-Apocalyptic Novel*, claims that the telos, which was originally meant to be utopian, has been inverted into "oppressive power dynamics: the elect versus the rest, us versus the other, insiders versus outsiders" (12), adding that "those who posit a telos to history use it to legitimize their often oppressive deeds" (17). In McCarthy's *The Road*, the imperative of the *telos* has been internalized.

14. The intermittent anthropological light can also be seen in McCarthy's short paragraphs flashing or flickering against the page as they focus on perception, thought, and sparse dialogue.

15. Aitor Ibarrola-Armendariz, "Cormac McCarthy's *The Road:* Rewriting the Myth of the West," *European Journal of American Studies* 6, no. 3 (2011): 3, accessed 1 July 2024, http://journals.openedition.org/ejas/9310.

16. McCarthy, *The Road*, 104.

17. Ibid., 49.

18. Ibid., 24, 182.

19. Ibid., 4.

20. Ibid., 85.

21. Ibid., 287, 30.

22. Ibid., 122–23.

23. Ibid., 88–89.

24. Cormac McCarthy, *The Passenger* (London: Picador, 2022), 137.

25. McCarthy, *The Road*, 95.

26. Ibid., 89.

27. Ibid., 273.

28. Ibid., 155, 102.

29. Ibid., 68.

30. Ibid., 54.

31. Ibid., 7, 4, 29, 88, 189.

32. Ibid., 6, 120.

33. Ciarán Dowd, "The Hum of Mystery: Parataxis, Analepsis, and Geophysiology in *The Road*," *The Cormac McCarthy Journal* 11, no. 1 (2013): 23–43.

34. McCarthy, *The Road*, 11.

35. Ibid., 12.

36. Ibid., 47.

37. Ibid., 11, 192.

38. Ibid., 4.

39. Ibid., 24.

40. Ibid., 26, emphasis added.

41. Ibid., 139.

42. McCarthy, *The Passenger*, 147.

43. Lydia R. Cooper, *Cormac McCarthy. A Complexity Theory of Literature* (Manchester: Manchester UP, 2021), 149.

44. Ibid.

45. Yuliya A. Tsutserova, "Seeing Nothing: Making Phenomenological Sense of the Counterspectacle in McCarthy's *The Road*" in *Philosophical Approaches to Cormac McCarthy: Beyond Reckoning*, ed. Chris Eagle (2017; repr. New York: Routledge, 2020), 193–94.

46. McCarthy, *The Road*, 131.

47. The same applies to the function of religious terminology, which, according to Patrick O'Connor's *Cormac McCarthy: Philosophy and the Physics of the Damned* (Edinburgh: Edinburgh UP, 2022), "operates to make the empty material universe more palpable," 124.

48. Holloway, *Late Modernism*, 149.

49. McCarthy, *The Road*, 129, emphasis added.

50. Tsutserova, "Seeing Nothing," 187.

51. O'Connor, *Cormac McCarthy*, 128.

52. Ibid., 131.

53. Cristofaro, *Contemporary Post-Apocalyptic*, 81.

54. McCarthy, *The Road*, 130, 183.

55. Ibid., 189.

56. Ibid., 191.

57. Ibid., 160.

58. Ibid., 275.

59. Ibid., 277.

60. *The Road*'s open ending flows into the third trout fable reading like a parable and insisting that the maps and mazes of the world which could be read on the trout's backs were of "a thing which could not be put back. Not be made right again" (287). As suggested earlier in *The Road*, "the intestate earth" (130) has left no will; nor can it be disposed of by will. Like the intestate earth, the novel leaves no will, no historical legacy, preferring the ahistorical parable to a narrative telos making it impossible to open up alternative possibilities.

61. Gary Saul Morson, Narrative and Freedom: The Shadows of Time (New Haven: Yale UP, 1994), 38–39, as quoted in Cristofaro, *Contemporary Post-Apocalyptic*, 16–20.

62. McCarthy, *The Road*, 75.

63. McCarthy, *The Passenger*, 235.

64. McCarthy, *The Road*, 279.

65. Ibid.

66. Ibid., 282.

67. Ibid., 286.

68. For further exploration of anthropological linguistics, see François Rastier, "Anthropologie linguistique et sémiotique des cultures," in *Une introduction aux sciences de la culture*, eds. François Rastier and Simon Bouquet (Paris: PUF, 2002), 243–67. See also "Le langage comme milieu: des pratiques aux œuvres," *Texto!* (Dec. 2003), accessed 1 July 2024, http://www.revue-texto.net/1996-2007/Inedits/Rastier/Rastier_Langage.html.

69. O'Connor, *Cormac McCarthy*, 135.

70. Here, I am referring to twisted instrumentalizations of Darwin's theory, especially to the confusion between species and individuals within species.

71. For similar arguments, see Cooper, *Cormac McCarthy*, 150.

72. O'Connor, *Cormac McCarthy*, 137.

73. One of the major reversals operated by neoliberalism simultaneously lies in the identification of formerly progressive crowds as conservative masses, and the promotion of neoliberal leaders to the position of reformers, thus "assigning [the latter's] opponents either to reaction, or to preservation of acquired rights, or else to a nostalgic yearning for a return" (my translation of "condamnant ses adversaires soit à la réaction, soit à la conservation des avantages acquis, soit à l'espérance nosalgique d'un retour") in Stiegler, "*Il faut s'adapter*," 18–19.

74. Stiegler, "*Il faut s'adapter*," 94–130.

75. Ibid., 124–27.

76. John Dewey, *The Public and Its Problems* in *The Later Works*, vol. 2, *1925–1953* (1927; repr. Carbondale: Southern Illinois UP, 2008), 290.

77. O'Connor, *Cormac McCarthy*, 131.

78. McCarthy, *The Road*, 17, emphasis added.

79. Ibid., 236.

80. Ibid., 96.

81. Ibid., 109.

82. Ibid., 24.

83. Ibid., 17.

84. Ibid., 91.

85. Ibid., 191.

86. Ibid., 116.

87. Ibid., 218.

88. Holloway, *Late Modernism*, 163.

89. The now well-known concept comes from *Blood Meridian, or the Evening Redness in the West* (1985; repr. New York and London: Picador, 1989), 247.

90. Holloway, *Late Modernism*, 168–74.

91. Ibid., 173.

92. Jarring opposites may appear in the same context, as in the following defamiliarizing, undistinguishing occurrences: "he just sat there holding the binoculars and watching the ashen daylight congeal over the land" (5), where /hot/ from "ash" and /cold/ from the Latin etymology "congelare"—thickening by cooling down—are coupled; "the gray shape of the city vanished in the night's onset like an apparition" (9), with "vanish"/end/ and "apparition"/beginning/ apparently clashing through etymology; "the blackened shapes of rock standing out of the shoals of ash and billows of ash rising up and blowing" (14), with the land being compared to a sea of ash, a prefiguration of the reversed discovery of the sea as gray, "dull and leaden" as the land (215).

7

DIAMONDS, DRUGS, AND THE DIGITAL AGE

Global Capitalism in Cormac McCarthy's *The Counselor*

Lydia R. Cooper

In a scene near the beginning of Cormac McCarthy's *The Counselor* (2013), the unnamed Counselor visits a diamond merchant in Amsterdam to purchase an engagement ring stone for his fiancée, Laura. As the Counselor peruses diamonds, the merchant begins to muse about the nature of moral virtue, economic value, and determinism. The merchant concludes his speech with an assertion about the frailty of the transitory, sublunary world. "En este mundo nada es perfecto," he says.[1] In response, the Counselor offers a guess about his interlocutor's ethnic and religious identity: "You are Sephardic." The Counselor deduces that this diamond merchant is a Sephardic Jew based solely, one assumes, on the single Spanish phrase and on the Counselor's association of Jews with diamond dealing.

Such a caricatured portrayal of a Jew—and moreover the Counselor's assumption of an innate relationship between Semitic blood and ancient sources of wealth—is troubling, particularly considered in the context of the recent rise in anti-Semitism in Europe and the United States.[2] This resurgence of anti-Semitism has emerged alongside global shifts toward isolationism, nationalism, and neo-fascism. Such trends ostensibly push against the tide of globalism, but without challenging the systems that underlie the increasing rarefication of capital on a global market. As David Harvey points out in *The New Imperialism* (2003), the rise of a "world-wide anti-globalization movement" began to ally itself in the early twenty-first century with populist movements that together, he says, "threaten to transform grassroots resistance into a series of . . . intensely nationalist" movements.[3] The almost casual allusion to anti-Semitism in that early scene in *The Counselor* thus begins to seem a prescient conjuring of the racial animus allying itself with rising populism in the United States. In fact, McCarthy's *The Counselor* provides a keen-eyed exposition of the dangers of late capitalism in the United States in the first decades of the twenty-first century. And what may seem a bit of casual racial stereotyping provides the first visual reference to the narrative's exposition of the rapacious appetites of global capitalism, its history of violent dispossession, and, most significantly, capitalism's mythic narrative of inevitability.

The film based on McCarthy's screenplay, *The Counselor*, directed by Ridley Scott, was released in 2013 to high expectations. A visually flashy crime drama, the film was nevertheless panned by critics. *The Counselor* follows an unnamed cartel lawyer (the Counselor) as he enters into an agreement with a cartel-affiliated nightclub owner, Reiner, and Reiner's dangerous former call-girl partner, Malkina. Reiner and the Counselor plan a drug deal along with Reiner's more reluctant associate, Westray. The Counselor makes little attempt to separate his deepening involvement with the cartel from his Catholic, wholesome fiancée, Laura, and when the drug shipment is found and stolen by unknown parties, Westray warns the Counselor that the cartel will hunt them all down. Laura gets kidnapped as punishment for the Counselor's failure to return on the stolen goods; she is later executed, a snuff film of her brutal murder given to the Counselor as notice of her death. Malkina, meanwhile, has determined that Westray made off with the funds from the drugs, and she hunts him down in London, hires a hit-woman to kill the man, and decrypts his bank accounts to steal the money back.

While the film did not perform well in the box office, its failures as a visual narrative are not necessarily failures of theme or content. Populated by characters consumed by competition, aggression, and greed, the film also poses a series of brutal, vivid visual metaphors, each one representing distinct movements in the history of market capitalism, the system that famously finds competition, aggression, and greed "good."[4] First, the Jewish diamond merchant in Amsterdam conjures the ancient histories of oppression behind an economic system created and driven by Western European elites whose hands, as the Jewish merchant points out, "are always dripping blood."[5] Subsequent references to black-market drug dealing, sex trafficking, and computer hacking represent global capitalism's shifts in the late twentieth and early twenty-first centuries. Somewhat tongue-in-cheek, Jacob Agner calls *The Counselor* a "trashy spectacle" of a film.[6] Agner specifically analyzes the visual emphasis on trash in *The Counselor* in the context of postmodernism and late capitalism. In such a context, he argues, "what triggered the critical gag-reflex" in the film was ultimately its point—a vivid articulation of the "limits of genre pleasure."[7] Yet this screenplay's project is even more ambitious than that, although certainly it does critique the American entertainment industry. The seemingly isolated scene in Amsterdam at the beginning of *The Counselor* is a critical interpretive key to the narrative's major project: a critique of the history and ethical implications of market capitalism and its most dire iteration in the twenty-first century.

The vivid and prolific scenes of trash that Agner identifies suggest the importance of the theme of overconsumption—of which "trash" is an inevitable consequence. Beyond actual trash, however, the more blatant scenes of hunting, killing, and eating provide a stunning visual metaphor for a global economic system based on predation and overconsumption.[8] More specifically, *The Counselor* constructs an impressionistic history of the monstrosities of global capitalism and gestures toward the looming crisis of late capitalism. Its most telling critique, however, lies in its narrative strategy in which a crucial absent plot point reveals the fundamental justifying myth of global capitalism—that it is inevitable, and that no alternative exists that can be imagined. In the film, the preconditions for the staged drama are already set: the damaging consequences of rapacious exploitation roll on, and any alternative choice is already too late. While many authors offer literary critiques of neoliberalism, warn of its excesses, or mourn the reduction of the working class to global human capital,[9] McCarthy's *The Counselor* forces viewers to confront the preconditions of their own participation in the assumed inviolability of capitalism. Is it, indeed, already too late for any alternative system of value?

McCarthy's works have provided many critical examinations of the antihuman and ecologically disastrous imperatives driving global capitalism, of course. His first novel, *The Orchard Keeper* (1965), offers brutal images of consumerism and rampant industrialization fostered by the American market economy in the nineteenth and early twentieth centuries. In fact, three of

McCarthy's early Appalachian novels (*The Orchard Keeper*, *Child of God*, and *Suttree*) describe the disenfranchisement of exchange-based local economies in 1930s–1950s rural communities in eastern Tennessee by the Tennessee Valley Authority, the federal program devoted to economic development of the region. Nearly all of his subsequent works, too, depict the catastrophic ecological and social effects of mechanization and industrialization. In *No Country for Old Men* (2005), late market capitalism in the United States wreaks havoc on the Texas–Mexico border, and *The Road* (2006) provides a postapocalyptic critique of overconsumption ravaging human societies, as well as the more esoteric notion of humanity. It is no surprise that *The Counselor* picks up these themes. *The Counselor*'s rendering of the perils of market capitalism is notable because it is the most comprehensive, if not the most aesthetically realized, critique of late capitalism in McCarthy's works to that point.

Specifically, *The Counselor* offers a fragmentary and imagistic contemplation of the human cost of capitalism, presented as a sort of collapsed history concluding with an apocalyptically dire vision of late capitalism. Yet this compressed history occurs within a narrative that pivots around a single crucial absence. *The Counselor*'s narrative erases the moment of choice—the moment in which the Counselor must have become complicit or actively adopted the tenets of neoliberalism. In other words, *The Counselor* erases the one moment that must have generated the action of the film. By erasing this all-important moment, the drama exposes perhaps the most pernicious aspect of neoliberal philosophy: its implicit assertion of inevitability.

In order to explore why capitalism is described with such a sense of inevitability, it may be helpful to begin with a brief discussion of what is meant by "late capitalism" for the purposes of this study. "Late capitalism" refers to the shift from traditional market capitalism, which was driven by international trade but primarily located in national centers, to transnational or "global" capitalism in the digital age. Global capitalism, with its diffusion of manufacturing around the world and the concentration of capital surplus funneled through a worldwide financial marketplace to an increasingly small number of power brokers and economic elites, provides an easy target for critique.[10] Its justifying philosophy of neoliberalism, which reduces the human laborer to a labor commodity on the global marketplace, is an equally easily criticized worldview. Yet critique itself is of little value if an alternative system cannot be imagined. And the imaginative failure to construct viable alternatives to global capitalism lies at the heart of its hegemony.

Ellen Meiksins Wood's *The Origin of Capitalism* criticizes economic theorists' failures, even in socialist accounts of the market, to de-naturalize capitalism. Overwhelmingly, capitalism continues to be understood as a function of innate human nature—the *homo economicus* imagined by Adam Smith, John Stuart Mill, and other eighteenth- and nineteenth-century political economists. In short, Wood says, "the conviction that there is and can be no alternative [to capitalism] is very deeply rooted, especially in Western culture."[11] Mark Fisher, co-opting that oft-cited aphorism from Fredric Jameson and Slavoj Žižek that it is easier to imagine the end of the world than the end of capitalism, names this myth of inevitability "capitalist realism." The power of this constructed sense of the "real," Fisher says, "derives in part from the way that capitalism subsumes and consumes all of previous history."[12] He references apocalyptic literatures, such as P.D. James's *The Children of Men*, which attempt and, to an extent, fail at this very project; their failure, Fisher contends, demonstrates our need to challenge the fatalism driving neoliberal justifications for market capitalism. *The Counselor* seems intent on exposing this very problem: the failure to imagine any alternatives to capitalism, or any alternatives to neoliberal justifications for value systems imposed by a free market. Yet instead of creating a fictional universe alternative to our "real" one, McCarthy's narrative lays bare the absurdity of a collective failure to question that assertion of "capitalist realism."

Sephardic Jews, Diamonds, and the Rise of Global Capitalism

The Counselor introduces its compressed history of capitalism through that first shorthand reference to the troubled origins of global capitalism: a transnational economic system born out of the systematic alienation and oppression of Jewish communities in Western Europe. German economist and sociologist Werner Sombart's *Jews and Modern Capitalism* (1913) famously makes a case for the significant and unique role that Jewish banking communities had in laying the fiscal groundwork for capitalism in the fifteenth and sixteenth centuries in Western Europe. Sombart tracks Jewish economic practices—an interest in unlimited competition, speculation and market share bargaining, and international banking—to the two unique aspects of Sephardic Jewish life in Western Europe in the late Middle Ages: first, Jews were excluded from the commercial centers of European communities, forcing them to create their own practices and build their own capital; and, second, they were expulsed from nearly every European state throughout the fourteenth and fifteenth centuries. "The rise to economic importance," Somberg writes, "of the [European] countries and towns whither the refugees fled, must be dated from the first appearance of the Spanish Jews."[13] That Sombart went on to write works praising the rising National Socialist Party in Germany indicates the problematic nature of economists' enthusiastic reception of his earlier work.

Yet he was not entirely wrong. It is a commonplace that Jewish communities lent money at interest while anti-usury laws for Christians were more or less consistent across Christendom. Maristella Botticini, examining Italian census records from the fifteenth century, argues for the unique role that Jewish communities played in medieval and Renaissance Italy's national market. A catasto (census) from 1427 suggests that "Jewish loans amounted to roughly 10 percent of the total debt of all households" in and around Tuscany, a significant proportion of the credit market considering the relative proportion of the Jewish population.[14] Because they tended to deal with liquid wealth rather than property (which they were often forbidden from owning) and because of the tight bonds of the Jewish community, even when they were geographically dispersed, Jewish lenders were able to offer competitive rates and were often less affected by local shocks to the market.[15]

With the birth of the diamond and other precious gem trade in the sixteenth century, Jewish communities found an early foothold in the industry, as its newness made the industry free of guild restrictions that excluded Jews from owning and operating businesses in many other sectors of the European economy. In Europe, Italian merchants in Venice and Sephardic Jewish merchants in Amsterdam gained dominance in the industry refining and selling diamonds shipped from India. Amsterdam quickly became a major hub of the diamond trade, and Jews monopolized the cutting and processing of raw diamonds throughout the lowlands.[16] Later, Antwerp would supersede Amsterdam in preeminence. Today, of course, centers of diamond dealing have been globally dispersed; and in cases where an individual wishes to purchase a particular stone, online trade is more common than in-person overseas shopping. So why does McCarthy's Counselor show up in Amsterdam, specifically, to discourse with a Sephardic Jew about the death of cultures and heroes while also buying a diamond for his fiancée in this twenty-first century narrative?

On the one hand, the Jewish diamond merchant in Amsterdam may seem like a collision of obvious stereotypes, but it is not necessarily the inevitable shorthand reference to the diamond mercantile industry. For if all the script needed to do was force a connection between Jewish communities and the diamond industry, it need have traveled no further than New York City, whose Orthodox Jewish community's control of that city's diamond industry is well documented.[17] It is therefore worth noting that the Counselor simply appears, with no depiction of travel, in Amsterdam, speaking with a Sephardic Jewish diamond merchant who "knows Spain" even though Spain exiled its Jewish community in 1492—a temporal distance that would logically suggest that the Jewish diamond merchant's knowledge of Spain is mere coincidence, rather than personal diaspora.[18] Yet the diamond merchant describes his "knowledge" of Spain in terms of exile: "At one time," he explains, "I thought that she [Spain] would return from the grave. But that is not to be. Every country that has driven out the jews [sic] has suffered the same fate."[19] This cryptic pronouncement of economic and cultural karma suggests that Spain's current failure to recover from the global economic crisis in 2008 somehow resulted from the expulsion of Jews in 1492. From a purely rational or historical viewpoint, this statement is absurd.

Yet if this scene is read as an atemporal metaphor, the Sephardic Jewish diamond merchant posits, metonymically, a fascinating critique of capitalism. As we have established, the rise of capitalism in Western Europe was influenced by the growth of Jewish lending, and Jewish lending was largely successful precisely because Jews were denied rights to own valuable physical property in medieval Europe. The "grave" in which Spain lies now, of course, must be understood to be economic. Spain suffered the ravages of the global financial collapse in 2007–08 particularly harshly. The financial crisis of 2008 was largely due to two incompatible fiscal endeavors colliding—the bundling and sale of mortgages for middle- and low-income Americans by international banks enjoying an era of historic deregulation and consumer overconfidence.[20] To put it even more abstractly, capitalism was born as a system that required an "other"—a class of people disenfranchised from property ownership and from centers of political and economic power. It is a system, moreover, that renews itself through fiscal crisis. The most recent crisis disenfranchised working-class property owners throughout the developed world while concentrating even more surplus capital in the ever-smaller class of global economic elites. As Harvey reminds us, "Put in the language of contemporary postmodern political theory, we might say that capitalism necessarily and always creates its own 'other.'"[21] For Harvey, capitalism's increasing reliance on what he calls "overaccumulation through dispossession" is the ethical crisis of the twenty-first century.[22]

Thus the Jewish diamond merchant warns the Counselor that the diamond—valuable because it is rare—represents the nature of value itself. In a capitalist market system, financial value is based on accumulation and dispossession; capital must be coalesced so as to be rare—the dispossession of the many in favor of the few who possess ever more. But the Jewish merchant reminds the Counselor that there are other value systems, such as non-materialistic religious and ethical paradigms that place enormous value on abstractions such as love and life—rare because they are fragile and brief in a metaphysical rather than material sense. "At our noblest," he says, "we announce to the darkness that we will not be diminished by the brevity of our lives."[23] In a speech composed primarily of short, rhetorical questions and lengthier, seemingly unrelated musings on the nature of gods and mortals, the Jewish diamond merchant manages to convey without clarity the critical foreshadowing of the drama: Western culture is dying because it no longer values its hero, the prophet. And what is the nature of the prophet? The prophet is a "penitent."[24]

The Counselor, of course, does not reflect on that telling word, "penitent." Nor does he grasp the larger and more obvious metaphor of the diamond. After all, he recognizes that Laura, his beloved, is not materialistic—a fact he tells the merchant, while nevertheless attempting to buy an expensive diamond for her. In a sexist attempt at humor, the Jewish diamond merchant suggests that she may be more "courageous" than the Counselor imagines—courageous enough to wear a larger stone, he means.[25] In the story, of course, Laura will prove to be courageous in a different way entirely. She is the wiser and more virtuous of the pair, and the Counselor's inability to extricate himself from his deal with the cartel will result in her murder. In this scene, then, the Counselor participates in the Western European cultural tradition of "buying" a woman's body and valuing her virtue with a precious stone. That is, in its historical context, the diamond engagement ring, popularized in the nineteenth century, symbolizes a woman's compensation for virtue: if the engagement is broken off, she keeps the ring as recompense for her damaged reputation, since her reputation on the marriage marketplace lies in her sexual purity, and an engagement draws that purity into question.[26] The Jewish diamond merchant's reminder of more humane definitions of the value of a person—not that she is chaste, but that she simply is—falls on deaf ears, as the Counselor demonstrates his full submersion in the capitalist ideal: all human beings' values and virtues are made material, and all of human history is subsumed in the rendering of all value systems subordinate to an insatiable market.

The diamond merchant, in fact, explicitly announces this scene's role as thematic foreshadowing—"I suppose every diamond is cautionary," he says.[27] His cautionary tale commences with his metaphorical and allusive discourse on the purity of the stone under examination. Explaining that the first facet cut on a diamond creates an ineradicable change in the stone, he suggests that the first cut represents the first step in all human endeavors. "We see a troubling truth" in the metaphorical first cut, he says, "in that the forms of our undertakings are complete at their beginning."[28] The caution in this scene—and the heavy-handed use of the metaphor of diamond cutting—seems obvious, yet it is less so upon examination. What, after all, is the first "cut" that the Counselor makes? What choice took the Counselor down this road? The thing that matters—the choice about which the merchant cautions—is entirely absent from their dialogue. It is absent as well from the screenplay as a whole.

It is here in this missing element—the Counselor's missing motivation—that we begin to understand why the diamond merchant identifies the "penitent" as the hero lost to Western civilization. Since, as the diamond merchant's father told him, there is nothing perfect in this world, audiences are meant to recognize that humanity itself is flawed. Yet in the Jewish and Catholic traditions of penitence, the penitent is a person who, recognizing their corruption, seeks to make right the wrong they have done and to be forgiven and reincorporated into the civic or religious community they have wronged. Penitence, in other words, is the key to reincorporation into solidarity. Yet penitence commences with confession; only with the naming of the sin can the sinner make an act of contrition and be forgiven. The diamond merchant spends a great deal of time expounding on the nature of flaws in diamonds, ostensibly to draw attention to the nature of flaws in humanity; he then calls on the Counselor to recognize the importance of the "penitent" as a salvific figure. Yet because the Counselor's "sin"—the single act or choice that turned him down this wrong path—is never named, the screenplay conjures a world in which penitence, contrition, and reconciliation are not, in fact, possibilities. Without choice (an act of will), redemption is impossible.

Of course, the mystical allusion to the penitent as the true hero of Western mythology seems like a momentary departure from the main narrative thrust. The Counselor buys his diamond and goes on his way, and the scene cuts to the American southwest, where the Counselor's complicity in a drug-dealing scheme is revealed. The shift from diamond merchants in Amsterdam to Mexican cartels and drug dealing in the United States in the twenty-first century seems abrupt, but the narrative's thematic throughline has already been established: the history of global capitalism explicates the market forces driving the illegal drug industry. Arundhati Roy's well-known piece in *The Nation* argues that America's neo-imperialism takes up the mantle of capacious global appetites for the natural resources (oil, minerals—and diamonds) of older forms of capitalism-driven empires, but with the capacity to operate digitally. "The New Imperialist doesn't need to trudge around the tropics risking malaria or diarrhea or early death," Roy writes. "New Imperialism can be conducted on email."[29] While Roy focuses on the war in Iraq as the exemplar of this neoliberal "new imperialism," in which the neoliberal empire (the United States) engages in voracious consumption of a global underclass, the War on Drugs is an equally apt example—and one that McCarthy has explored before.

The War on Drugs and the Neoliberal Penal System

Stephen Tatum, for example, argues that *No Country for Old Men*, which takes place along the Mexico-Texas border in 1980, can be read as a morality tale about the neoliberal policies driving the War on Drugs—or, more accurately, driving the illegal drug trade between Central and North America. Tracing themes and imagery in the novel that evoke similar rhythms and themes in narcocorridos, Tatum argues that the "drug economy at the time of *No Country for Old Men* [1980] appears as the illegal image of a globalizing world system in transition to a post-Fordist mode of production."[30] According to Dominic Corva, the rise of "hyperpunitive criminal justice practices" in the United States in the 1970s illuminates the relationship between neoliberal global economic policies and the creation of a global "underclass"—a criminal class.[31] Corva describes the convergence of Republican and Democratic penal policies from Ronald Reagan's War on Drugs to Bill Clinton's "tough on crime" policies as fueled by "late 20th century capitalist media practices oriented towards producing social spectacles for profit, and the depoliticization of social relations that produce 'crime' and 'criminals' by their transformation into bipartisan electoral capital."[32]

In *The Counselor*, a thin storyline creates an explosive, violent array of images that expose and exploit the market forces driving the flourishing drug cartels along the Mexico-US border in the early twenty-first century. The Counselor performs a deed that seems initially like an act of mercy—he pays off the $400 ticket of a young man whose mother, Ruth, is already in prison and who the Counselor represents. That young man will become the courier (known as "the Green Hornet") who links the drug shipment to its delivery center because of the debt he owes to the Counselor. The young man's role in the narrative is primarily as a victim of criminal circumstance, yet it is important to unpack what his story represents.

Ruth explains to the Counselor that her son was bringing her $12,000 but because he was speeding, US police pulled him over and confiscated his money. The Counselor points out the legality of this theft: the US government can legally seize any cash in excess of $10,000 found in the process of an arrest or investigation. "Welcome to America," the Counselor quips cynically.[33] Of course, because his money was confiscated, the young man cannot now post bail, rendering him a willing victim to the Counselor's offer to post bail—for a favor. In other words, legal theft on the part of a US police force that arrested the young man precipitates his involvement in a criminal enterprise from which he is unable to extricate himself. His story presents a concise description of the fiscal processes by which the criminal justice system in the United States creates a persistent criminal underclass, without which the entire system's financial infrastructure would collapse.

In the *University of Chicago Law Review*, Blumenson and Nilson explain how this very policy underlies the categorical failure of the War on Drugs. Forfeiture provisions authorizing law enforcement agencies to seize drug-related assets, including any money over $10,000, have encouraged the many budget-restricted agencies around the country to "use the proceeds for their budgetary needs."[34] The economic stimulus given to law enforcement agencies by this provision, then, ensures that this "war" must continue in order for law enforcement agencies to function. *The Counselor*, in fact, explicates this process to audiences in case they have missed the narrative's underlying critique, in the scene in which Westray explains the caper to the Counselor. Westray describes the "six hundred and twenty-five kilos. Pure uncut" that will be brought in the sewage truck across the border. He provides the financial breakdown of the scheme: "[Cocaine] goes for about fifty dollars an ounce in Colombia and the street price in Dallas can be as high as two grand."[35] They will sell the drug up in Chicago. The Counselor, reflecting on this venture's financial rewards, remarks, "If the drug wars stop this will dry up, right?"[36] In other words, US policing and penal systems are driven by the financial incentive to arrest and imprison bodies. And so long as the policing and penal systems profit off the illegality of the product, the illegality of the product drives up the profitability of trafficking in that product's sale.

In addition to underscoring the financial processes by which policing in the neoliberal United States manufactures its own products through creating and perpetuating crime and criminal classes, *The Counselor* also underscores the humanitarian crisis at the heart of neoliberal economics—the dehumanization of the masses reduced simply to being "human capital." A failure to recognize and respect the dignity of others lies at the heart of Westray's admission of his own guilt and his indication of what he perceives as the Counselor's complicity as well. Westray tells the Counselor that Mexican cartels are depraved; hundreds, "thousands, more likely" of young girls are killed "for fun. Snuff films."[37] Westray explains that he hates his own corruption; he "could live in a monastery," except for his fatal weakness: "women."[38] By implication, of course, his weakness lies in his taking sexual pleasure from the use and abuse of women. Westray then recites a fragment from a famous nineteenth-century poem, "Tom Gray's Dream," by Retta Brown: "the only thing ultimately worth your concern is the anguish of your fellow passengers on this hellbound train."[39] The poem is about an alcoholic man (Tom Gray), who wakes up on a hell-bound train, and the devil says as all of the train's passengers plead to get off that they condemned themselves to this hell-bound ride by scorning justice, trampling the "laws of nature," taking advantage of the weak, and so forth. According to Westray, the only truly valuable occupation in the material world is an immaterial act—concern for the "anguish of your fellow passengers."

Westray here draws attention to the quandary at the heart of *The Counselor*. He recognizes his moral turpitude in finding sexual gratification in trafficked women and is lured into complicity with the cartels because of his desire. He recognizes this cycle of supply and demand as innately corrupt, and he can recognize the alternative—a value system based on compassion for others—but he cannot or does not separate himself from this destructive system.

The most explicit image of the dehumanization of "innocents" in the course of the pursuit of material gain, of course, is the murder weapon that Reiner tells the Counselor about, and which Malkina later employs: a "bolito"—a "mechanical device" that forms a noose that, once dropped over a victim's head, tightens "until it goes to zero."[40] In other words, McCarthy crafts for this narrative a murder device that, first, operates mechanically after being initially started by a human and, second, reduces its human victims from being (1) to nothingness (0).

Digital Technology and the Global Economy

That metaphor—the binary system as a description of a human being reduced to an object (a corpse)—is no accident, of course. In *The Counselor*, inhumanity and violence characterize the War on Drugs, just as the War on Drugs characterizes the inhumanity and violence inherent in the neoliberal policing system in the United States in the late twentieth and early twenty-first centuries. But *The Counselor* turns its attention in its final act from the War on Drugs to an even more recent symbol of global capitalism: digital capital.

Perhaps the most perplexing scene in the screenplay is the script's closing narrative arc in which Malkina meets with Lee, a "twenty-five year old Chinese American" whose expertise lies in computer hacking—specifically, hacking bank encryption through the creation of viruses.[41] Seb Franklin argues that networking, hacking, and computer viruses are all potentially radical disruptions to the new and exploitative forms of "computer-enabled" global capitalism. The role of informatics and computational technologies in the form and function of global capitalism in the twenty-first century cannot be overemphasized. It is not just labor itself that has become de-located; in the contemporary world, information "replaces material goods as the principle commodity."[42] For Franklin, modes of computational activity such as hacking or the creation of computer viruses are potentially disruptive because "they retain a connection with the Romanticist notion of the individual or group that is undercut by the predominance of the dividual [the de-humanized laborer in the digital marketplace] and the data bank characteristic of control societies."[43] That is, hacking and open-source networking offer the possibility of a global system in which information technology lies in the hands of the workers. Franklin cites Alan Turing's famous assertion in 1950 that a computing machine, properly constructed, possesses a "control unit" that obeys the instructions of the programmer automatically.[44] Properly run, computation is simply a single human command replicated automatically—much like the function of the "bolito." Hackers and creators of computer viruses, Franklin says, are agents who intervene in automation. In other words, hacking interrupts or subverts the intended command of the programmer—and thus represents that Romantic ideal of the individual counter to the global market.

In addition to noting hacking as a source of reallocation of global power, Sara Schoonmaker focuses on the creation of open-source or free software as a critical intervention in neoliberal politics—a form of "globalization from below."[45] Schoonmaker identifies Brazil as one of the most progressive nations in terms of its legislation on Internet technologies. Since 2003, Brazil has "promoted the shift from proprietary to free and open source software" and thus poses a political alternative to neoliberal policies that exacerbate "global inequalities" through restricting digital capacities to economic powerhouses, as the United States does.[46] The significance of hacking and open-source software, of course, is that proprietary control of informational technology is quickly becoming the source and substance of much of the surplus capital in developed nations. Yet both Schoonmaker and Franklin, while discussing the radical potential of global communication, networking, and computer programming, nevertheless remind readers that the dominant use of informatics in global capitalism is still controlled by transnational corporations. That is, despite its radical potential, digital capital operates primarily in service of the economic hegemon.

Malkina represents both the possibilities and the failures of these disruptive digital technologies. For example, Malkina answers Lee's question about her nation of origin by claiming "Soy pura Portena," identifying herself as possibly from Buenos Aires, as she claims rather unreliably while she is "confessing," but perhaps simply identifying herself as a creature always on the move—and one moreover who emerges from the global south.[47] She also predicts the collapse of the European Union and the rise of China in a new era of globalization. Malkina physically represents the disruptive south—a perpetual immigrant from South America who operates through disruptive technologies that liberate capital from the banking centers of the Northern Hemisphere. Yet she represents not so much a disruption, or the rise of the Global South, but rather the system replicating itself. Malkina, like the Counselor, fails to imagine a value system apart from the market forces of capitalism—apart, that is, from the accumulation of wealth at the expense of others, the men she betrays, the lives she destroys.

The scene in *The Counselor* in which Malkina and Lee discuss their course of action reads like an incoherent list of technical words regurgitated by an author more comfortable with an Olivetti typewriter than with twenty-first century digital technology:

LEE: What do you have? Do you have the CAs?

MALKINA: I have two of them.

LEE: Can you get the other two?

MALKINA: Yes. I've got a search engine downloading them out of another computer. . . .

MALKINA: I'll have everything by tomorrow that there is to get. What we don't have we'll just have to figure out. I've got the routing numbers and the account numbers. I've got the source code but we'll have to have a compiler to translate everything into machine-readable code. It's all doable.

LEE: VPNs and routers.

MALKINA: Yes.[48]

In other words, Malkina promises that she has or can acquire four certification authorities—an encryption that authenticates a user and authorizes a transfer of digital information. There may be some rationale for opening a scene with this level of unnecessary jargon. But the scene continues in rapid exchanges of technobabble, replete with anomalies that create a level of verisimilitude equal to low-budget nineties hacking heists, such as Malkina's "CA" that is apparently downloading for the duration of the scene, or Malkina's need to explain to a computer hacker that she is capable of downloading her desired data onto a USB memory stick. Like the Sephardic Jewish diamond merchant's technical description of how to determine the grade of a particular diamond, in other words, this scene sounds like a "how-to" guide to digitally stealing money from offshore accounts but includes little enough underlying accuracy or explication to be informative. Instead, this scene functions as a visual metaphor accomplished with little aesthetic flair.[49]

At the end of the screenplay, Malkina offers a poetic monologue on the beauty of watching predators slaughter prey. "The hunter has a purity of heart that exists nowhere else," she says, referring obliquely to her pet hunting cheetahs.[50] Yet humanity, she notes, is different from other predators of the animal kingdom. "I suspect that we are ill-formed for the path we have chosen," she says, indicating that humans have chosen a path of relentless predation, yet are hindered by their own qualms—perhaps by compassion, or by a moral system that values something other than the "hunt," concluding that, despite the weakness—the doubts that societies have about the moral failures of their predatory systems—they persist in predation anyway: "The slaughter to come," she says, "is probably beyond our wildest imagining." In

The Counselor's concluding line, Malkina tells a paid sex worker that she is "famished."[51] Malkina's voracious appetite—her sexual, physical, and material hunger—represents her role as a willing participant in the rampant consumerism of late capitalism. Yet she also suggests both the failure of those who would critique late capitalism, and the reason for such a corrupt system's persistence: a failure to imagine the human cost of global capitalism as well as a failure to imagine a way out.

After all, in the screenplay's closing dialogue between the paid "escort" and Malkina, the latter completes the metaphoric circle by indicating that she will translate her non-material digital wealth into diamonds, "the easiest way to compress wealth" since diamonds "weigh nothing at all."[52] On the one hand, her claim is technically untrue, since the original form of that wealth was digital—a medium that literally weighs nothing. But diamonds, as the novel's earlier scene has indicated, represent material history. As pure carbon, super-compressed, they provide a visual metaphor for the temporal compression of the history of capitalism, humankind's most comprehensive expression of insatiable consumption. In the full extension of this metaphor, the only form of wealth purer than digital wealth is compressed carbon—a single human life.

Malkina tells the escort that the one thing she wants more than anything is to possess her own life: "I imagine that I would like my innocence back," she says, "But I would never pay the price which it now commands on the market." Her paid escort, a man whose body has been ceded to her as a commodity, nods, understandingly, and says, "Your own life."[53] These two characters exchange here a recognition of the cataclysmic cultural and individual loss conjured by the Sephardic Jew: the loss of penitence, or of the penitent. In the Catholic tradition, acts of penitence ready the penitential for reconciliation, for reincorporation into the corporate body. It is not obvious that, as the Jewish diamond merchant claims, the "heroes" of Christianized Western civilization have been penitents at any point. But here at the drama's conclusion, McCarthy tips his hand: if the "good" is a sort of spiritual possession of one's own life—a state of autonomy that is achieved through moral or ethical "innocence," in which the individual is incorporated into a healthy communal life—then that good has been stripped away from individuals and societies through the pernicious exploitation of global capitalism. Greed and consumption become the only virtues of a capitalist system, and once an individual has become complicit in the global exchange, it no longer matters whether they are a part of the system or a disrupter of the system.

Here the ominous metaphorical warning of the Jewish diamond merchant echoes from that earlier scene. "Once the first facet is cut there can be no going back," the merchant has instructed the Counselor.[54] Yet while audiences tuned in to this heavily metaphorical script will immediately recognize this assertion as symbolic, it is not precisely "foreshadowing"—since by the time the Counselor proposes to Laura, he is already embroiled in his illegal venture. In other words, the audience is warned at the beginning of *The Counselor* about the critical importance of choice—of choosing to "opt in" to the value system imposed by global capitalism. Later, Reiner repeats this warning with greater clarity: "You pursue this road that you've embarked upon," he tells the Counselor, "and you will eventually come to moral decisions that will take you completely by surprise."[55] Yet both times, the temporal mode of the warning misses its mark. The Counselor has obviously already made the decision since he is, after all, meeting Reiner to discuss their "caper" in this latter scene.

Alyssa Pelish, in her review of the film, points to the film's visual emphasis on that critically missing moment of choice. There is no precipitating event in the film. "Even before the opening credits have rolled," she explains, "we see a motorcyclist burning down a road, the sound of his engine fading in the distance as we drift on high to the Counselor and his beloved in their bed of white linens. The motorcyclist, we will realize later, is already heading toward what the Counselor has set in motion."[56] Not only is the moment of choice and the precipitating action visibly erased from the film, but the rationale for that choice is likewise obscured. Reiner at one point confronts the Counselor about his motivation. Reiner asks the Counselor why he chose to embark on their fated venture. The Counselor says, "Same as you. Greed." But Reiner objects: "I don't think so. . . . I tried to appeal to your greed two years ago. No deal. Now it's too late."[57] According to Reiner's fragmentary dialogue, two years ago, the Counselor was unmoved by greed. The intervening years and, most importantly, the actual motivation are elided.

By removing the protagonist's motivation in the narrative, the text exposes the fragile artifice of the film's MacGuffin. The technical MacGuffin are the kilos of cocaine, which audiences see only once, toward the end of the action. But the cocaine, audiences realize, could be any substance—diamonds, oil, drugs, even bitcoin. The failure of capitalism is not tied to a particular product, or process of profitability. Capitalism itself is an inherently corrupt system, a system that is fundamentally based on greed yet driven by some need deeper than greed, as the Counselor's dubious admission of guilt regarding his own avarice suggests. The failure of capitalism lies not in the system's easily corruptible nature, its literal banking on human avarice and turpitude, but rather on several societies' persistent failures of imagination—both a failure to imagine the extent of the human cost of rapacious economic practices and a failure to imagine an alternative.

As is typical of McCarthy's work, characters in this narrative infrequently engage in any imaginative exercise. Their behaviors appear unpremeditated, as if they operate some predetermined trajectory without the capacity or possibility of reflection. Yet—as is also typical of McCarthy's work—subtle clues to alternatives to this failure of imaginative or reflective mental work seed the text. In a scene near the end, where the Counselor attempts to bargain for Laura's life with a cartel "jefe," the jefe reminds the Counselor (and the audience) of that crucial missing scene in which a choice was made. The Counselor has already made his choice, the jefe claims, and now must endure the consequences: "There is only the accepting," he says. "The choosing was done long ago."[58] The jefe then references Antonio Machado's poems in *Campos de Castilla* (1912), a collection grieving the death of the poet's wife. He interprets Machado's love poetry as substantiating his claim that "there is no rule of exchange" in the practice of love or the experience of loss: "Grief transcends every value," the jefe says. "A man would give whole nations to lift it from his heart. And yet with it you can buy nothing."[59] In this aphoristic description of grief, the jefe also obliquely references the famous verse in the Hebrew Bible's Song of Songs, in which the Beloved tells her Lover that "love is strong as death," a verse that is answered with an assertion about the nonmaterial nature of love: "if a man would give all the substance of his house for love," the Lover claims, "it would utterly be condemned."[60]

The jefe, in other words, has seen through the absent choice in the film's plot to the underlying flaw in the Counselor's narrative: it is not a single moment or choice that has condemned the Counselor. It is rather his worldview, a philosophy in which all things, including human beings, are material goods in a cosmic exchange. Just as he attempts to put a diamond on Laura—metaphorically as well as literally—so also the Counselor here at the end fails to realize that he has been attempting to give his material possessions, even his body, in exchange for a person. Instead, all that had been required of him was to love that person.

The Counselor sits at the nexus of McCarthy's persistent critique of the moral failures of market capitalism as that economic system has been practiced in Western, and particularly US, society. Yet throughout his corpus, posed counter to violent and violating images of neoliberalism—embodied in such dramatic forms as cartel hitmen and cannibal hordes in *No Country for Old Men* and *The Road*, respectively—are images and scenes of alternative economies of exchange and subsistence and value systems separate from commercial or material gain. In profit-driven economic systems, the motivating principles that drive those societies are, by and large, antithetical to the veneration of beauty for its own sake, or to ecologically sustainable existence—images that are hallowed in McCarthy's *The Stonemason* (1994) and the Border Trilogy (1992–1998), for instance. While the capacity of humankind to ever achieve some ecologically balanced pastoral ideal is treated with profound skepticism, McCarthy's persistent denaturalization of neoliberal philosophies of production and value suggest that any hope lies in humanity's capacity to imagine an alternative. In *The Counselor*, McCarthy confronts his audience with the absurdity of their own failure to do so; and, more importantly, the Counselor's failure of imagination suggests the terrible weight resting on our own capacity to critique global capitalism's myth of inevitability.

In 2013, when this graphic and more than a little misogynistic "trashy" screenplay and film came out, the fragmented scenes evoking the specter of anti-Semitism and Chinese computer hacking framing a narrative about the threat posed by drug cartels in the American southwest seemed disconnected, if not irrelevant. It is difficult, more than a decade after the film's release, not to read those elements as almost startlingly prescient. This drama is not so much prophetic, however, as it is visionary. McCarthy's narrative pivots around an absurdity: it is a story about the consequences of a fatal choice that was made. It would, perhaps, be wise to note the absurdity of this missing chance at some alternative to catastrophe. McCarthy's imaginative critique of global capitalism and his subtle, brief gestures toward alternative value systems of mutual care and concern may, in the end, be one of his most significant contributions to the twenty-first century.

Notes

1. Cormac McCarthy, *The Counselor: A Screenplay* (New York: Vintage, 2013), 17. I have chosen to cite from McCarthy's screenplay rather than the film since this analysis contextualizes *The Counselor* within McCarthy's corpus; the focus is therefore on McCarthy's authorship rather than Ridley Scott's interpretation, although Scott's film adheres closely to McCarthy's script.

2. The figuration of a diamond merchant as Jewish holds symbolic as well as historical weight.

I will explore the relationship of this image to the history of capitalism later, but here note that, more than simply a "lazy" authorial move, this image represents a codified social history in which Jews are the brokers of wealth—a codification always implicated in the most virulent forms of anti-Semitism. Moreover, given the role that Henry Ford played in the dissemination of the conspiracies of Jewish global dominance through his dissemination of *The Protocols of the Elders of Zion* in the United States, we can detect the connection between perpetrators of capitalist ideology and a persistent configuring of the Jew as both the manipulator and the downfall of global capitalism. Nor is that particular coded symbol—the Jew as the purveyor of diamonds—as outdated as one might think. Late American televangelist Pat Robertson joked on a 2014 episode of his television program *The 700 Club* that Jews are not car mechanics because they are too busy "polishing their diamonds." See Elias Isquith, "Pat Robertson Wants to Know Why Jewish People Are So Rich," *Salon*, 31 March 2014, accessed 1 July 2024, https://www.salon.com/2014/03/31/pat_robertson_wants_to_know_why_jewish_people_are_so_rich/.

3. David Harvey, *The New Imperialism* (Oxford: Oxford UP, 2003), 74.

4. Gordon Gekko's famous "greed is good" speech from Oliver Stone's 1987 film *Wall Street* echoes here, of course.

5. McCarthy, *The Counselor*, 19.

6. Jacob Agner, "Salvaging *The Counselor*: Watching Cormac McCarthy and Ridley Scott's Really Trashy Movie," *The Cormac McCarthy Journal* 14, no. 2 (2016): 204–26.

7. Ibid., 214.

8. Malkina is introduced with her pet cheetahs strolling around her, a tattoo of "an Egyptian cat" on her neck. The tattoo is likely meant to be an image of the cat goddess Bast—the goddess of warfare. Malkina's cheetahs recur as suggestive metaphors throughout the screenplay, hunting prey in the background. Malkina is thus associated with warfare and desert predators. Additionally, scenes not involving actual killing usually involve people eating in restaurants—the Counselor and Laura get engaged in a restaurant; Malkina and Laura meet in a café at a shopping mall (combining an image evoking the excesses of capitalism with actual food consumption), and so forth.

9. Literary texts that engage with and critique the effects of capitalism are in generous supply, but some notable examples that express the breadth and diversity of such texts include Don DeLillo's *White Noise* and *Cosmopolis*; Ngûgi wa Thiong'o's *The Devil on the Cross*; China Miéville's urban fantasies; and Mohsin Hamid's *How to Get Filthy Rich in Rising Asia*.

10. See Harvey, *New Imperialism*, 73; and Robert J. S. Ross and Kent C. Trachte, *Global Capitalism: The New Leviathan* (Albany: SUNY Press, 1990), 6.

11. Ellen Meiksins Wood, *The Origin of Capitalism* (New York: Monthly Review Press, 1999), 2.

12. Mark Fisher, *Capitalist Realism: Is There No Alternative?* (2008; repr. Hampshire: Zero Books, 2014), 4.

13. Werner Sombart, *The Jews and Modern Capitalism*, trans. M. Epstein (Boston: E.P. Dutton, 1913), 14.

14. Maristella Botticini, "A Tale of 'Benevolent' Governments: Private Credit Markets, Public Finance, and the Role of Jewish Lenders in Medieval and Renaissance Italy," *Journal of Economic History* 60, no. 1 (2000): 164–89.

15. Ibid., 171.

16. Karin Hofmeester, "Shifting Trajectories of Diamond Processing: From India to Europe and Back, from the Fifteenth Century to the Twentieth," *Journal of Global History* 8, no. 1 (2013): 25–49.

17. Barak D. Richman, "Community Enforcement of Informal Contracts: Jewish Diamond Merchants in New York," Harvard Law School, Discussion Paper no. 384 (Sept. 2002): 1–57.

18. McCarthy, *The Counselor*, 18.

19. Ibid.

20. Carl Levin and Tom Coburn, "Wall Street and the Financial Crisis: Anatomy of a Financial Collapse," *Majority and Minority Staff Report*, Permanent Subcommittee on Investigations, United States Senate, 13 Apr. 2011, accessed 1 July 2024, https://www.hsgac.senate.gov/subcommittees/investigations/library/files/report-psi-staff-report-wall-street-and-the-financial-crisis-anatomy-of-a-financial-collapse/.

21. Harvey, *New Imperialism*, 141.

22. Ibid., 156.

23. McCarthy, *The Counselor*, 20.

24. Ibid., 19.

25. Ibid., 14.

26. See Margaret Brinig, "Rings and Promises," *Journal of Law, Economics, and Organization* 6, no. 1 (1990): 203–15.

27. McCarthy, *The Counselor*, 20.

28. Ibid., 17.

29. Arundhati Roy, "The New American Century," *The Nation*, 9 Feb. 2004: 11–14.

30. Stephen Tatum, "'Mercantile Ethics': *No Country for Old Men* and the Narcocorrido," *Cormac McCarthy: All the Pretty Horses, No Country for Old Men, The Road*, ed. Sara Spurgeon (London: Continuum, 2011), 77–93.

31. Dominic Corva, "Neoliberal Globalization and the War on Drugs: Transnationalizing Illiberal Governance in the Americas," *Political Geography* 27 (2008): 176–93.

32. Ibid., 178.

33. McCarthy, *The Counselor*, 70.

34. Eric Blumenson and Eva Nilson, "Policing for Profit: The Drug War's Hidden Economic Agenda," *University of Chicago Law Review* 65, no. 1 (1998): 35–114.

35. McCarthy, *The Counselor*, 53.

36. Ibid., 56.

37. Ibid., 58–59.

38. Ibid., 61.

39. Ibid., 62. See also Stacey Peebles, *Page, Stage, Screen: Cormac McCarthy and Performance* (Austin: Univ. of Texas Press, 2017), 173, where Peebles further notes that the Brown poem is often recited at Alcoholics Anonymous meetings. By implication, Westray describes the drive to exploit the vulnerable as a type of compulsion. The comparison to alcoholism perhaps illuminates a distinction between the compulsion driving excessive or exploitive consumption and the innate myth of neoliberalism. If exploitive consumption can take the form of a disease like alcoholism, then it may seem to have certain "innate" characteristics but is nevertheless innate only insofar as it is a predilection, a possible illness that may manifest, typically due to the compounding force of certain external factors, rather than being an essential characteristic of the species ("homo economicus").

40. McCarthy, *The Counselor*, 35–36.

41. Ibid., 167, 171, 173.

42. Seb Franklin, "Virality, Informatics, and Critique; or, Can There Be Such a Thing as Radical Computation?," *WSQ: Women's Studies Quarterly* 40, nos. 1–2 (2012): 153–70.

43. Ibid., 156.

44. Ibid., 164.

45. Sara Schoonmaker, "Globalization from Below: Free Software and Alternatives to Neoliberalism," *Development and Change* 38, no. 6 (2007): 999–1020.

46. Ibid., 1001.

47. McCarthy, *The Counselor*, 169, 83.

48. Ibid., 167–69.

49. Ibid., 14–16.

50. Ibid., 183.

51. Ibid., 184.

52. Ibid., 178.

53. Ibid., 182.

54. Ibid., 17.

55. Ibid., 34.

56. Alyssa Pelish, "The Moment of Choice: Cormac McCarthy's 'The Counselor,'" *Los Angeles Review of Books*, 2 Nov. 2013, accessed 1 July 2024, https://lareviewofbooks.org/article/on-cormac-mccarthys-the-counselor/.

57. McCarthy, *The Counselor*, 119–20.

58. Ibid., 147.

59. Ibid., 148.

60. Songs of Songs, the Judeo-Christian Bible, King James Version 1611, Song 8:6–7.

8

NECROCAPITALISM AT THE END OF THE WORLD

The Economics of Death in *The Counselor*

Vernon W. Cisney

> No man can serve two masters: for either he will hate the one, and love the other; or else he will hold to the one, and despise the other. Ye cannot serve God and mammon.
>
> *Matthew 6:24*

"But for those with the understanding that they're living the last days of the world, death acquires a different meaning." So says Rubén Blades's Jefe in the 2013 Cormac McCarthy-Ridley Scott collaboration *The Counselor*, a film that is, ultimately, a work of eschatological fiction.[1] As a meditation on the end of days, crystallizing the late stages of North American capitalist development, the film echoes Fredric Jameson's oft-cited proclamation, "it is easier to imagine the end of the world than to imagine the end of capitalism."[2] The next line of Jameson's piece, quoted far less frequently, is: "We can now revise that [notion] and witness the attempt to imagine capitalism by way of imagining the end of the world." That is, capitalism itself, in its latter days, becomes apocalyptic in its logic, indistinguishable from the most gruesome hellscapes of the dystopian phantasmagoria it has produced. To be sure, *The Counselor* is a dystopian work, "arguably McCarthy's bleakest work since *Blood Meridian*."[3] But its dystopic lens casts not a vividly visualized future, extrapolated from an unsettling element of the present, but, rather, an unvarnished view of the world we already inhabit, a dystopia to which we all contribute, even accede. If it is hellish, it is a hell of our own creation, an expression and reflection of the very soul of America itself.

The bleakness of the film likely accounts, at least partly, for its meager reception. *The Counselor* was nearly universally panned by critics; moviegoing fans, who are often more forgiving than film critics, appreciated it even less. Indeed, it bombed spectacularly at the box office, grossing a mere $16.9 million in the United States. Citing the metaphysical nature (or even the sheer volume) of the dialogue, many critics characterized the film as ponderous and clumsy.[4] Some saw it as tawdry or trashy, even noting the ubiquity of sewage, garbage, and excessive depictions of sexuality (one involving a woman masturbating to orgasm with a Ferrari's windshield). Jacob Agner, writing on the "trashiness" of the film in a compelling effort to "salvage" it, notes that "*The Counselor* baffled, if not outraged, opening audiences with its lengthy ruminations on the weight of greed, desire, and choice in the face of grisly cartel violence. Perhaps due to its strange mixture of the philosophical and the pulpy, the film became one of 2013's most unconventional and puzzling mainstream films."[5]

How, then, are we to understand this film in retrospect? Citing McCarthy himself, Stacey Peebles argues that the work can be understood as a fairly formulaic Aristotelian tragedy, one in which the protagonist is "a kind of 'man in the middle,'" neither morally pure nor wholly evil, who "does what he does out of hamartia, a much-discussed term that has been translated in many different ways, most commonly as 'tragic flaw,' but also, as Julian Young notes, as 'fault,' 'mistake,' 'fallibility,' 'frailty,' and 'error.'"[6] Russell Hillier, too, characterizes the work as "a cautionary fable that depicts the depraved and ultra-violent world of narcotics and portrays characters whose poor moral choices and thoughtless complicity in vice result in the ruin of their own lives and the lives of others."[7] This tragic dimension is undoubtedly prevalent in the film, and in that specific respect the work can be situated fairly closely to *No Country for Old Men*, both involving a protagonist who executes a single, fateful act in the world of the international drug trade, and is ultimately brought to ruin.

In this chapter, however, I want to extend beyond the tragic dimension and explore the economic landscape that sets the stage for our hero's fall. *The Counselor* has as much to do with the world *around* the protagonist as it does with his individual moral failings: the economic milieu that understands life as mere commodity, eminently disposable if the price is right. The Counselor haughtily believes, against the many warnings of his associates, that he can traffic in this milieu for a one-and-done venture without getting his hands dirty or incurring any losses. But his action ultimately takes him into the black heart of contemporary neoliberal economics that, following Sunny Singh and Subhabrata Bobby Banerjee, I shall refer to as "necrocapitalism."

Singh succinctly defines necrocapitalism as "a form of capitalism where a country's trade and industry are founded on, linked to, and dependent directly or indirectly upon death and the profits accruing from it."[8] Banerjee likewise defines the concept as "contemporary forms of organizational accumulation that involve dispossession and the subjugation of life to the power of death."[9] Finally, Achille Mbembe writes, characterizing what he calls "necropolitics," "Nearly everywhere the political order is reconstituting itself as a form of organization for death."[10] Bringing such concepts into a discussion of Cormac McCarthy, I will first develop this understanding of necrocapitalism as it unfolds from within the logic of neoliberalism itself. I will then elaborate upon the apocalyptic characteristics of American necrocapitalism that *The Counselor* addresses in order to show how the film presents viewers with a decisive indictment of this system. But the film does not merely show us a world *out there*, untouched by the everyday life of the average American citizen. Rather, it reminds us that we are all consumers in this necrocapitalist system, and that "the consumer of the product is essential to its production," such that none are innocent.[11] Or, as Lydia Cooper argues in her brilliant analysis of the film, "*The Counselor* forces viewers to confront the preconditions of their own participation in the assumed inviolability of capitalism."[12]

A New Faith: To Change the Heart and Soul

I begin with neoliberalism and the elaboration of necrocapitalism. In *The Communist Manifesto*, Karl Marx and Friedrich Engels famously write that under capitalism, particularly in its twilight stages, "All that is solid melts into air, all that is holy is profaned, and man is at last compelled to face with sober senses, his real conditions of life, and his relations with his kind."[13] The lifeblood of capital being the ever-expanding accumulation of wealth, it necessarily requires its markets to constantly extend into new regions. These regions are geographical, as markets shatter national and political borders in search of new corners of the world to drain for raw materials, commodities, consumers, and laborers. But such regions are also onto-ethical, meaning that the logic of the market must eventually hollow out and infect domains of everyday human life that were previously considered off-limits to the transactional, competitive forces of the market—areas such as education, healthcare, justice, defense, and so on.

Even among theorists who write on neoliberalism, there is dispute over when, precisely, to locate its emergence.[14] Most point to the 1979 and 1980 elections of, respectively, Margaret Thatcher in the UK and Ronald Reagan in the US as the pivotal moment. And this is indeed when the logic and rhetoric of neoliberalism suddenly, explicitly, and almost universally enters the public lexicon of the West, when the policies of unprecedented tax cuts for society's wealthiest citizens, coupled with the ethos of free international trade and deep austerity measures for public services, are widely implemented. But we might then inquire further back, to the anti-inflation austerity measures instituted by President Jimmy Carter after appointing Paul Volcker to the Federal Reserve in 1979—a "draconian shift," as Harvey puts it, that exacerbated the cultural despair and the seismic wave of resentment that helped usher in the folksy cowboy persona of Reagan, who would charm the nation with a wink and a smile and promise to "make America great again" by limiting the reach of "big government."[15]

But the "Volcker shock" hearkens to the earlier crisis of "stagflation," an unusual period of high unemployment paired with high inflation. This period helped produce the 1975 New York City fiscal crisis, which altered "the politics in the city in profound ways without ever talking about race or class explicitly," thus acting as a template for the political strategy of the nation's wealthy later in the 1980s.[16] But what about the 1973 CIA-backed coup in Chile, deposing and assassinating socialist President Salvador Allende and instituting US-friendly autocrat Augusto Pinochet, who built an entire cabinet of neoliberal economic advisers—intellectual followers of Milton Friedman—from the University of Chicago and implemented some of the world's first robust experiments with neoliberal policies?[17] What about the gradual diminishment of the power of labor unions in the United States as early as the 1960s? What about the effectiveness of the "Red Scare" and Wisconsin Senator Joseph McCarthy's communist witch hunts in the 1950s that helped deepen the rhetoric that would later be used to dismantle social programs? Searching for the putative origins of neoliberalism, we discover a labyrinth that reaches back almost to the Great Depression itself.

Indeed, as a theoretical apparatus, neoliberalism gestated alongside the societal implementation of Keynesian economics, in part as a response to and break with this "embedded" form of market liberalism so called in order "to signal how market processes and entrepreneurial and corporate activities were surrounded by a web of social and political constraints and a regulatory environment that sometimes restrained but in other instances led the way in economic and industrial strategy."[18] The Keynesian framework of embedded liberalism employed a "demand-side" economic model in order to stimulate the flows of capital by aiming at fiscally strengthening the populace so that citizens would have greater access to social mobility and would be better situated to purchase consumer goods, thus driving increased industrial productivity and creating further employment. It emphasized full employment by almost any means necessary and relied upon a heavily variegated system of progressive taxation, providing revenues which were to be reinvested into the public in the forms of state and municipal parks, infrastructure, education, healthcare, and pensions.[19]

While acknowledging the good intentions of such initiatives, the neoliberal theorists saw these programs as destined to lead to incrementally greater degrees of government intervention that would ultimately result in a new form of "serfdom," a rigidly planned economy wherein the most ambitious tyrants would rise to power and, concerned only with their own gain and not the needs of the public, would be certain to manage things inefficiently, failing to meet human demands for basic necessities and resulting in overall immiseration and inequality. The neoliberals strove, therefore, against the Keynesian embedded liberal model almost from its inception, championing instead a "supply-side," market-driven approach to the economy.

Neoliberal thought thus emerged, like Keynes himself, as an alternative path forward from the pitfalls of classical liberalism, which had culminated in the stock market crash of 1929, a post-classical, post-*laissez-faire* (hence "neo") liberal alternative that, like Keynes, rejected the dogma of unfettered *laissez-faire* economics: "While Keynes would later become the favourite target of neo-liberals, it should not be forgotten that Keynesianism and neo-liberalism for a time shared the same concern: how to save from liberalism itself what could be salvaged of the capitalist system."[20] We need look no further than the heralding prophet of neoliberal thought, Friedrich von Hayek, whose 1944 book *The Road to Serfdom* served almost as Gospel to college-age conservatives in the 1950s and 1960s, many of whom would end up in the halls of United States Government one or two decades after first encountering Hayek. "The liberal argument [soon to be called neoliberalism] is in favour of making the best possible use of the forces of competition as a means of co-ordinating human efforts, not an argument for leaving things just as they are," argued Hayek. "It is based on the conviction that where effective competition can be created, it is a better way of guiding individual efforts than any other."[21]

This new liberalism, Hayek argued, is *not laissez-faire*, but operates on the "conviction" that competition must be "created," wherever possible, as the best way to guide human endeavors. Such creation is to be the primary role of the neoliberal state. Milton Friedman, even more explicitly than Hayek, refers to the tenets of neoliberal thought as "a new faith," and claims that "the liberal tradition regards freedom of entry and of competition as basic; it therefore justifies state action to preserve competition and to make selling a product of higher quality or at a lower price the only means whereby existing enterprises can prevent new enterprises from being established": market forces, driven by competition, fostered by the state.[22] For the neoliberals, in fact, this is the state's *raison d'être*. The state exists not to stimulate demand or ensure full employment, but to acculturate its citizenry in the ethos of competition and to bolster the forces of the market.

From this background, we can highlight the components of neoliberal thinking essential to the account of necrocapitalism and our engagement with *The Counselor*. First, in place of the classical liberal understanding of the ethos of exchange, neoliberalism institutes the ethos of competition, and not just as the underlying principle of the market, but as the most effective ontological motor of humanity. Second, where classical liberalism had understood certain domains of life, in particular, those pertaining to morality, ethics, and the public good, as off-limits to the logic of the market, neoliberals would hold that "effective competition" is the most efficient and dynamic way of guiding all human endeavors; thus market logic should be extended into all areas of life, "a strictly economic interpretation of a whole domain previously thought to be non-economic," as Michel Foucault noted.[23] Or, to put the point more explicitly, there is and ought to be no arbiter of value *beyond* the competitive forces of the market and the "right" of the individual to enter that market.

Third, where classical liberals would treat *political* liberty as primary (at least in theory), with market freedom being a subfield of that freedom, neoliberals will hold the inverse, that "economic liberalism is . . . an indispensable prerequisite for political freedom."[24] Through the 1970s, in fact, Hayek would act as an avid apologist to the West for the authoritarian Pinochet regime in Chile, going even so far as to justify dictatorships more generally, provided they preserved economic liberalism: "It is possible for a dictator to govern in a liberal way. And it is also possible for a democracy to govern with a total lack of liberalism. I personally prefer a liberal dictator to a democratic government lacking liberalism."[25] Finally, the indispensable role of the state is to *ally* with the competitive forces of the market, buttressing them as needed, fostering and stimulating their activity through public policy, through targeted injections of capital, through political rhetoric and initiatives in education. As Margaret Thatcher famously said, "Economics are the method; the object is to change the heart and soul."[26] To that end, neoliberalism is not simply an undoing of post-depression Keynesian initiatives; it is nothing short of a radical reorientation of the whole of society toward an atomizing and totalizing deference to market forces, the insinuation of competition as the principle of life, and of the "best practices" of business efficiency as the arbiters of all human activity.

Capitalism Functioning Very Well

Necrocapitalism is the logical terminus of this rationality. In the short run, the loosening of market regulations and the decrease in tax rates for America's wealthiest *did* produce the facade of net positives in the economies of the West, particularly the United States—a thriving real estate market, reduced inflation, an overall increase in the standard of living, and the general visage of a consumer's paradise. Bolstered by such gains, Reagan took credit for the fact that it was "morning again in America," and the nation thanked him with a landslide reelection.[27]

Of course, there was a dark and often violent underbelly to such "Reaganomics," which would not become apparent to the American working and middle classes for a few decades. Fast forward to today—past the mass incarcerations, economic recessions, and mass shootings that characterized the 1990s and the early 2000s, past a global financial collapse in 2008-09 that increased the wealth inequality gap in the West, past a growing climate crisis that is likewise killing flora and fauna the world over, past finally a global pandemic, the mitigation of which investors insisted must not take precedence over the economy, no matter how many corpses the virus produced—and it has become clear exactly what the goal of neoliberal capitalism has always been: "This bloody and ongoing legacy is not an aberration of capitalism," noted Asma, "it is not proof that 'capitalism is broken,' but, rather, it is evidence that it is functioning very well."[28]

As Asma suggests, necrocapitalism is not *simply* the logical terminus of capitalism, waiting to unmask itself only in capitalism's final stages; it is, rather, capitalism's ever-present *sine qua non*. This is a truth that Marx uncovered back in the nineteenth century: "Capital is dead labour which, vampire-like, lives only by sucking living labour."[29] The COVID-19 pandemic merely exposed what many scholars *and* workers have implicitly known all along: that the market is satisfied with nothing less than its subjects working themselves, literally, to death. Capitalism generates profit by consumption; it feeds on nature and human labor, ultimately, on life itself. "The truth, however, is that the litany of the dead produced by both the emergence and consummation of capitalism is innumerable," continues Asma. "We are tasked with itemizing a seemingly infinite graveyard, which began with slavery and colonial genocide, the millions simultaneously worked to death in Western Europe, and every mass murder since then."[30]

Indeed, *The Counselor* reveals to us that even at its most successful, capitalism today just is necrocapitalism. We proceed from the film's hero, the titular Counselor himself, into his milieu. Early in the film, a Jewish diamond dealer (Bruno Ganz) tells the Counselor that "The heart of any culture is to be found in the nature of the hero. Who is that man who is to be revered?"[31] This framing invites our consideration, suggesting that the hero of *our* narrative is likely expressive of a broader commentary on the nature of the culture in which he exists. The jeweler proceeds:

> In the classical world it is the warrior. But in the western world it is the man of God. From Moses to Christ. The prophet. The penitent. Such a figure is unknown to the Greeks. Unheard of. Unimaginable. Because you can only have a man of God, not a man of gods. And this God is the God of the jewish people. There is no other God. We see him—what is the word? Purloined. Purloined in the West. How do you steal a God?[32]

Through the mouth of the madman in the marketplace, Friedrich Nietzsche in the nineteenth century famously proclaimed that "God is dead."[33] The Jewish jeweler, however, claims not that God is dead but that he has been "purloined." *How do you steal a God*, he asks? "The jew beholds his tormentor dressed in the vestments of his own ancient culture. Everything bears a strange familiarity. But the fit is always poor and the hands are always dripping blood."[34] One steals a God first by appropriating him, *bearing a strange familiarity* to the prophet himself, and then warping him, mangling him into a mutilated and obscene idol, a hollow sarcophagus of his former self, "revealing the contemporary confusion of the sacred and the profane."[35]

The "hero" of our work is the unnamed Counselor. The term "counselor" has connotations pertaining to wisdom or advice, and viewers' attention is explicitly drawn to these connections a number of times throughout the film. The Counselor's "wisdom," however, is certainly not of a moral nature, for not only does he appear to be entirely lacking in such wisdom himself; he obstinately and repeatedly refuses to accept the experienced counsel of Westray (Brad Pitt) and Reiner (Javier Bardem), both of whom caution the Counselor explicitly against his foray into the drug world: "You pursue this road that you've embarked upon and you will eventually come to moral decisions that will take you completely by surprise. You wont see it coming at all."[36] In other words, neoliberalism—which is to say necrocapitalism—has encoded such immorality, such impossible choices, in its own DNA. Reiner appeals to this moral sense while Westray appeals to the Counselor's existential sense, both elaborating in gory detail the horrors for which drug cartels are responsible; and both appeals fall on deaf ears for a competitor who fails to understand this encoding until he has lost everything.

More specifically, the term "counselor" is connected to its namesake's occupational status as an attorney, and within the framework of neoliberalism, the attorney is an indispensable knower and guardian of the law. The proliferation of competition as the guiding social ethos under neoliberal policy requires the institution and ongoing negotiation of a vast system of rules, rules designed to help adjudicate in matters pertaining to the bloodsport of economic competition. Thus, despite the pervasive "small government" rhetoric of many Americans of both major political parties, the expansion of neoliberal reason is accompanied by a drastically increased role of law and of the intervention of the court system:

> Whereas economic regulation takes place spontaneously, through the formal properties of competition, the social regulation of conflicts, irregularities of behavior, nuisance caused by some to others, and so forth, calls for a judicial interventionism which has to operate as arbitration within the framework of the rules of the game. If you multiply enterprises, you multiply frictions, environmental effects, and consequently, to the extent that you free economic subjects and allow them to play their game, then at the same time the more you detach them from their status as virtual functionaries of a plan, and you inevitably multiply judges.[37]

We recall, though, the core of the neoliberal "faith" from both Hayek and Friedman, that economic competition provides the ideal method of coordinating *all* human behavior, and that economic liberty is more fundamental than political liberty. Wendy Brown thus presses Foucault's argument even further. "More than simply securing the rights of capital and structuring competition, neoliberal juridical reason recasts political rights, citizenship, and the field of democracy itself in an economic register," Brown writes. In so doing, neoliberalism "disintegrates the very idea of the demos."[38] In a system where "Law" is synonymous with "the rules of the game," where the "game" is the interplay of economic forces, and where economic forces act as the guides for all human behavior, the "Law," founded in principle on justice, becomes little more than a justification for the worst forms of exploitation; and the Counselor, unlike the prophets of old, little more than a player in and beneficiary of that exploitation.

It's All Shit

The Counselor's milieu is the international drug trade. More generally, it is the border separating the United States from Mexico; and even more generally, it is the nature of the exploitative relation of the borders between the global north and the Global South. *The Counselor* thus takes direct aim at America's southern border and at the exploitation associated with this border as it has intensified tremendously under neoliberalism. But these lines of separation are in many senses fictive as well, signifying categories having more to do with socioeconomics than with geography. As Daniel Melo writes, "the US border has always existed as a contradiction—a simultaneous closing off from the world, of protecting the nation-state and those it allows to labor under it, while also demonstrating limitless power, influence, and expansion."[39] It is a world of terror, where bodies are beheaded and displayed publicly as a mere show of power—a world that the global north helped to create but against which it pretends to be immune and for which it claims to bear no responsibility.

The paradoxical solidity and tenuousness of this separation are witnessed in the opening moments of the film, as we see the Green Hornet tearing down the highway on his sport bike from Ciudad Juárez into El Paso, Texas; the camera then cuts to a shot out the condominium window of the Counselor from which, in the distance, we see the glimmers and hear the roar of the motorcycle, highlighting the proximity of the two worlds. The camera then tracks to the bed, where a pristine white sheet completely covers the Counselor and his girlfriend, Laura. Beneath the sheet, the afternoon sunlight casts a heavenly glow, the fine fabric once more creating the illusion of separation, the apparently insular world of the privileged inhabitants of the global north. McCarthy's screenplay makes this explicit, stating that the "*dialogue is muffled at times by the bedcovers and it therefore appears in* SUBTITLES *on the screen*."[40]

This tenuous separation is then immediately duplicated, as we watch the sewage tanker truck, which, in addition to being filled with literal feces, we know to be carrying the cartel's cocaine, as it crosses the border into the United States; and then cut to a shot from the high desert where Reiner and Malkina (Cameron Diaz) sit, drinking Manhattans and watching two cheetahs on the hunt. Again, in the distance, we see the tanker truck traversing the desert highway, the apparent separateness of the two worlds attenuated by their physical and socioeconomic proximity.

Just moments before, in a scene that is *not* in the screenplay, we are inside the truck itself, where the couriers catch a glimpse ahead of undocumented immigrants entering the country with as much of their worldly possessions as they can carry in-hand. The driver shouts, "Ilegales! Bienvenida a los Estados Unidos!" The passenger briefly lifts his head from his slumber, sliding his sunglasses down his nose to see the migrants more clearly, then dismissively waves his hand and returns to his nap. The dismissive hand wave resembles that of an apathetic employee shirking their official duties, suggesting that the cartel mules *might* have done something to interfere with the passage of the migrants, but elected against doing so—this time. Its brevity notwithstanding, this scene invokes much of the injustice and brutality surrounding the plight of undocumented immigrants making their way into the United States.

Migration across the US southern border has been an integral component of the US economy almost since the beginning. Melo writes, "while there are competing, sometimes contradictory, forces at work, the pervasive need for cheap labor within the capitalist system largely dictates the need for control over immigrant rights and immigration flows."[41] The service industry jobs these laborers tend to work—construction, restaurants, meatpacking, agriculture, housekeeping—not only constitute the scaffolding of the American economy, they also very often fall outside the purview of many labor laws, making them low-paying, grueling, easily exploitable occupations, avoided by most Americans. This is by design: "A *dual labor market* developed in which some workers . . . become upwardly mobile and enjoy the benefits of industrial society, while others were legally and structurally stuck at the bottom."[42] Neoliberalism has severely worsened this exploitation in a number of ways. The implementation of "free trade" agreements, such as the 1994 North American Free Trade Agreement (NAFTA), resulted in the export of many American factory jobs while simultaneously increasing pressures on laborers from Latin America, further catalyzing migratory movements north: "NAFTA flooded Mexico with cheap imported goods, decimated manufacturing and small farming, drove millions from their land and pushed them northward towards available work."[43] So while, for over a century, the extralegal dimension of this labor force was quietly welcomed as an integral component of the US economy, the ravages of neoliberal deindustrialization have intensified the sense of economic desperation for a large portion of the American population, helping facilitate an increased cultural antipathy toward "illegal immigration," under the deluded assumption that immigrants are responsible for the loss of American jobs. Like neoliberalism, the critique of such "illegal" immigration cuts across political parties in the US and Europe. By the time Donald Trump launched his presidential campaign focused on the issue of immigration, for example, Barack Obama had already carried out unprecedented numbers of deportations and overseen the construction of internment camps at the borders: "Trump, if anything, was a latecomer to the end of the world."[44] Even as American economic forces push Latin American immigrants into the welcoming arms of the US economic structure, the political apparatus makes their existence even more precarious. This in turn makes them more exploitable, pawns in every sense of the term.

Furthermore, because they lack even the most basic human protections, undocumented immigrants are often the victims of kidnapping, frequently at the hands of cartel "coyotes": "Known as coyotes, the human smugglers used to work independently or in small groups. But as the cartels became bigger and more violent, they made the coyotes work for them, and took the lion's share of profits. Today if migrants try to cross the border without paying, they risk getting beaten or murdered by cartel goons."[45] Once kidnapped, they may be robbed, raped, murdered, turned over to the cartels, sold into trafficking—the hellish possibilities are virtually limitless. The insignificance and disposability of the immigrant is further represented in the scene containing the delivery of drugs to the Chicago buyer wherein "Coverall Man" identifies the fourth drum in the tanker as likely carrying the body of an immigrant:

COVERALL MAN

Yes. There is always somebody you wish for him to go away. So you send him to America.

BUYER

Do you know who he is?

COVERALL MAN

No. Of course not. He is a pasajero.

BUYER

A passenger?

COVERALL MAN

Yes. An immigrant.

BUYER

It's just a way to get rid of a body.

COVERALL MAN

Yes. Just a way. Somebody you dont want around.

BUYER

From Mexico.

COVERALL MAN

From Columbia.

BUYER

He came from Columbia.

COVERALL MAN

Yes. Of course.

BUYER

What will you do with him?

COVERALL MAN

Nothing. He goes back in the truck.

BUYER

He goes back in the truck.

COVERALL MAN

Of course.

BUYER

And then what?

COVERALL MAN

Nothing. It is normal. Well. Not so normal I suppose. They think it is funny. A sort of joke. You have to have a sense of humor in this business.

BUYER

So what happens to him?

COVERALL MAN

Nothing. The truck goes back together. They paint it. He is inside.
He rides around. Maybe they sell the truck. At auction maybe.
It's all the same. He rides around some more. Sucking up the shit.
Welcome to America.[46]

Bienvenida a los Estados Unidos. The constitutive exploitation embedded within American neoliberalism is all evoked with the seemingly minor, dismissive handwave of the Mexican drug courier in the opening moments of the film, implying that on another day, perhaps, depending on their mood, the couriers might well have taken some or all of the immigrants captive, subjecting them to such unspeakable horrors.

Nowhere are these horrors of the necrocapitalist machine more salient than in the film's treatment of women as utterly disposable instruments of pleasure. In the first conversation between the Counselor and Reiner, Reiner asks the Counselor whether his fiancé, Laura, knows about their upcoming drug deal, confessing that his own partner, Malkina, is aware of it. When the Counselor asks if Reiner trusts Malkina, he responds, "Jesus, Counselor. She's a woman. . . . I dont mean it to sound that cold. I just mean that where men are concerned they've got their own agenda. I always liked smart women. But it's been an expensive hobby." He characterizes women as "lacking any moral sense," suggesting that perhaps that is why they are drawn to morally complicated men and claims that women "just want to be entertained."[47]

Reiner's juvenile misogyny assumes a far more sinister valence when the Counselor meets with Westray. In his efforts to impress upon the Counselor the brutality of the drug trade, Westray draws attention to the phenomenon, which has drastically accelerated during the neoliberal era, of the widespread kidnapping, torture, rape, and murder of young women in parts of Mexico, in particular Ciudad Juárez.[48] When the Counselor asks why the young girls are murdered, Westray responds, "Who knows. For fun. Snuff films. You'll see. Those will start turning up. Anyway, what do you do with a fifteen year old girl that you've just violated with a tiretool?"[49] The content of one such snuff film is described in gruesome detail later, after the Green Hornet has been beheaded and the shipment stolen: "He said that the girl was beheaded with a machete. She was about fourteen and she was being sodomized by a hooded figure and looking into the camera and crying when her head fell off."[50] He stresses that the women in these films are selected for their youth and beauty, so that they can be, quite literally, consumed and destroyed. Both Westray and the Counselor agree that they would never watch a snuff film because "the consumer of the product is essential to its production. You cant watch without being implicated in a murder."[51] The culpability for this violence, however, is not limited merely to the specific acts of violence committed by specific men against specific women—nor even simply to the person who pays for and watches the snuff film—but to every beneficiary of neoliberalism, the system that has weakened the local economies of these regions and attenuated local community ties, creating vast populations of transient human beings, and, just as we saw with the issue of immigration, intertwined the legal structures of these nations with their extralegal[52] counterparts, to the point that the line between legality and criminality, like the border itself, is impossible to discern: "The notion that there is a clear division between state forces and crime groups—that corruption and collaboration are the work of a few bad apples—is a hegemonic idea promoted by nation-states and the mainstream media. . . . The provision of impunity to armed actors who are politically aligned with capitalism is part of a modern nation-state's *raison d'etre*."[53] Tijuana activist, Sayak Valencia, argues that "ever since the end of the 1970s, the Mexican state cannot be thought of as a state *per se*, but rather as a web of political corruption that has followed the orders of drug traffickers in the management of the country."[54] Or, as Westray says to the Counselor, "I've pretty much seen it all, Counselor. And it's all shit."[55]

Yet, despite his seasoned familiarity with this brutality, and in spite of his own apparent self-awareness (more vivid in the screenplay than in the Scott film), Westray is incapable of pulling himself away from the trade until the moment when it becomes absolutely imperative that he do so. And why? "In a word? Women."[56] He refuses to leave his lifestyle behind because it brings him into contact with his own assortment of women to use and discard. This trait will ultimately be his downfall when, just after the deal goes bad, just after leaving the US, when circumstances dictate that he should exercise extreme caution, Westray hits on a young woman at a hotel counter, initiating a one-night stand that will soon get him killed: the woman had been hired by Malkina to seduce him and steal his financial information. Malkina, finishing her business with the woman the next day, says that what she admires most about Americans is that "You can depend on them," referring to the utter predictability of Westray's character that allowed her to easily ensnare him.[57]

Likewise, the Counselor himself: in spite of so many warnings, both moral and existential, in spite of the depictions of the brutality and the savage treatment of young women, the Counselor expresses no qualms at all about entering into this world, demonstrating a willed obtuseness to the incalculable victimization that results from this trade. While we are not privy to the precise catalyst for the Counselor's decision to enter his Faustian pact, we can surmise that it has *something* to do with the diamond that he has purchased for his beloved, given that just after this purchase the Counselor contacts Reiner to indicate his willingness to do business. As Cooper puts it, "The Counselor buys his diamond, and the scene cuts abruptly to the American southwest, where the Counselor's complicity in a drug-dealing scheme is revealed."[58] The purchase of the diamond, along with the financial investment required for the club he is opening with Reiner, appear to be "investments" in preparation for his coming marriage to Laura. Yet he has overlooked the parting truth that the Jewish jeweler had left with him: "To enhance the beauty of the beloved is to acknowledge both her frailty and the nobility of that frailty."[59] The Counselor foolishly believed that he could conduct commerce in a world of disposable women, that he could profit from this world, without incurring loss, without endangering the singular woman that he loved. He believed in the border, in the sheet separating their "heaven" from the rest of the world. Instead, Laura is kidnapped in the airport parking garage as she is preparing to travel to Boise to reunite with the Counselor. He is then brought face to face with the horrifying banality of his own loss when, leaving a Mexican café late at night, he stumbles into an organized demonstration, occupied by throngs of persons holding signs depicting their missing loved ones, reading "¿Me has visto?"/"Have you seen me?"[60] The anxiety of his own complicity in this horror quickly overtakes him, and he rushes away from the crowd to his motel room. Later, a boy delivers to his motel room a package containing a burned DVD. In a shot rife with revelation, the camera very clearly shows us the reflection of the Counselor's face in the surface of the DVD, and just moments after he realizes that the DVD contains Laura's snuff film on it, we see her headless body, recognizable thanks to the bold red dress she was wearing when she was kidnapped, dumped in a Juárez landfill.

What Do You Know About Malkina?

By way of conclusion, I want to tarry with the one character of the film who, from the morass of violence and treachery, emerges victorious. As a character, Malkina has a great deal in common with Ellen Ripley, the female protagonist of Ridley Scott's sci-fi/horror classic film *Alien* (1979). Part of the brilliance of this earlier film involves the way it subverts viewer expectations in its character development. Early in the film, we're introduced to such recognizable male thespian talents as John Hurt, Tom Skerritt, and Harry Dean Stanton, and we reasonably assume that the story is theirs. But as, one by one, each of the male stars is brought down due to their pride, carelessness, or fear, it becomes clear that the hero of the film was never Dallas or Kane, but rather was Ripley all along, played by a then-little-known Sigourney Weaver.

Malkina has a very similar arc. From the beginning of *The Counselor*, we are primed to believe that we are in a man's world. The sealing of the drums, the binding and filling of the tanker, the driving of the truck, the border officer accepting the suspicious envelope, the delivery and purchase of the drugs—all these tasks are performed by men, a fact of which we are reminded as the driver of the truck urinates over the side of a cliff. We have already discussed the dismissive and exploitative ways in which women are treated by every male character involved in the trade. Then we have our main characters: Reiner, the dealer; Westray, the liaison; and the Counselor, the neophyte investor. Our initial introductions to Malkina give the illusion that she is little more than the for-now love interest of Reiner, a more world-wise version of Laura, perhaps, but with no real part to play in the plot. But one by one, the male figures are brought down, until finally, Malkina is the only one standing. The difference between Ripley and Malkina is that where Ripley is undeniably the hero of the *Alien* franchise, Malkina is obviously the villain of our tale.

Or is she? In a technical, narrative sense, to the extent that our "hero" (the namesake of the film, after all) is the architect of a plan for which Malkina is (unbeknownst to all the male characters) the antagonist, then, yes, she is the villain, a veritable *femme fatale*. But in a world where everything is "shit"—where, in spite of their pretense of friendship, the male protagonists openly threaten each other (as Reiner does to the Counselor during his efforts to deter him), where even our "hero" is willing to engage in a necrocapitalist world of torture, murder, mutilation, and human trafficking—where do we even begin to draw the line between a hero and a villain?

Indeed, given the basic principles of necrocapitalism, it would seem that in this story there are no heroes and villains, only winners and losers. By the unforgiving rules of necrocapitalism, Malkina is, incontestably, the winner of this specific competition.

But "What do you know about Malkina?" Westray asks the Counselor at one point. Our first encounter with Malkina occurs very early in the film, in the high desert where she and Reiner watch cheetahs chase down jackrabbits. One of the most striking and revelatory exchanges occurs when Reiner asks Malkina, "Do I remind you of someone else?" She replies, "Yes. You do." Reiner then asks her if this person is someone she misses, to which Malkina responds, "Someone who is dead. I dont think I miss things. Things are here and then they are gone. I think to miss them is to hope they will come back. But they are not coming back. I've always known that. Since I was a girl." Reiner then asks her, "You dont think that's a bit cold?" to which Malkina responds, "I think truth has no temperature." In the screenplay, Reiner gives no response to this remark, and in the film, he responds with only a look of startled but reluctant acceptance of her mantra, one forged in the fires of personal suffering.[61]

The accusation of "coldness" suggests a detachment in Malkina's character, an inability or unwillingness to care about or connect with others. And the apparently casual way that Malkina betrays Reiner, her lover, and Laura, her apparent friend, as well as Westray, seems, at first, to confirm such a callous detachment. But there is far more depth to Malkina. In that very same conversation, immediately prior to this exchange, Reiner says to Malkina, speaking of the desert vista, "You like it because it reminds you of Argentina," to which Malkina responds, "It is like Argentina. The Pampas. But that's not why I like it. I like it for itself." Reiner then says, "It doesnt have to be like something else."[62] Like so many other interactions in the film, this one reflects on the meaning of value. Neoliberalism holds that there is and ought to be no arbiter of value beyond the competitive forces of the market, recognizing that the market seeks only to amass more wealth even as it expands "freedom." But in a world where the only real value is wealth, the value of which, after all, is nothing more than its limitless capacity for exchange, *nothing*, strictly speaking, has value. Already, from the opening of the film, Malkina reveals that she does not subscribe, at least not wholeheartedly, to this philosophy. She values the desert landscape for itself; it doesn't have to be like something else. In fact, given the determination and clarity with which Malkina expresses her views on these things, we might even say that, more than any other character in the film, Malkina has a very clear sense of what she values and why. This appears to be confirmed when we learn of Malkina's pregnancy at the end of the screenplay.

Reiner, however, and men in general, are purely instrumental to her. Like the landscape, Reiner reminds Malkina of something (someone) else, but unlike the landscape, she makes no claim to value him for his own sake. He reminds her of someone she has lost—but someone she explicitly does not miss. In fact, the later episode with the windshield of Reiner's car suggests just the opposite: that his "value" to her is of a sort that she can just as easily derive from an inert, material object, an object, we should note, that Reiner himself values highly. But the act that she performs with the windshield, including the understanding of the effect that it will have on Reiner, suggests also that he "values" her in a similar, instrumental manner. Forcefully pressing her labia against the glass directly in front of Reiner, in a manner that he describes to the Counselor as "too gynecological to be sexy. Almost," suggests that Malkina recognizes what he values most about her—her sexuality—and her ability to use this to reduce him to stunned incapacitation suggests a power in her awareness.[63] Indeed, every single conversation that Reiner has about women, including about Malkina herself, revolves around sexual objectification. Malkina does not make the mistake of assuming or desiring there to be anything more to his infatuation with her.

What do we know about Malkina? She seems to genuinely crave human connection. Her desire to speak with the priest suggests a will to interact with another human being, to speak to and be genuinely heard by another, apart from any suspicion of manipulation or exploitation: "All you would have to do is listen" she says to the priest.[64] But when she refuses to leave the confessional, he storms out, frantically blessing himself as he hurriedly makes his way up the aisle of the church. Moreover, given that this scene immediately precedes the one in which Malkina corresponds with Jaime (the man who arranges the assassination of the Green Hornet), we cannot help but wonder if things might have gone differently if the priest had listened.

In her conversation with the priest, we learn that Malkina lost her parents as a child, likely the moment when she learned the hard lesson, expressed to Reiner, that the dead do not come back: "I never knew my parents. They were thrown out of a helicopter into the Atlantic Ocean when I was three."[65] Given Malkina's age (late 40s?) and her country of origin (Argentina)—and given the magnitude of her parents' murder (being thrown from a helicopter)—it is very likely that Malkina's parents were political victims of

Operation Condor. That is to say: the US-backed coup in Chile in 1973 was but one component of a wider strategy on the part of the United States that sought to prevent leftist governments from forming, even democratically, in Latin and South America, for fear that they would nationalize their natural resources, many of which were controlled by US corporations. "Operation Condor was organized from within this developing system of cross-border coordination," writes J. Patrice McSherry in reference to Argentina specifically. "In fact, the Latin American militaries, encouraged and assisted by their US partners, began to collaborate to repress leftists and even oust leftist governments long before Condor was officially instituted and named."[66] Argentina was one of the nations whose political structure was worst affected by this operation: "Between 1976 and 1979 a wave of terror swept the country. The activities of the repressive apparatus were basically secret, making it difficult to establish the number of victims. They were part of a group for which Argentina became tragically famous: *los desaparecidos* (the missing ones), those about whom nothing was ever heard again."[67] And as we saw with the case of Chile, these countries provided a laboratory for neoliberal policies. Malkina is thus one of the early victims of necrocapitalism.

But she refuses to remain a victim of this system, mastering its rules in order to overpower it and emerge victorious. Like the Counselor himself, we are not certain of the motives that compelled Malkina to attempt to steal the shipment of drugs, but the revelation in the end of the screenplay that she is carrying a child, "*about five months pregnant, just noticeable*" along with her expressed commitment to love the child unconditionally suggests that her actions were for the sake of her child.[68] Russell Hillier has persuasively argued that Malkina, at least in McCarthy's screenplay, is motivated by revenge, by the multiple implications that Westray is the father of her unborn child, and thus, when she ultimately hires the blonde woman to seduce Westray (or rather, to trick him into seducing her), it is in order to steal back what rightly belongs to their son: "What Malkina appears to want are Westray's assets, which amount to her child's future birthright."[69] Having Westray killed in the process, on this understanding, is necessary, because a failure to do so will likely result in harm to her or her child or—and perhaps worse in the form of Westray's confiscation and corruption of Malkina's son, perpetuating the very culture of necrocapitalism that he embodies: "I think that Freud is right in that a son who is worshipped by his mother will never doubt himself. But a contentious father can undo that."[70]

In this respect, Malkina is decidedly *not* Anton Chigurh, "the ideal neoliberal subject, a *Homo economicus* in the purest sense: a subject whose entire identity is reducible to market logic."[71] Chigurh might be characterized as what Sayak Valencia calls an "Endriago Subject," "a new creature, an amalgam of *economic entrepreneur, political entrepreneur,* and *violence specialist*."[72] Malkina, however, states quite explicitly that all she wants is "My own life. I own very little. Some jewelry. A few clothes."[73] Her employment of the rules of necrocapitalism derives, not from her identification with its logic, but from her conviction that failure to do so will result in her destruction: "There are times when I imagine that I would like my innocence back. If I ever had it. But I would never pay the price which it now commands on the market."[74] That price, which we see paid by Laura, is to be chewed up and spit out by the system, particularly if one is a woman, which is why Malkina says to the escort at the end of the screenplay that if her unborn child had been a girl, she would have aborted it. But I have argued that Malkina has a very clear sense of value, her cruelty notwithstanding:

> When the world itself is the source of your torment then you are free to exact vengeance upon any least part of it. I think perhaps you would have to be a woman to understand that. And you will never know the depth of your hurt until you are presented with the opportunity for revenge. Only then will you know what you are capable of.[75]

Malkina is born from the necrocapitalist world of late twentieth century US imperialism, tangled in the narco-state politics of US relations with Mexico and with Central and South America, the politics for which *The Counselor* provides a stunning indictment. She adapts the rules of that system to her own ends, to be free of that system and to provide a loving and stable future for her son. She makes her way to the heart of the empire, only to take from it what belongs to her, and to ultimately leave it behind in the hope of building a new world for her son. She, not the Counselor, is the hero of the story, and her odyssey contains multiple hints of a messianic hope. Hillier reminds us that the name, "Malkina," is etymologically connected to the sense of a woman from the lower classes. Like Mary the mother of Jesus, Malkina comes from nothing, an orphan in a despotic state. The child she carries has no father, and she intends to raise him apart from the fragile egos of masculinist power. Armed only with the love that she has promised to give absolutely to her son, Malkina may hope for a new world and a new humanity, beyond the blood-soaked ashes of necrocapitalism. But only because she has faced down and fully taken stock of the evils of that system is she able to triumph: "We would like to draw a veil over all that blood and terror. That have brought us to this place. It is our faintness of heart that would close our eyes to all of that, but in so doing it makes of it our destiny. Perhaps you would not agree. I dont know. But nothing is crueler than a coward, and the slaughter to come is probably beyond our imagining."[76] *The Counselor* is McCarthy's unvarnished attempt to show us the necrocapitalism at the heart of modernity, as it is only in the recognition of our servitude and complicity that there is hope of renewal. *Are you awake?*

Notes

1. Cormac McCarthy, *The Counselor: A Screenplay* (New York: Vintage, 2013), 151. See also, *The Counselor*, directed by Ridley Scott, Blu-ray, 20th Century Fox, 2013. I am calling it a "collaboration" in the sense that I am treating the two components of the work—the screenplay and the film—as independent but mutually reinforcing parts of the whole, as offering slightly different elements and interpretations of the story, and in the sense that McCarthy himself advised in the production of the film. Throughout this piece, I will be very clear about which aspect of the work I am referencing.

2. Fredric Jameson, "Future City," *New Left Review* 21 (June 2003): 65–79.

3. Steven Edward Knepper, "*The Counselor* and Tragic Recognition," *The Cormac McCarthy Journal* 14, no. 1 (2016): 37–54.

4. Peter Travers (Rev. of *The Counselor, Rolling Stone*, 24 Oct. 2013, accessed 1 July 2024, https://www.rollingstone.com/tv-movies/tv-movie-reviews/the-counselor-109718/) calls the film "a droning meditation on capitalism." Mick LaSalle ("'*The Counselor*' Review: A Lawyer Crosses the Line," *The San Francisco Chronicle*, 24 Oct. 2013, accessed 1 July 2024, https://www.sfgate.com/movies/article/The-Counselor-review-A-lawyer-crosses-the-line-4923728.php) writes, "'The Counselor' is about as nihilistic as McCarthy's 'No Country for Old Men,' but without the Coen brothers' sense of humor, or sense of drama"; and *The New Yorker's* Richard Brody argues that the film's "dialogue alternates between throwaway snark and pseudo-philosophical criminal cant; each scene serves as little more than an index card for the mechanistic plot, which Scott films in a glossy and fluid style befitting an industrial promotion for the movie's high-tech weaponry." Richard Brody, Rev. of *The Counselor, The New Yorker*, 4 Nov. 2013, accessed 1 July 2024, https://www.newyorker.com/goings-on-about-town/movies/the-counselor-2.

5. Jacob Agner, "Salvaging *The Counselor*: Watching Cormac McCarthy and Ridley Scott's Really Trashy Movie," *The Cormac McCarthy Journal* 14, no. 2 (2016): 204–26.

6. Stacey L. Peebles, *Cormac McCarthy and Performance: Page, Stage, Screen* (Austin: Univ. of Texas Press, 2017), 5. Peebles is here quoting Julian Young's *The Philosophy of Tragedy: From Plato to Žižek* (Cambridge: Cambridge UP, 2013).

7. Russell M. Hillier, *Morality in Cormac McCarthy's Fiction: Souls at Hazard* (London: Palgrave Macmillan, 2018), 231.

8. Sunny Singh, "The End of Necro-Capitalism (But Not Necessarily Capitalism)," *Media Diversified*, 7 Nov. 2017, accessed 1 July 2024, https://mediadiversified.org/2017/11/07/the-end-of-necro-capitalism-but-not-necessarily-capitalism/.

9. Bobby Banerjee, "Necrocapitalism," *Organization Studies* 29, no. 12 (Dec. 2008): 1541–63.

10. Achille Mbembe, *Necropolitics*, trans. Steven Corcoran (Durham: Duke UP, 2019), 7.

11. McCarthy, *The Counselor*, 112.

12. See Lydia R. Cooper, *Cormac McCarthy: A Complexity Theory of Literature* (Manchester: Manchester UP, 2021), 116. Cooper reads the film in the context of a global history of capitalism, tracing it from the expulsion of the Jews from Spain and Portugal up through the digital capitalism of the 21st century. Her argument is thorough and incisive and my own account is indebted to hers.

13. Karl Marx and Friedrich Engels, *The Communist Manifesto*, ed. Frederic L. Bender (1848; repr. New York: W. W. Norton, 2013), 64.

14. The term "neoliberalism" is itself controversial, derided by many commentators and pundits. Daniel Altman, for example, writes that "real neoliberals don't seem to exist" ("Neoliberalism? It Doesn't Exist," *The New York Times*, 16 July 2005, accessed 1 July 2024, https://www.nytimes.com/2005/07/16/business/worldbusiness/neoliberalism-it-doesnt-exist.html), while Jonathan Chait writes in *New York* magazine ("How 'Neoliberalism' Became the Left's Favorite Insult of Liberals," *New York*, 16 July 2017, accessed 1 July 2024, https://nymag.com/intelligencer/2017/07/how-neoliberalism-became-the-lefts-favorite-insult.html) that "Neoliberalism is held to be the source of all the ills suffered by the Democratic Party and progressive politics over four decades, up to and (especially) including the rise of Donald Trump. The 'neoliberal' accusation is a synecdoche for the American left's renewed offensive against the center-left and a touchstone in the struggle to define progressivism after Barack Obama." These two pieces embody the stereotypical criticisms of the neoliberal taxonomy, namely, that the word "neoliberalism" is an empty signifier, little more than a sweeping terminological gesture employed by leftist ideologues as a cudgel against anything that they happen to dislike.

15. David Harvey, *A Brief History of Neoliberalism* (Oxford: Oxford UP, 2005), 23.

16. Kim Phillips-Fein, *Fear City: New York's Fiscal Crisis and the Rise of Austerity Politics* (New York: Metropolitan Books, 2017), 8.

17. See Sebastian Edwards, *The Chile Project: The Story of the Chicago Boys and the Downfall of Neoliberalism* (Princeton: Princeton UP, 2023), and Philip J. O'Brien and Jacqueline Roddick, *Chile: The Pinochet Decade; the Rise and Fall of the Chicago Boys* (Shropshire: Latin America Bureau, 1983).

18. Harvey, *Brief History*, 11.

19. We must be cautious, however, not to fall into the trap of romanticizing the period of embedded liberalism, as liberals often do. In spite of all its merits, this era was also a time of severe oppression, both of women and of racial minorities. It was also the adolescent phase of the American military-industrial complex.

20. Pierre Dardot and Christian Laval, *The New Way of the World: On Neoliberal Society*, trans. Gregory Elliott (London: Verso, 2017), 38.

21. F. A. Hayek, *The Road to Serfdom* (1944; repr. New York: Routledge, 2006), 37.

22. Milton Friedman, *The Indispensable Milton Friedman: Essays on Politics and Economics*, ed. Alan O. Ebenstein (Washington, D.C.: Regnery, 2012), 6, 18.

23. Michel Foucault, *The Birth of Biopolitics: Lectures at the Collège de France, 1978–79*, trans. Graham Burchell (London: Palgrave Macmillan, 2008), 219.

24. Friedman, *Indispensable*, 14.

25. Friedman in a 1981 interview given to *El Mercurio*, a Chilean magazine. See Bruce Caldwell and Leonidas Montes, "Friedrich Hayek and his visits to Chile," *Review of Austrian Economics* 28, no. 3 (2015): 261–309.

26. Margaret Thatcher quoted in Ronald Butt, "Mrs. Thatcher: The First Two Years," *Sunday Times*, 3 May 1981, Margaret Thatcher Foundation, accessed 1 July 2024, https://www.margaretthatcher.org/document/104475.

27. The line is from Reagan's famous 1984 campaign advertisement.

28. M. I. Asma writing group (J. Moufawad-Paul, et al.), *On Necrocapitalism: A Plague Journal* (Montreal: Leftwingbooks/Kersplebedeb, 2021), 10.

29. Karl Marx, *Capital: A Critique of Political Economy*, trans. Ben Fowkes (1867; repr. New York: Penguin Books, 1981), 342.

30. Asma, *On Necrocapitalism*, 22.

31. McCarthy, *The Counselor*, 19.

32. Ibid.

33. Friedrich Nietzsche, *The Gay Science: With a Prelude in Rhymes and an Appendix of Songs*, trans. Walter Kaufmann (1882; repr. New York: Vintage, 1974), 125.

34. McCarthy, *The Counselor*, 19.

35. Bryan Giemza, *Science and Literature in Cormac McCarthy's Expanding Worlds* (New York: Bloomsbury Academic, 2023), 132.

36. McCarthy, *The Counselor*, 34.

37. Foucault, *Birth of Biopolitics*, 175.

38. Wendy Brown, *Undoing the Demos: Neoliberalism's Stealth Revolution* (New Haven: Princeton UP/Zone, 2017), 151–52.

39. Daniel Melo, *Borderlines: The Edges of U.S. Capitalism, Immigration, and Democracy* (Hampshire: Zero Books, 2021), 47.

40. McCarthy, *The Counselor*, 3.

41. Melo, *Borderlines*, 8.

42. Aviva Chomsky, *Undocumented: How Immigration Became Illegal* (Boston: Beacon Press, 2014), 9.

43. Melo, *Borderlines*, 35.

44. Oswaldo Zavala, *Drug Cartels Do Not Exist: Narcotrafficking in US and Mexican Culture*, trans. William Savinar (Nashville: Vanderbilt UP, 2022), 81.

45. Ioan Grillo, *Blood Gun Money: How America Arms Gangs and Cartels* (New York: Bloomsbury, 2023), 156.

46. McCarthy, *The Counselor*, 155–57.

47. Ibid., 30–33.

48. The statistics are staggering. This phenomenon, known as "femicide," is worse in Latin American countries than anywhere else in the world. See Mark Ensalaco, "Murder in Ciudad Juárez: A Parable of Women's Struggle for Human Rights," *Violence Against Women* 12, no. 5 (2006): 417–40.

49. McCarthy, *The Counselor*, 59.

50. Ibid., 112–13.

51. Ibid.

52. In 1996, journalist Gary Webb—see *Dark Alliance: The CIA, the Contras, and the Crack Cocaine Explosion* (New York: Seven Stories Press, 1999)—famously wrote a series of controversial articles for the San Jose Mercury News, under the heading of "The Dark Alliance," later expanded and compiled into a weighty tome. Providing extensive documentation, the pieces argued that, beginning in the early 1980s, the CIA helped orchestrate massive influxes of Colombian cocaine into

the ports of Los Angeles, creating the supply network that would make the United States the largest customer in the world of Latin American narcotics. In his own exhaustive account of the history of the Mexican drug trade, Benjamin T. Smith—*The Dope: The Real History of the Mexican Drug Trade* (New York: W. W. Norton, 2022)—appears to corroborate Webb's findings, pointing out that the CIA's complicity was instrumental in helping supply money to the Contras in their battle against the Sandinistas: "The CIA was, of course, keen to deny this. And it did so repeatedly. But over the next decade, the connection between the CIA and the Contras became increasingly transparent. CIA insiders, shady contract pilots, disillusioned DEA agents, and a handful of traffickers all testified that the Company had sought to get around the U.S. Congress's ban on Contra funding by establishing a drugs-for-arms racket. Traffickers would bring drugs to CIA-protected airstrips in the United States. They would exchange cocaine for repurposed Vietnam-era assault rifles and cash, then return with their haul and split it between the Contras and the Colombian cocaine lords" (354).

53. Dawn Paley, *Drug War Capitalism* (Chico: AK Press, 2014), 17.

54. Sayak Valencia, *Gore Capitalism*, trans. John Pluecker (Los Angeles: Semiotext(e), 2018), 47.

55. McCarthy, *The Counselor*, 61.

56. Ibid.

57. Ibid., 164.

58. Cooper, *Cormac McCarthy*, 119–20.

59. McCarthy, *The Counselor*, 20.

60. Several women's movements have arisen in Mexico in response to the crisis, and in particular in response to the abject failure on the part of law enforcement to pursue justice for the victims. See Ensalaco, "Murder in Ciudad Juárez."

61. The entire exchange quoted in this paragraph is from McCarthy, *The Counselor*, 21.

62. Ibid.

63. Ibid., 93.

64. Ibid., 85.

65. Ibid.

66. J. Patrice McSherry, *Predatory States: Operation Condor and Covert War in Latin America* (Lanham: Rowman & Littlefield, 2005), 35–36.

67. Juan Carlos Torre and Liliana De Riz, "Argentina Since 1946," *The Cambridge History of Latin America,* ed. Leslie Bethell (Cambridge: Cambridge UP, 1991), 8:159.

68. McCarthy, *The Counselor*, 176.

69. See Russell Hillier, "'Nor Hell a Fury': Malkina's Motivation in Cormac McCarthy's *The Counselor*," *The Explicator* 72, no. 2 (2014): 151–57.

70. McCarthy, *The Counselor*, 180–81.

71. Jonathan Elmore and Rick Elmore, "Human Become Coin: Neoliberalism, Anthropology, and Human Possibilities in *No Country for Old Men*," *The Cormac McCarthy Journal* 14, no. 2 (2016): 168–85.

72. Valencia, *Gore Capitalism*, 64.

73. McCarthy, *The Counselor*, 181.

74. Ibid., 181–82.

75. Ibid.

76. Ibid., 183–84.

9
THE ARCHAEOLOGY OF NEOLIBERALISM

Brian James Schill

In the first book of his sweeping three-volume exploration of twentieth century governance, *Law, Legislation, and Liberty*, Austrian economist Friedrich August von Hayek describes the "spontaneous" order that emerges in societies naturally over time as both desirable and as a reflection of Nature's own production of ordered structures, from flocks of geese in flying-V to the arrangement of iron filings subject to electromagnetism.[1] Such natural order had long fascinated the godfather of neoliberal capitalism, who had by the 1970s dedicated several pages to theorizing the phenomenon in human communities, seeing Nature herself as the standard by which political and economic systems should be judged. As early as 1936, Hayek noted that the "spontaneous" action of individuals will, "under conditions which we can define, bring about a distribution of resources which can be understood as if it were made according to a single plan, although nobody has planned it."[2] Three decades later, Hayek was still arguing that government is unlikely to outmaneuver the natural world, which in every case should remain the standard for civilized societies. In this latter case, he turned to a much smaller example: the hydrocarbon. "We can never produce a crystal or a complex organic compound by placing the individual atoms in such a position that they will form the lattice of a crystal or the system based on benzol rings which make up an organic compound," insisted Hayek in 1973. "But we can create the conditions in which they will arrange themselves in such a manner."[3]

Forty-five years following Hayek's ode to libertarianism, this same referent—the hexagonal C_6H_6 benzene molecule—served for American novelist Cormac McCarthy as the best point of entry for problematizing the grip on knowledge that the unconscious continues to exert in hominid societies, millennia after the eruption of language. Cursing his inability to puzzle out the structure of the molecule he'd dedicated years of his life to understanding, German chemist Friedrich A. Kekulé nodded off in front of the fire one icy London night, recalls McCarthy in his essay "The Kekulé Problem," whereupon he dreamed the ouroboros.[4] "I was sitting, writing at my textbook; but the work did not progress. . . . I turned my chair to the fire and dozed," wrote Kekulé himself of his eureka moment, remembering how "atoms were gambolling" beneath his drooping lids. "My mental eye, rendered more acute by repeated visions of the kind, could now distinguish larger structures of manifold conformation: long rows, sometimes more closely fitted together; all twining and twisting in snake-like motion. But look! What was that? One of the snakes had seized hold of its own tail, and the form whirled mockingly before my eyes." Waking with a start, "as though struck by lightning," Kekulé "spent the rest of the night working out the results of my hypothesis."[5]

For McCarthy, this embellished anecdote illustrates the central problem still facing not only scientists and economists but artists across media in the Anthropocene: accounting for the "natural" influence of the unconscious on human thought and action. "The problem of course—not Kekulé's but ours—is that since the unconscious understands language perfectly well, or it would not understand the problem in the first place, why doesn't it simply answer Kekulé's question with something like: 'Kekulé, it's a bloody ring,'" McCarthy writes. "To which our scientist might respond: 'Okay. Got it. Thanks.' Why the snake? That is, why is the unconscious so loathe to speak to us? Why the images, metaphors, pictures? Why the dreams, for that matter."[6] Answering his own question, McCarthy posits that language is little more than a cute strategy humans invented some 100 millennia ago and disseminated "with considerable speed" in an effort to help manufacture the order Hayek later saw in Nature and sought in manmade economic systems.[7]

Exploring the nature of consciousness in greater detail in his final novel

Stella Maris, which resurrects the Kekulé anecdote, McCarthy—who despite writing that "language had acted very much like a parasitic invasion" later claimed not to have read William S. Burroughs's *The Ticket That Exploded*, which notes how "The word may once have been a healthy neural cell. It is now a parasitic organism"[8]—gives math whiz and University of Chicago dropout Alicia Western space to wax poetic on not only mathematics but the unconscious and language. In so waxing, Alicia references Austrian philosopher Ludwig Wittgenstein more than once, grinning appreciatively when her psychiatrist catches her reference to the philosopher's *Tractatus Logico-Philosophicus*.[9] For Alicia, which is to say McCarthy, Wittgenstein remains relevant decades after his death not only for his contributions to logic and mathematics but to linguistics and consciousness, for recognizing that, as Alicia puts it,

> the actual issue is that someone a hundred thousand years ago stood up and said Holy Shit. Sort of. He didnt have a language yet. But what he had just understood is that one thing can be another thing. Not look like it or act upon it. Be it. Stand for it. Pebbles can be goats. Sounds can be things. The name for water is water. What seems inconsequential to us by reason of usage is in fact the founding notion of civilization. Language, art, mathematics, everything.[10]

Despite Wittgenstein's eventual rejection of his *Tractatus*, this notion of the world-in-a-word, Alicia suggests, was embedded in Wittgenstein's logic long before Noam Chomsky commandeered linguistics as a field in the 1950s with his suggestion that language learning was innate—even structural—to the human brain.[11] "One name stands for one thing, another for another thing, and they are combined with one another" such that the infinite number of word combinations a speaker might produce is responsible for the world itself, Wittgenstein had argued in anticipation of both Chomsky and Alicia Western. To wit, as the philosopher eventually concluded, "*The limits of my language* mean the limits of my world."[12]

For McCarthy, who not only gives Wittgenstein ample space in *Stella Maris* but includes the philosopher among the very few names he cites as influences,[13] this notion is the heart of "The Kekulé Problem," wherein McCarthy opposes anonymous "influential persons," who imagine language to be less innate than evolutionary in nature. These influential persons "have actually claimed that language could be up to a million years old," McCarthy groans, despite the fact that these persons "haven't explained what we have been doing with it all this time."[14] It's hardly a gamble to imagine that at least one of the persons McCarthy has in mind was perhaps not Hayek, who like McCarthy was very interested in Darwin and Wittgenstein, then Chomsky, who eventually inched away from his theory of the anatomical "language acquisition device" in the brain in favor of the "uncontroversial" fact of evolution in language.[15] But while the mature Chomsky's scholarship—and that of other advocates of language evolution such as Steven Pinker[16]—may not have struck a chord with the American novelist, the younger Chomsky had long ago won over the Austrian economist, who was Wittgenstein's "second cousin once removed"[17]: "In the field of social phenomena only economics and linguistics seem to have succeeded in building up a coherent body of theory," grinned a self-satisfied Hayek in 1967, referencing Chomsky's *Syntactic Structures*, which Hayek says helped linguistics take flight by "abandoning the striving after an inductivist 'discovery procedure' and substituting for it the search after an 'evaluation procedure' which enables [Chomsky] to eliminate false theories of grammars."[18]

Chomsky, Pinker, and Wittgenstein notwithstanding, the study of evolution in language did find allies at the Santa Fe Institute (SFI), which for years has provided ongoing support for the Evolution of Human Languages project and once humble-bragged that its "unparalleled atmosphere of transdisciplinary collaboration" put SFI in position to achieve "a new and concrete understanding of the cultural origins of our species."[19] The appeal of structural and evolutionary linguistics to the institute that served as a second home to Cormac McCarthy rests comfortably in the fact that such disciplines today overlay almost too neatly with, as Hayek implied, the complexity systems science that has been SFI's *raison d'être* from day one. McCarthy's closest followers already know, of course, that complexity science has interested McCarthy for a very long time.[20] It thus takes no great imaginative leap to read McCarthy's twin novels from 2022, which focus on mathematical theory, physics, language, the unconscious, and madness, as a contribution to complexity theory itself, which emerged almost directly out of the braiding of economics, epistemology, quantum physics, and even linguistics in the last century. Many early reviewers of *The Passenger* and *Stella Maris* noted the meandering, "rhizomatic," and ultimately complex quality of the novels, with one reader observing how "Some keen online defenders have suggested that the project is so complex and esoteric that it will take years for its true significance to become apparent, making any present attempt at evaluation pointless."[21]

Indeed, the interwoven tales of siblings Alicia and Bobby Western certainly seem designed to pin down the books' typically intangible subjects: quantum entanglement, uncertainty, spooky action at a distance, and, yes, the "spontaneous" order that emerges from complex systems, whether a mental hospital, American city, or offshore oil rig. No surprise, then, for the reader following the pattern laid out above, that none other than Hayek (whose Mont Pèlerin Society served as the neoliberal alternative to the Vienna Circle that was populated by Alicia Western's influences Kurt Gödel and Wittgenstein) played a foundational role in theorizing complexity by inaugurating the aforementioned braiding in the previous century. In fact, the economist's now classic 1964 essay "The Theory of Complex Phenomena," which praised not only then-recent advances in physics but Chomsky's linguistics, Karl Popper's logic, and Darwin's natural history, argues that as "new patterns" and the interplay between them emerge in the social sphere, new and often untestable theories of the complex whole will be required in order to "determine the particular form which the pattern described by the theory will assume in the given circumstances."[22] For Hayek, that is, the study of complexity just is the study of economics, physics, language, the unconscious, evolution, and government, and the increasing complexity of the modern global economy mattered then as now insofar as it had and has profound consequences for human freedom and the future of civilization.

Hayek's almost instinctive understanding of the interoperability of economics, language, physics, and the unconscious all begs, finally, the question: did McCarthy realize that he was chasing Hayek time and again as he scribbled out his thoughts on the unconscious and Wittgenstein, language and complexity, evolution and mechanics? Assuming this pattern of overlays by historical contemporaries was unintentional, or perhaps the serendipitous result of a certain spontaneous order, what appears at first as an uncanny concordance provides instead a crucial clue to what lies at the heart of McCarthy's entire project: Given that the novelist was always-already thinking about socioeconomics and science, even unconsciously, as he recreated the world through violence and dreamscape, madness and mathematics, this concordance demonstrates the degree to which McCarthy's fiction has, since the 1970s, functioned as not merely a commentary on Hayek's own attempt to resuscitate capitalism and reshape reality through neoliberal reason, but as *the archaeology of neoliberalism* itself. Doing to Hayek's neoliberal political economy the very thing Hayek did to capitalism, that is, McCarthy's literary fiction, in the end, doubles as a genealogical project dedicated to speculating upon the new liberalism, challenging its discourses, assumptions, and operations by imagining its logical conclusions and anticipating the predictable effects those conclusions will have on neoliberalism's increasingly "abject" subjects, as Judith Butler once put it, in the postindustrial West. And as we shall see, in the last analysis it is this commitment to archaeology and genealogy that returns, in the end, to grasp McCarthy by his own tail.

The Pretense of Knowledge

Consider first Hayek the intellectual. Any reader engaged in even a quick scan through Hayek's many works cannot help but admire the breadth of knowledge he brought to bear on a variety of problems: ethics, psychology, and government, neurological anatomy, world history, and botany. His early work in particular makes clear that the concern animating his thought, perhaps over and above economics, is the problem of knowledge: how knowledge or its lack produces order or its opposite in increasingly complex communities; how knowledge affects human choice in the marketplace or a dynamic social environment; how knowledge influences phenomena as disparate as presidential elections and natural selection. This interdisciplinary interest in epistemology and what was yet to be called "complexity" probably came naturally to the son of a physician-cum-university lecturer, whose grandfathers were an economist and a biologist, respectively. Earning two doctoral degrees at the University of Vienna, Hayek spent time in an anatomist's lab "tracing fiber bundles of the brain" before assisting Ludwig von Mises on his legal and economic work for the Austrian state and working with New York University professor Jeremiah Jenks on a project for the US Federal Reserve.[23] After founding and directing the Austrian Institute for Business Cycle Research in the late-1920s, Hayek became faculty at the London School of Economics, where his reputation as a critic of economist John Maynard Keynes grew.[24] Hayek's first major public statement in this regard came in a speech given to the London Economic Club in 1936, which, in exploring the need for equilibrium in market economies, argued that the "division of knowledge," as opposed to division of labor, was the "central problem of economics as a social science." "The problem," Hayek mused, "is how the spontaneous interaction of a number of people, each possessing only bits of knowledge, brings about a state of affairs . . . which could be brought about by deliberate direction only by somebody who possessed the combined knowledge of all those individuals."[25]

Describing what he was by then calling "catallactics," a term derived from the Greek *Katallattein* meaning both "to exchange" and "to convert an enemy into a friend,"[26] Hayek went on to argue that nation-states should hardly try to correct but must *accept* disequilibrium in knowledge among market actors in so far as imperfect information and knowledge spontaneously produces—without state manipulation—a "natural" distribution of resources and thus social order.[27] Or, as Hayek put it soberly in a speech entitled "The Pretense of Knowledge," given the day he accepted the Nobel Memorial Prize in Economics in 1974, "The recognition of the insuperable limits to his knowledge ought indeed to teach the student of society a lesson of humility which should guard him against becoming an accomplice in men's fatal striving to control society."[28] Making such arguments alongside the major twentieth century discoveries in psychology and quantum physics—the unconscious, uncertainty, electromagnetism—Hayek was admitting grudgingly to the influence of not only his fellow Austrians Freud and Wittgenstein (plus Chomsky), but at least classical physics on his own thinking, writing in 1973 how "the physical sciences" provide a useful example for the managers of society. Specifically, the second law of thermodynamics, "according to which the tendency of the molecules of a gas to move at constant speeds in straight lines produces a state for which the term 'perfect disorder' has been coined," wrote Hayek, is applicable to human communities, whose own entropy shifts in relation to the relative order and freedom of its own decision-making molecules: "Similarly, it is evident that in society some perfectly regular behaviour of the individuals could produce only disorder."[29]

In this brief reference lies the core of what Hayek would later develop into a robust theory of how to better manage human action by reshaping classical liberalism to produce an economy wherein states not merely back off the economy and the behavior of individual entrepreneurs—after establishing a set of ground rules up front—but actively intervene *on capital's behalf* to solidify the functioning of free, fluid, unregulated markets across sectors managed collectively by countless individuals-atoms possessing only incomplete knowledge of the whole. This limited state action would act as an antidote against the various populisms—fascism and the growing state socialisms—that were then creeping across the globe. And because no state or global institution has enough knowledge of any industry to act upon it in a non-destructive way, Hayek felt, states should resist the urge to intervene in economies and allow markets—which is to say people—to order themselves without any coercion by government, except that which is necessary to maintain free and open markets and the free action of the individuals in those markets, who shall be solely responsible for their choices within the system. And make no mistake: all choices are economic, or should be understood as such, whether the decision involves one's health, education, or career, leisure, worship, or courtship. What Hayek and his supporters sought was the generalization of competition and individual action/choice to all systems and domains, public and private. Even more, where possible the public sphere should simply be eliminated.[30] In his update to Adam Smith's notion of the "invisible hand," in other words, Hayek felt that when every choice every individual agent makes can be quantified and "economized" in an expanded private sphere, social order and the increase in prosperity were the most likely results, if for no other reason than forcing the "Logic of Pure Choice" and rational self-interest upon all agents all the time would prime the pump for socioeconomic gain broadly, and better keep both rational and irrational citizens-entrepreneurs in line.

To summarize the logic at play over the course of Hayek's career, then: attempts to order society from above are tyrannical and must be abandoned; as with ecosystems or organic structures, order emerges spontaneously from the actions of countless individuals within a given society acting in their own self-interest in a free, competitive environment of which their knowledge is incomplete; because the free market polices these individuals without coercion, it is a highly effective force for social order; and so should government limit its work to enabling free markets (often aggressively) and enforcing market rules. Even more, as individual agents-entrepreneurs were set free by this market logic—which was increasingly competitive, ubiquitous throughout society, and both required and produced "decentralized planning by many separate persons"—the individual, as the CEO of her own enterprise-of-one, was the sole party responsible for her fate in an environment wherein every choice was an investment in the self's portfolio and every relation an economic one.[31] Ignoring the uncharitable pitch of this rising-tide-lifts-all-boats logic, Hayek concludes the third volume of *Law, Legislation, and Liberty* by calling redistributionist bleeding hearts and religious prophets "mostly reactionaries" whose evangelizing has obstructed the development of a free market.[32] Instead, "It was the thousands of individuals who practised the new routine more than the occasional successful innovators whom they would imitate that maintained the market order," Hayek argued, paving the way for Gordon Gecko's "greed is good" mantra. "[Capitalism's] mores involved withholding from the known needy neighbours what they might require in order to serve the unknown needs of thousands of unknown others. Financial gain rather than the pursuit of a known common good became not only the basis of approval but also *the cause of the increase of general wealth*."[33]

Encoded within these cognitive gymnastics was not only a serious interest in epistemology, political economy, and ethics as disciplines, but a recognition of the hidden (collective) unconscious that would capture McCarthy. Well aware of his readers' suggestions that he was overlaying a sort of Freudianism upon the economy, Hayek insisted that his theory of spontaneous order was in no way "connected with the conception of an unconscious or subconscious mind underlying the theories of psychoanalysis or 'depth-psychology'" of which Hayek's ideas "are in fact wholly different."[34] Even so, Hayek had by this time already acknowledged, while discussing the price system on durable goods, that the ironic "misfortune" of the spontaneous order produced by neoliberal reason "is the double one [in] that it is not the product of human design and that the people guided by it usually do not know why they are made to do what they do."[35] Admitting, rather, that human subjects are bound by this self-regulating "unconscious" system—or should be—Hayek went on to defend "social Darwinism" as both a good, real-time version of the unconscious at work in the natural world and as an awkward phrase in so far as it jumbled the order of things: Darwin developed his ideas on the natural world *after* having witnessed such evolution in the social sciences.[36]

Describing all of this in the 1970s, Hayek was doubling down on arguments he had been making since the 1930s. In so doing, he all but invented complexity theory. As Hayek had already concluded in "Complex Phenomena," it was not the physical sciences so much as the social sciences—economics and linguistics in particular—that "may well have achieved a very elaborate and quite useful theory about some kind of complex phenomenon . . . [for which] we do not know of a single [physical] law . . . which this kind of phenomenon obeys."[37] All of this—epistemology and evolution, psychology and taxonomy, physics and linguistics, neuroscience and, above all, complexity—demonstrate the degree to which Hayek was less a practitioner of what Popper's antagonist Thomas Kuhn called "normal science"[38] than a paradigm-shifting philosopher of order and uncertainty who set himself the task of reconstructing a world economic system that had been all but obliterated in the twentieth century not only by two World Wars but the collapse of empire and its attendant decolonization, universal suffrage in the Global South, and the ostensible threat to freedom represented by various Marxisms and fascisms. Hayek's goal as a theorist of information, probability, and knowledge was nothing less than an exhuming and resuscitation of a reformed capitalism, which, by the century's second half, he had largely manifested—in conjunction with a host of Western leaders and their advisers. In so doing, Hayek accomplished what Michel Foucault would have called an *archaeology of capitalism*: analyzing, developing, collating, and distributing an entire discourse of market economics—white papers, legislation, news briefs, public speeches, ethical maxims, analytical methodologies, and financial institutions—designed reify and universalize in a positive way the heretofore "unconscious" and highly complex functioning of a market-oriented global political economy. Or, as Hayek put it in a throwaway line at a cybernetics conference in 1968, borrowing in advance from Foucault's *The Order of Things* (1966), "order is not an object"; it is an "event."[39]

Accordingly, it is easy to imagine Hayek's complexity project as Foucauldian in scope well in advance of the French philosopher himself. As Quinn Slobodian put it of Hayek's contribution to the drafting of what became the General Agreement on Tariffs and Trade (GATT), "What we recover in the writings of the Hayekians at the GATT is a genealogy of thought that linked the neoliberal world economic imaginary from the 1920s to the 1990s."[40] The word "genealogy" was well-applied to a philosopher-historian whose essay "Facts of the Social Sciences" predated Foucault's "archaeology of the human sciences" *The Order of Things*[41] by more than a decade; who insisted that "what we call historical facts are really theories which, in a methodological sense, are of precisely the same character as the more abstract or general models which the theoretical sciences of society construct"[42]; and whose life work consisted of recording, producing, and trying to anticipate the discursive practices of a system of thought that had been operating largely unconsciously for more than a century even as it produced a novel subjectivity: *homo economicus*. In this way, Hayek seemed to be trying to analyze what he called the "particular conditions" that produce actions by economic actors, and how (the probability of) those decisions, in Hayek's analysis of the Pure Logic of Choice, are based on imperfect information, which is also the result of the discourse of capitalism itself: commercial news reports and industry journals, monetary policy and financial technology, advertising and trade secrets.[43] Anticipating Foucault, that is, and borrowing from Heisenberg, Wittgenstein, and Chomsky, Hayek produced a history of (spontaneous) order itself. "Just as the existence of a common structure of thought is the condition of the possibility of our communicating with one another, of your understanding of what I say," he argued in advance of Foucault, "so it is also the basis on which we all interpret such complicated social structures as those which we find in economic life, or law, in language, and in customs."[44] In so arguing, Hayek was again tipping his hat to his cousin, who once wrote, in a phrase that resonated as much with Hayek as it did with Foucault, "no part of our experience is at the same time a priori. Whatever we see could be other than it is. Whatever we can describe at all could be other than it is. *There is no a priori order of things.*"[45]

The Order of Things

All of this matters in the reading of Cormac McCarthy, who, while never referencing Hayek by name nonetheless grappled with and lived through the reification of Hayek's ideas for decades both as a novelist writing in a competitive literary marketplace and a human being subject to neoliberal reason. As we have seen, the effect of neoliberalism and what Wendy Brown calls the economization of the subject are at the core of *Blood Meridian* and the Border Trilogy, *No Country for Old Men* and *The Road*, *The Gardener's Son* and *The Counselor*. And the origins and outcomes of neoliberalism are certainly evident throughout *The Passenger* and *Stella Maris*, whose schizophrenic subject Alicia Western attended the University of Chicago simultaneous to the tenures of Hayek and his American analogue Milton Friedman. When McCarthy grapples with Hayek, though, he does so often *through* Michel Foucault, that reader of Hayek who served as a model for McCarthy's midcareer work in multiple ways and upon whom McCarthy's own archaeology relies.

To begin the analysis of McCarthy's archaeology of neoliberalism, we should recall that McCarthy was reading Foucault in the 1970s. Both *Blood Meridian, or the Evening Redness in the West* (1985) and *Suttree* (1979) contain barely paraphrased lines and scenes lifted from the Frenchman's reputation-establishing exercise in discourse analysis *Madness and Civilization* (1961), which is referenced in McCarthy's *Blood Meridian* notes and drafts. As Michael Crews confirmed, when McCarthy describes Judge Holden and the imbecile trekking across the desert, Foucault is there.[46] The philosopher's description of the transformation of European art during the Renaissance—"Things themselves become so burdened with attributes, signs, allusions that they finally lose their own form"—becomes, for McCarthy's wanderers, "Like things so charged with meaning that their forms are dimmed."[47] Even more, says Crews, Foucault's rendering of the depiction of madness in Renaissance painting by the likes of Bosch and Breughel—"Impossible animals, issuing from a demented imagination, become the secret nature of man," Foucault writes, "and when on the Last Day sinful man appears in his hideous nakedness, we see that he has the monstrous shape of a delirious animal"[48]—become Suttree's typhoid hallucination: "At the door of the Huddle folk from the looms of McAnally are convened," McCarthy writes of his eponymous protagonist's own impossible animals. "First among these is the beardless Celt, with spattle skin and rebate teeth. Three eyes in his head he has and he is covered over all with orange hair like unto a Cathay ape. At his elbow a stripling with a small foxy face let into the lower part of a bulbous skull."[49]

We need not go so deep into *Suttree* to recognize McCarthy's debt to *Madness*, though, for Cornelius Suttree's very being as an itinerant river rat, living often on a boat at the fringe of bourgeois society, seems modeled on Foucault's early description of the medieval *Narrenschiff*, that Ship of Fools or drunkards' boat "that glides along the calm rivers of the Rhineland and the Flemish canals," which "conveyed their insane cargo from town to town."[50] In this way does Suttree—himself housed temporarily in a Foucauldian medical institution late in the novel—become less Charon ferrying the dead to the underworld than a caretaker of the *living* whose task it is to "rid the city of a madman who walked about the streets naked" and, later, becomes something of a madman himself.[51] Echoing Foucault's description of the decaying asylum of the middle age—"There prevailed, then, a sort of undifferentiated image of 'rottenness' that had to do with the corruption of morals as well as with the decomposition of the flesh, and upon which were based both the repugnance and the pity felt for the confined"[52]—McCarthy notes carefully Suttree's reaction to the "old drooling derelicts bent above their basketry, their fingerpaints or knitting" in the Knoxville madhouse whose "walls reek with the odors of filth and terminal ills they've soaked up these hundreds of years."[53] Or, as the author had noted as early as *Child of God* (1973), after Lester Ballard's commission to the state hospital at Knoxville perhaps familiar to Suttree and being "placed in a cage," Lester eventually acquires pneumonia, likely the result of the hospital's wretched conditions. Following his convalescence at the University Hospital to which he had been sent, Ballard "was returned to the state hospital at Lyons View and two mornings later was found dead on the floor of his cage."[54]

In crafting such scenes concomitant or subsequent to his reading of Foucault's *Madness*, McCarthy took inspiration not only from the former's prose, but his *method*. Developing over the course of several publications a new approach to historiography he called "archaeology," Foucault moved intentionally away from the traditional academic's recording of history that focused on the progressive, deliberate continuity of events and dates—great men and their works taking shape slowly and emerging in a steady and predictable way on the quilt of time—and toward an emphasis on the discontinuity of discourses and statements, on the spasm of systems of thought and the speech, knowledge, and subjects they produce: Which discourses generated, or were generated by, institutions like the state prison? What conditions of being produced the mental hospital as a clinical site of knowledge and what effect did such facilities have on the relations of even the "sane" women and men in whose neighborhoods such hospitals were built? How does the physician's palpation and pidgin affect social space itself through the production of novel analytical subjects and novel forms of inquiry? Such questions sought to "define a method of analysis purged of all anthropologism," claimed Foucault in *The Archaeology of Knowledge* (1969), "to analyse history in the discontinuity that no teleology would reduce in advance; to map it in a dispersion that no pre-established horizon would embrace; to allow it to be deployed in an anonymity on which no transcendental constitution would impose the form of the subject."[55] Based on the analyses of unconscious structures and the "discursive formations" that define systems of thought in a given linguistic, political, or socioeconomic regime, and in a given historical epoch, archaeology was coined, wrote Foucault,

> to suggest that the kind of analysis I was using was out-of-phase, not in terms of time but by virtue of the level at which it was situated. . . . Why, for instance did madness become, at a given moment, an object of knowledge corresponding to a certain type of knowledge? By using the word 'archaeology' rather than 'history,' I tried to designate this desynchronisation between ideas about madness and the constitution of madness as an object."[56]

Employing also the term "genealogy" to his method, insofar as the concept allowed Foucault to "set out from a problem expressed in the terms current today" and allowed him to develop his "history of the present,"[57] the philosopher sought not only to identify and challenge power in all its forms but, in a blurb that ought to adorn the back cover of *Blood Meridian*, to "cleanse [history] of all transcendental narcissism."[58]

This, at least, must have been McCarthy's reading of *Madness and Civilization*. Not only do *Suttree* and *Blood Meridian* (and arguably the Border Trilogy) double as such cleansing—the former of the twentieth century American South in general and Knoxville, Tennessee, in particular; the latter of both Manifest Destiny as a nightmare and of the West as a mystification—but, as I have written elsewhere, *Blood Meridian*, as discourse itself, functions as an exercise in Foucauldian archaeology, excavating the unconscious assumptions, thoughts, ideologies, discourses, and structures of the American myth—that is, the discursive practices of an entire *episteme*—and laying them out for a chalky swallowing by consumers of the cultural dominant.[59] In so doing, the novel served, at the very moment neoliberal capitalism was reinforcing its own mythologies under an American president who himself had played a cowboy in Hollywood, as a history of the present and as an allegory of the madness and senescence of the West that was by then already underway.

Consider the novel's sixteenth chapter. After Glanton's gang passes a crumbling church harboring a handful of nearly feral men and discovers the roasted bodies of four of their mates, and after Glanton's horse causes a ruckus by biting the ear off a Chiricahua chief's horse, the group takes refuge in the presidio at Tucson. Settling down in a cantina, the gang is confounded at the segregationist barkeep Owens's refusal to serve the black John Jackson. Insulted on Jackson's behalf, and at having himself been mistaken for black by Owens, Brown tosses a pistol to the barkeep, enabling Jackson to kill Owens in "self-defense." The murder triggers an investigation by the presidio's Lieutenant Couts, who meets with Judge Holden as soon as the latter claims to be Glanton's bona fide representative in all matters financial and legal. "[Couts] and the judge sat together and the judge went over points of law with him," McCarthy writes of what becomes a rather one-sided discourse. "The lieutenant nodded, his lips pursed. The judge translated for him latin terms of jurisprudence. He cited cases civil and martial. He quoted Coke and Blackstone, Anaximander, Thales."[60] Case dismissed. Avoiding an official indictment for the killing, the gang resumes its debauchery and a child goes missing. Before leaving town the next day, the gang retrieved its fresh horses from a farrier named Pacheco, who uses for an anvil a massive iron meteorite. Grasping the meteorite on a wager, the judge "raised it overhead and stood tottering and then lunged forward." Easily throwing the great gray nugget over the several lines drawn in the sand by various speculators, Holden, riding off with his gang, "shared with no one the specie piled on the saddleblanket at the farrier's feet."[61]

Compressed into this short chapter set in a lawless, unfenced American Southwest—racism, random and ratified acts of brutality, sexual violence and drunken games of chance, the crumbling of Christianity as an institution, the impotence of federal government, a rogue attorney's slick justification of crime via reference to both historical tradition and the actual letter of the law, and survival of the fittest—is a concise history of both North America since 1492 CE and of the West in its phantasmagoric singularity. This radical unearthing of the true history of "the West" as a category in all its density and depravity is not only archaeological in its recovery of an explicitly American narrative that no teleology could reduce in advance, as Foucault posited; it is genealogical in less a Nietzschean than Foucauldian sense in that it tells not a history of the past than of the present, asking how the conditions of possibility as they were in 1848 generated the political economy, the ideologies, the violence that were still with Americans in the 1980s and remain with us today, as the West continues its long sunset. McCarthy's accomplishment in *Blood Meridian*, then, rests in his unflinching documentation of Walter Benjamin's notion that "There is no document of civilization which is not at the same time a document of barbarism," in showing readers that such horrors were and remain encoded in the genetics of the world's "last best hope."[62]

In demonstrating how all of the above—the speech, thoughts, and actions of filibusters and federales, merchants and mercenaries—was part of the era's conscious and unconscious discourse, was in fact enshrined in US Code, McCarthy was certain to ruffle a few feathers. Indeed, few critics embraced the book whole-heartedly in 1985. In *Blood Meridian*, "The grim and patient character development, the crisp narration of the earlier novels are junked; what's left is hyperbolic violence, strained surrealism, and pseudo-philosophic palaver," chuffed Terence Moran in his *New Republic* review, apparently hoping to read in *Blood Meridian* more of McCarthy's trademark Southern Gothic. Instead, writes the reviewer, McCarthy's attempt:

> to extend and deepen his exploration of the beastly potential inherent in the American character . . . convinces only when it is acutely dramatized in the lives of small characters and in the empty concreteness of their country. But in *Blood Meridian* McCarthy ends up merely toying with his language and ideas. We are neither afraid to look at what he sees, nor moved to think about his vision of America. This novel, despite its chronicling of appalling horrors and its straining for apocalyptic effects, is boring."[63]

For fans of *Blood Meridian*, and of Foucault, it's hard to read reviews like

Moran's as anything less than evidence of a mission accomplished. Indeed, had McCarthy's archaeology of Manifest Destiny and American political economy not triggered such reactions among readers and writers of the establishment press, among the defenders of American power, the book would have failed its task. These squint-eyed rebukes verify what Foucault meant when he described his method as anxiety-inducing in that it deprives the gatekeepers of ideology and culture of their self-serving sense of purpose. "I understand the unease of all such people," shrugged Foucault in 1970. "They have probably found it difficult enough to recognize that their history, their economics, their social practices, the language that they speak, the mythology of their ancestors, even the stories that they were told in their childhood, are governed by rules that are not all given to their consciousness." Wrinkling their noses at seeing their own history, their own value systems, laid bare, says Foucault, such readers contort their brains in an often vain effort to "preserve that tiny fragment of discourse—whether written or spoken—whose fragile, uncertain existence must perpetuate their lives."[64]

McCarthy, it seems, couldn't agree more. Taking further Foucault's admission that he has "never written anything but fictions,"[65] the novelist reminds reviewers of even his last novels that:

> You think that you can create a history of what has been. Present artifacts. A clutch of letters. A sachet in a dressingtable drawer. But that's not what's at the heart of the tale. The problem is that what drives the tale [or the book review] will not survive the tale. As the room dims and the sound of voices fades you understand that the world and all in it will soon cease to be. You believe that it will begin again. You point to other lives. But their world was never yours."[66]

Or as Alicia's co-resident at Stella Maris, Jeffrey, puts it to Bobby in *The Passenger*, the notion that "history" is ever anything but ideology is simply naive. "All physical history eventually turns out to be a chimera," Jeffrey quotes Alicia. "She said that even if you place your hands on the stones of ancient buildings you'll never really believe that the world which they've survived had at one time the same reality as the one you're standing in. History is belief."[67] Which is McCarthy's way of echoing Foucault in suggesting that even history is a fiction.

The Archaeology of Neoliberalism

In assuming both Foucault's archaeological method and his attitude toward historiography, and thus triggering the return of the repressed noted above, McCarthy also assumed the philosopher's oblique critique of (neoliberal) capitalism. Even more, in offering readers not just *Blood Meridian* as an illustration of the flaws embedded within Hayek's thinking on knowledge and competition applied to the population at large (e.g., Holden's notion that whatever exists outside his knowledge exists outside his consent[68]); in producing the Border Trilogy as an archaeology of America's shift from industrial to postindustrial capitalism; in *No Country*, which offers the world, in Anton Chigurh, neoliberal reason anthropomorphized; in giving us *The Road* to illustrate the outcome of the absolute financialization of human beings; and in writing *The Counselor* for the screen in an effort to shock a mass audience into a recognition of the at times comic horror of neoliberal business-as-usual in the new century, McCarthy achieved an archaeology of neoliberalism writ large, unearthing the often unconscious functioning of a structure that rather than freeing individuals to pursue their own interests amid an embarrassment of social, political, and economic riches also fragmented communities and lives by producing greater sociopathy and precarity systemwide.

Despite this towering accomplishment, however, McCarthy, like Foucault, failed to escape neoliberalism-as-ideology. Even more, McCarthy arguably took to *courting* and amplifying neoliberal reason, as his final novels confirm, eventually assuming Foucault's complicity in advancing the neoliberal agenda. Concerning the latter, after distancing himself from both his former Maoism and the term "archaeology," the philosopher, sensing an intellectual consanguinity in Hayek's genealogy of capitalism, undertook a yearlong seminar in 1979 on what he teased would be a course in "biopolitics" but really ended up being a rudimentary archaeology of neoliberal capitalism.[69] Turning his growing interest in "governmentality" toward economics proper, Foucault, in his 1979-80 seminar at the Collège de France, described how a certain "regime of truth," coupled with a set of discursive practices, produced a global postwar structure that "was able to make what does not exist . . . nonetheless become something that continues not to exist" even as it remains visible and almost tangible.[70] That something is a novel subjectivity that generates a creature which, in its ubiquitous financialization and economization, is always-already a market agent who, like it or not, is less a partner in some exchange than a permanent "entrepreneur of himself" subject always to an inescapable competition.[71]

Insofar as the Enlightenment's *laissez-faire* liberalism had failed—given its inability to prevent the Great Depression and not one but two World Wars and the rise of fascism, Leninism, and other social upheavals—the new theorists of capitalism, said Foucault, envisioned instead a market-based society predicated less on free exchange than a robust and pervasive competition. As Foucault put it, giving much space in his seminar to Hayek and von Mises, Walter Lippmann and Milton Friedman, "this uncoupling of the market economy and *laissez-faire* policies was achieved . . . when the neoliberals put forward a theory of pure competition in which competition was not presented as in any way a primitive and natural given" but as a well-designed, disciplinary structure "that assured, and could assure, economic regulation through the price mechanism," in order to maintain the market economy *sans laissez-faire*.[72] This is how liberals renewed capitalism in the wake of World War Two, Soviet socialism and, later, May '68, Foucault says, using policy itself to enable not only "free" and competitive markets, but to insert market logic into the public sector as social policy to better manage agitated populations of all types in an effort to prevent further international conflicts and eruptions of unseemly behaviors such as ethnic chauvinism, religious fundamentalism, and political populism of all stripes. "This means that what is sought is not a society subject to the commodity-effect, but a society subject to the dynamic of competition," claimed Foucault. "Not a supermarket society, but an enterprise society."[73]

Such an analysis, which was surprisingly courteous toward its subject, came not long after Foucault had begun acknowledging openly his admiration for American culture and thought, especially as it manifested in one of neoliberalism's post-Chile testing grounds: California. Having first taken in the Golden State in 1975—when Foucault dropped acid with Simeon Wade in Death Valley—the philosopher returned to France with a radically new perspective, scrapping his draft work on the history of sexuality, and in many ways his earlier self, itching to "begin again" as he later wrote Wade.[74] Adapting easily, that is, to California's climate, countercultural social milieu, and liberatory economic environment that promoted altered states of consciousness, uninhibited sexual practices, and the anti-institutional "self-care" movement—which were all themselves the product of a neoliberal reason that was at that moment being championed by Golden Staters across the political spectrum, from Richard Nixon and Ronald Reagan to Steve Jobs, Source Family founder James Edward Baker, and the founders of the deep state-affiliated Esalen Institute[75]—Foucault, in Wade's recollection, wasted no time during what was the first of many subsequent California junkets in developing an interest in yoga, psychedelics, and Wilhelm Reich's "orgones." "I produced a book of hatha yoga [a branch of yoga designed to preserve and channel power in the body] photographs," Wade recalls, describing how he prepared for his guest a marijuana cigarette. "Foucault went through [the book] assiduously and, pointing to a most difficult position of standing on one's hands with legs over the head, devilishly asked, with a broad smile displaying his large white teeth, 'Can you do that?'" Responding with a sheepish "no," Wade added that Foucault then recounted his visits to a variety of Folsom Street bars and that the honorarium he requested for his famous public debate with Noam Chomsky in Amsterdam in 1972 was a block of hashish, which the debate's organizers were more than happy to produce. "My students and I refer to it as the Chomsky hash," Foucault laughed, adding that he found Chomsky to be a "very agreeable man."[76]

As his voyages west began to increase in duration and frequency, Foucault—who eventually told Wade "I feel that I have to emigrate and become a Californian"[77]—began to write such lifestyling into his philosophizing, producing a series of "neoliberal" books on pleasure, self-care, and the "government of the self," which although often focused on antiquity were really describing the present.[78] Embedded within these then-private admissions is what eventually emerged publicly as Foucault's internalization of a rationality that saw the philosopher abandoning organized political projects—and the traditional Left in general—and moving instead toward the analysis of non-judgmental, non-normative, and non-moralizing governmentalities that he felt would be "capable of breaking with the structures inherited from Christianity and opening the space for new forms of subjectivity," as Mitchell Dean and Daniel Zamora put it.[79] Arguing in favor of the individual and the care of the self—and seeking out novel subjectivities not hemmed in by Western convention—Foucault began further exploring alternative forms of pleasure, political agency, and 'Being,' endorsing a lower age of sexual consent in France, supporting the revolutionary violence in Iran (even if it meant implicitly endorsing a crack-down on intellectuals, women, and the LGBTQ+ community), and arguing that since limits on resources and access cannot be established by the state with regard to healthcare, "It is clear that there is hardly any sense in speaking of a 'right to health.'"[80] Asked further whether individual citizens of a given state are justified in demanding from government the satisfaction of their health needs as they pursued, in the US at least, life, liberty, and happiness, Foucault added that, "It seems—if those needs are likely to increase infinitely—that a positive answer to this question could take no acceptable or even conceivable form."[81] Such are the arguments that prompted America's Central Intelligence Agency (CIA) to *celebrate* the mature Foucault for his success at undermining French Marxism in the wake of Sartre and Louis Aragon.[82]

All of this had been telegraphed by Foucault, whose guarded defense of neoliberalism in the late-1970s concluded with a reference to Adam Ferguson's allusion to the "spontaneous" order embedded in the North American Indigenous community. "Thus, without any settled form of government, or any explicit bond of union . . . [w]ithout police or compulsory laws, their domestic society is conducted with order," Foucault quotes Ferguson, wondering too if Hayek's new liberalism similarly represented humans' best chance at genuinely freeing themselves from excess government oversight and producing a greater tolerance of difference in the social sphere.[83] Indeed, Foucault went so far as to suggest that neoliberalism—at least as he had seen it manifested in California—might very well reduce racism, sexism, and homophobia in increasingly complex societies: "You can see that what appears on the horizon of this kind of analysis is not at all the ideal or project of an exhaustively disciplinary society in which the legal network hemming in individuals is taken over and extended internally by, let's say, normative mechanisms," claimed Foucault, doing his best high-wire act.

> On the horizon of this analysis we see instead the image, idea, or theme-program of a society in which there is an optimization of systems of difference, in which the field is left open to fluctuating processes, in which minority individuals and practices are tolerated, in which action is brought to bear on the rules of the game rather than on the players, and finally in which there is an environmental type of intervention instead of the internal subjugation of individuals.[84]

Borrowing explicitly from Hayek and Friedman, Foucault called this optimization of difference and tolerance of the other the result of the "spontaneous bond and spontaneous equilibrium" that neoliberal reason seemed poised to produce.[85]

Today, of course, the world knows better: neoliberalism has less lifted all boats than capsized the smallest among them after making the seas much more volatile. To take only a few examples, Thomas Picketty has documented how income inequality in the US has grown significantly since 1980 and purchasing power has declined.[86] Home ownership has thus *dropped* in the US since 2001—in large part as a result of the Great Recession in 2008-09 and the COVID-19 pandemic—meaning that four-plus decades of neoliberalism has produced *fewer* owners of private property rather than more.[87] Accordingly, as income inequality has increased, labor union membership plummeted, with overall union participation dropping by 50 percent between 1983 and 2023, resulting in less capacity for laborers to demand wages or health benefits that match inflation.[88] And as immigration swelled in the neoliberal era—as workers pursue capital flows across international borders, typically from the Global South to the North—so has human trafficking exploded: the US State Department notes that with more than twenty-seven million estimated victims of human trafficking worldwide in 2025 there are more "slaves" today trapped in indentured servitude, sexual slavery, or forced labor situations than there were in the nineteenth century.[89] Even more, a raft of studies over the past two decades has verified prophecies by Freud and Foucault, Deleuze and Guattari, concerning the "madness" and "schizophrenia" that are exacerbated by the new capitalism.[90] Finally, dozens of peer-reviewed analyses have confirmed the degree to which a deregulation-oriented neoliberal regime has accelerated climate change and the destruction of the natural world.[91]

None of this, of course, comes as a surprise to the architects of neoliberal reason, who understood such outcomes as an acceptable price to pay for the production of a certain type of global order that even as it enables government in certain ways nominally "limits" "our powers of control," as Hayek put it.[92] Living through such developments—and the extension of corporate control over entire communities—as he was drafting his midcareer novels and (screen)plays, and witnessing first-hand the slow dismantling of the American South and Southwest, McCarthy at least initially set about demonstrating how Foucault's Hayekian thinking was at best naive and at worst monstrously complicit in enabling the rise in social disintegration, mental illness, income inequality, and ecocide. But as he aged—as he was absorbed into the neoliberal status quo and the daily routine at SFI in New Mexico—McCarthy, while not abandoning archaeology, also seemed to fall into at least a nonalignment pact with neoliberal reason, if not a tentative endorsement of it. Of this there is no better example than McCarthy's final couplet.

The Möbius Loop

Animated by siblings Bobby and Alicia Western, the lapsed physicist and schizophrenic mathematician very likely named after the standard bob-and-alice quantum experiments that would have been familiar to their physicist father, *The Passenger* and *Stella Maris* bend and swirl around each other like the opposite sides of a Möbius loop. Published a month before its sister novel in late 2022, *The Passenger* follows Bobby, the ex-racecar driver and salvage diver whose exposure, in 1980, to a mystery involving a downed private jet in the Gulf of Mexico leads to his being questioned/tailed by, readers assume, federal agents. After the freezing of his assets and passport, and following repeat break-ins at his various flats, Bobby makes his way to Ibiza, Spain, to confront finally the death of his sister nearly a decade beforehand, whose italicized conversations with a gutter-mouthed, flippered Thalidomide Kid and his vaudevillian cohorts constitute one-quarter of the book. Alicia's suicide, in fact, serves as the reader's point of entry into these characters' thoughts and lives, and it is the weeks leading up to this suicide that constitute the diptych's corresponding panel *Stella Maris*, which is set in the Stella Maris mental hospital in Black River Falls, Wisconsin, in 1972—before the events of *The Passenger*—and is framed entirely as a dialogue between Alicia and her woefully overmatched therapist.

This structural complexity—the novels don't so much follow an obvious narrative arc or really even "end" as explore a variety of ontological and epistemological abstractions before looping around into the other to begin again—reinforces the novels' focus, which is complexity itself and the interrelation between everything from mathematics, madness, and global conspiracy to quantum physics, spacetime, cryptocurrency, history, the hydrocarbon industry, surveillance, language, love, the unconscious, and the divine. In this way, they/it function(s) as a different type of archaeology that exhumes less America's past than its present, specifically the outcome of the economization of the subject and the mutually-reinforcing consequences that Hayek's neoliberal economics and the siblings' father's quantum physics have on the subject—which is to say the reader—and her environment today. To wit, both *The Passenger* and *Stella Maris*, as objects, function as entangled particles telling the stories of the likewise entangled Bobby and Alicia whose physical and temporal distance not only doesn't impede but determines the velocity, position, and direction of their counterpart and those around them. To this point, the novels seem to have been anticipated by the

March 1998 issue of *Physics World* magazine, the cover of which featured a sharp-chinned man in profile, telephone receiver to his ear, gushing "Oh, Alice, you're the one for me" as a full-lipped blonde on the other end of the line thinks—as arithmetical equations-questions ("psi+ or psi-?") languish on the blackboard behind her—"But Bob . . . In a quantum world how can we be sure?" (See figure 1.)

Artwork by John Richardson originally published in Physics World March 1998. © IOP Publishing. Reused with permission.

This is all to say that the novels are, in the end, an effective meditation on complexity systems science. Remembering that Hayek was developing his notions of spontaneous order and the physics of "catallactics" at the very moment that Oppenheimer and crew were splitting the atom and McCarthy's future colleagues Richard Feynman and Murray Gell-Mann were theorizing quantum electrodynamics and quarks, quantum mechanics and neoliberal economics were always-already interlocked, developing in concert over the course of the twentieth century, courtesy of Hayek. Suttree's musings on a sunrise as he pulls his lines in from the cold October Tennessee River, for example, all but signals McCarthy's reverence for Hayek's spontaneous order in Nature, which is too converted into a "currency": "A rack of clouds troweled across the east grew mauve and yellow and the sun came boring up," McCarthy writes of Suttree's approval of the order embedded in Nature. "He was moved by the utter silence of it. He turned his back to the warmth. Yellow leaves were falling all through the forest and the river was filled with them, shuttling and winking, golden leaves the rushed like poured coins in the tailwater. A perishable currency, forever renewed."[93]

Such lines—nature as a currency "forever" renewed—all but anticipate the formal academic discipline—econophysics—then emerging around this overlay that almost certainly interested McCarthy and which found an obvious home at SFI.[94] "Because physics is traditionally a discipline that is strongly tied to empirical facts and experiments, the possibility of performing extensive data analyses has attracted many physicists toward [economic] problems," writes Fabrizio Lillo, referencing both a *Physics Today* piece that asked if economics just might be "the next physical science" and a *Physics World* story that wondered whether it was possible to "treat people as particles." "This data-driven motivation helps also to explain why many physicists have been so attracted by finance, given that in the last years there has been a significant increase in the quantity of available financial data and in their level of detail."[95]Like Foucault in California, then, McCarthy, rubbing elbows with contemporary thinkers in the American Southwest who since at least the turn of the century were explicit in combining physics with neoliberal economics, probably couldn't help but craft not merely *The Road*, which like a backhoe unearths in advance what Wendy Brown called the "ruins of neoliberalism," but also his final couplet, the narrative of which functions too as the excavation of complexity itself.

To take but one example from the latter novels, consider the job Bobby takes on, even after learning of his colleague Oiler's death on the ocean floor while welding pup joints for Halliburton Corporation, that brings him to an oil rig off the Florida coast. Ignoring here the ripe fruit of his employment by a petrochemical multinational, Bobby's solitary wayfaring through what amounts to the skeleton of industrial capitalism halfway through the novel quickly leads to his feeling that he has stumbled into a burial vault, desecrating a sacred space and thus conjuring up the boneyard's ghosts. "After a while [Bobby] went down to the galley and found some eggs and fixed breakfast and made a cup of tea and sat down at the table to eat," McCarthy writes. "Then he stopped. There was an empty coffeecup over on the counter. He didnt remember seeing it there before. Would he have noticed it? It must have been there. He got up and went over and took hold of it but of course it was cold."[96] Sensing nevertheless that "Someone was on the rig with him," Bobby retreats to his bunkroom, the door of which does not lock, and pushes the room's small desk up against the door before falling asleep, attempting first a reading of Hobbes's own competition-obsessed treatise on governmentality and the brutishness of humankind, *Leviathan*. "When he woke in the late afternoon the desk was backed away a good foot. The vibration of the rig was slowly walking it across the floor. He looked around the room. What else had walked?"[97] Taking a meat cleaver back to his room with him, Bobby, fighting off paranoia, is nonetheless relieved at the arrival of the rig's "skeleton crew" the next day.

It's hard to read this scene as anything other than McCarthy's version of a haunting, a visit from the specter of capitalism's past, the creaking corpse over which Bobby had stumbled in a book addressing the present. Back on the mainland, the question Bobby had asked himself on the rig—"What else?"—becomes the collective query of each of the novels' characters. Uttered dozens of times across both novels, the line is the nucleus around which the novels-particles orbit: What else contributes to and affects humans' perceptions of reality? What else produces the knowledge and structures through which subjects like Bobby, Alicia, Debbie, and Oiler slog and the velocity with which they do so? What else is at stake in every choice each of us make in our capacities as artists, physicists, economists, and bureaucrats, siblings and parents, children and grandparents, laborers and friends? What else determines the color and the shape of each life? By way of an answer, the novelist's legitimate-if-uninspiring restatement of the butterfly effect is, effectively, "everything." All creation is interconnected in a complex and open econophysical system: "Who are his clientele?" Bobby asks Jeffrey, referencing Alicia's dream of a document forger whose portfolio "had been fashioned from the hide of a heathen." "History is his clientele" quips Jeffrey, reminding Bobby just how radically indeterminate history, which is to say reality, truly is: "If you think that the dignity of your life cannot be canceled with the stroke of a pen I think you should think again."[98] Much in how Hayek had argued in "Complex Phenomena" that "There are, strictly speaking, no closed systems in within the universe,"[99] McCarthy too, in a pair of books about the complex interplay between physics, work, dreams, mathematics, love, presidential assassinations, spies, racecars, the mafia, gender dysphoria, and madness, concludes not only that "There's always something else" but that this radical openness means that, to again quote Walter Benjamin, every day is Judgment Day.[100]

This is why Bobby's lawyer's long monologue on the Kennedys, while something of a MacGuffin, matters. The multifarious machinations behind and aftermath of the assassinations of both John and Robert Kennedy—the CIA, the mafia, Cuba, Lee Harvey Oswald, Dallas, Jack Ruby, the defense industry, New Orleans, Edward Lansdale, Vietnam—are so convoluted in their construction, so impossible to unknot, Kline implies, that they serve as a prophetic case study of a neoliberal future that, in the early 1960s, loomed just over the horizon, a future overrun with mainstream conspiracy theories, fake news, revisionist histories, New Age self-care, artificial intelligence, deep fakes, and both virtual and simulated realities. As paranoid as it is impossible, rather, *The Passenger* demonstrates the degree to which conspiracy and anxiety are the result of complexity, the degree to which paranoia and isolation *just are* the neoliberal aesthetic. For who, really, is "after" Bobby? Although readers are led to believe that Bobby is being tailed by the American Internal Revenue Service (IRS) or CIA, the black-suited agents who freeze Bobby's bank account, cancel his passport, and lose his cat might as well be representatives of any of the global financial firms or multinational agencies whose job is enabling and restricting capital flows, managing stochastic dynamics, and determining the velocity and position of currency. That is to say, Bobby is being tailed, of course, by neoliberalism itself, whose agents are always-already everywhere, judging his economic, social, and political choices, which even Bobby admits are often lazy and not in his own self-interest. This is the same "they" who stole the elder Western's physics papers from both Princeton University and his parents' home. Why would the IRS—or CIA or World Bank or Google or IMF—want to steal papers from a physicist-mathematician? the reader is correct to ask (perhaps having not read much Philip K. Dick). Because they know that people are particles; that physics determines who controls economic information; and that physics determines economic, political, and social reality in its entirety. Because they know, like Oppenheimer, that physics is power and to understand and control the econophysics complex is to control not only the known world, but the unconscious, language, history, and everything else that we cannot even see.

Cargo Cult Fiction

All of this, then, is the problem. As Foucault's apologetics implied in advance, McCarthy's "what else?" is a sort of capitulation, another instance of the author's chasing of—but never really catching or burying—Hayek. Even more, McCarthy, like Foucault, seemed to openly buy into neoliberalism at the same time as he feigned a critique of it. In this case—what else?—the overdetermined and overused query serves as both the mystification of power and a concession to the technical and almost mystical discourse of complexity science and its amplifiers, which, increasingly, serve to mask the unsustainability of the neoliberal reason at the heart of complexity. The twenty-first century McCarthy, that is to say, seems to have repeated Foucault's mistakes, compounding the philosopher's cynicism by finding himself also taken with neoliberalism-as-ideology and the SFI-linked obscurantism that was to McCarthy what California, LSD, yoga, and self-care were to the late Foucault.

Several researchers have already demonstrated how the SFI in particular has succeeded in cultivating if not a replicable research model then considerable funding from the defense, finance, and tech industries, proliferating and norming neoliberalism in so doing.[101] The institute's roster of sponsors and benefactors, even if they are serious in their interest in complexity science, represents a veritable who's who of voices working hard to broaden late capitalism's reach and influence, including the US Department of Defense's Defense Advanced Research Projects Agency (DARPA), Google, billionaires Charles and David Koch, the late "financial manager" and sex trafficker Jeffery Epstein (whose partner Ghislaine Maxwell's sister is a former SFI trustee and father Robert was, Like Epstein, an SFI donor), and the John Templeton Foundation, a right-wing think tank "Grounded in the ideas of classical liberal political economy" that uses its resources to finance "education, research, and outreach projects to promote individual freedom, free markets, free competition, and entrepreneurship."[102] Speaking of the SFI's defunct Business Network for Complex Systems Research (BusNet), Fabrizio

Li Vigni documented how, in 2007, the institute retained fifty-five corporate partners from various sectors within its ken, including Deloitte, Lockheed-Martin, Cisco, Sun Microsystems, Barclays, Morgan Stanley, and Boeing.[103] This roster of advocates is what allowed David Kushner to get away with gushing in *Rolling Stone* magazine, in a 2007 piece that reads less like a feature story than an investment pitch, how "Google's honchos spent a few days wandering the Institute's sunlit halls, [becoming] so impressed by its unique mix of brains and natural beauty that they aspired to turn their company into the 'SFI of Silicon Valley.'"[104]

McCarthy, in his seventies by the time he was contributing to Kushner's article, seemed unfazed by any of the above, even as the cynical realpolitik and exercise of less-than-soft power Kushner described was facilitating the social collapse McCarthy wrote into *The Passenger*, accelerating the apocalypse McCarthy anticipated in *The Road*, and creating the economic conditions that all but forced a Vietnam veteran-turned-arcwelder to insert himself into a turf battle between a Mexican drug cartel and its corporate buyers in West Texas in *No Country*. Admitting to Kushner that he's attracted to SFI as an idea not only because of its rugged self-reliance in financial matters but because he feels at home among its intellectual "outlaws," McCarthy mused that "You have to go back to Elizabethan England or Periclean Athens to find this kind of extraordinary work being done."[105] Whether or not such a statement is objectively true, embedded in this fierce commitment to independence from the state and its bureaucracy—whose advocates are "always pushing creativity to its practical limits" and, as such, are "relentless at hammering down the boundaries created by academic disciplines and institutional structures," as McCarthy put it in the handwritten "Operating Principles" he developed for SFI[106]—all but demands autonomy from the gatekeepers of Kuhn's normal science, DARPA notwithstanding.[107]

This is, of course, the point, says SFI president David Krakauer. Promoting complexity science as the best approach to "understanding *and surviving the new world order* of large-scale autonomous networks," Krakauer all but waved away those Cassandras weeping over the crumbling of the public sphere and democracy as an institution that neoliberalism has wrought by suggesting that SFI at least was well-positioned to help guide this new order in a more "humanistic" direction: "It would be a significant and noble ambition for SFI science to contribute to rethinking society along lines faithful to the increasingly complex organization of the modern world, and several of our recent meetings and discussions, portend a move in this direction."[108] If accomplishing such a rethinking means "meetings and discussions" primarily with the defense, tech, and finance industries looking to aid in the production of commodifiable science and the expansion of corporate power in the neoliberal era, so be it, Krakauer implies: there is no alternative. Describing how SFI "administration and faculty have always had a very negative opinion of public funding, which they describe as too bureaucratic . . . too directive, old-fashioned, short-sighted, and rigid," Li Vigni adds that a succession of SFI leaders, Krakauer included, envisioned their institute as an eminently private space, explicitly hoping to bypass government rules and regulations and "blur the line between the scientific and the entrepreneurial—the ultimate state of asymmetric convergence where science works *with*, *like*, and *for* business."[109]

The reader needs little assistance at this point in understanding how and why this almost smirking disdain for collective, state-sponsored, and replicable efforts at basic science conducted within historically public, which is to say traditionally "nonmarket," institutions that almost pines for the premodernism of the ancient Greece that Foucault explored late in his career is the product of neoliberal reason itself, given neoliberals' bias toward the marketplace of ideas, financialized self-care, alternative intellectual methodologies, and the entrepreneurialization of human capital across industries. Calling his "initial misgivings" about SFI "justified," Baker, in his review of *The Passenger* and *Stella Maris*, recalled his own visit to SFI, which included both a pleasant exchange with McCarthy and a review of the institute's receipts. "Coming from the worlds of business, academia, and think tanks, SFI libertarians drew on the Institute's ideas—and sometimes its institutional resources—to paint a picture of economic and social 'self-organization' in which capitalism was natural, and entrepreneurs solved problems creatively and spontaneously," sighs Baker, referencing his earlier scholarship on the think tank's primary export: neoliberal ideology. "It became clear to me that despite its researchers' undeniable contributions to a wide range of scientific disciplines, SFI's self-portrait as the Island of Misfit Geniuses served primarily to mask its long-running and profound connections to the power centers of American and global capitalism."[110]

For any critic not enervated by the bromides alluding to the SFI's romantic outlaw status and enticing association with high profile intellectuals like Gell-Mann or, later, ex-CIA agent Valerie Plame, this provenance means that McCarthy's latter novels especially—wherein plucky cowboys cling to their independent and dignified rural enterprises in the face of encroaching federal agencies (or abscond to the continent's less rigid southern parallels); fathers and sons fight to keep the fire burning as the public mass of morally averse cannibals closes in; Vietnam veterans are forced to insert themselves in the (state-sponsored) drug trade simply to survive; and a pair of genius siblings who, being too smart to function within mainstream systems and institutions, are essentially forced into alternative social spaces, whether sanatoriums, French Quarter pubs, or leaky Spanish windmills—all but reinscribe, in, yes, magnificent sentences, the privatizing, atomizing, and economizing neoliberal ideology at the core of complexity and the SFI, even if they appear to critique that ideology.[111]

With all of the above roiling behind the scenes of McCarthy's late works, it is here that the real tragedy of Alicia and Bobby Western takes shape. Because having come of age in this environment—human capitalization, social atomization, Cold War anti-collectivism, ubiquitous privatization—McCarthy seems to have followed Foucault by internalizing neoliberal thinking by at least *Suttree*, to his characters' and readers' chronic disadvantage. The glut of McCarthy's writing from the late 1970s and after focuses, for instance, on ruggedly individualized, entrepreneurial, competitive agents who are highly suspicious of not just authority but government specifically—but rarely markets—and routinely pursue go-it-alone responses to socioeconomic, political, and social problems, be they in New Mexico or New Orleans, Texas or Tennessee. *The Road* (2006), *No Country for Old Men* (2005), *The Counselor* (2013), and even the Border Trilogy all feature stalwart and stolid, and at times necessarily aggressive, individuals who seek out self-made solutions to sociopolitical and economic problems via market mechanisms in an open, winner-take-all competitive arena, but never really challenge the social and economic Darwinism of their immediate environments. As the drifter tells Billy in the epilogue of *Cities of the Plain* (1998), for example, the shape of this world "was forced in the void at the onset and all talk of what might otherwise have been is senseless for there is no otherwise."[112] Even the *style* with which McCarthy communicates these stories, says David Holloway in this book's introduction, can leave the reader feeling as if there is no alternative: "The spiraling sentences in whose length and complexity the reader can feel simply locked, the irrefutable density of the words on the page, the reaching of narrators and protagonists for universal truths" communicate the fact that McCarthy's fiction itself is "ontological, immovable, carceral, an avalanche of language in which the reader may feel (and may derive pleasure from feeling) simply lost or overwhelmed."

Although many critics read many of McCarthy's stories as the author's *critique* of unfettered market capitalism—wherein the protagonists' individuation, competition, and refusal of community actually kills them in a world that has been demolished by late capitalism—the specific character of this critique remains ambiguous.[113] That is to say, it's not always clear if, by locating his characters in environments dominated by global markets and their agents and showing how characters participating in such markets almost always end up dead (including the animals and ecosystems "interpellated" by the market, as Louis Althusser might put it), McCarthy is challenging political economy or simply assuming, like Billy's drifter, that this landscape is all there is or ever will be, that there is no alternative. As Bobby puts it, "the bomb was always coming." The subtle commentary on racism in the banking system in *The Stonemason* (1994), the participation of the Houston-based Matacumbe Petroleum Group in *No Country*, the references to the "oilcompany map" in *The Road*, and the passing Halliburton reference in *The Passenger* typically remain just that: passing or stage-setting references delivered in a prose that, adds Holloway "cleaves so closely to the neoliberal world it accepts as ontology and reproduces as truth" that it comes across to the reader as less a critique than "a kind of super-identification with neoliberal capital." Or, as a resigned Ed Tom Bell puts it in *No Country*, "I know as certain as death that there aint nothin short of the second comin of Christ that can slow this train."[114]

Ridley Scott's film version of McCarthy's screenplay *The Counselor* is a useful case in point. Having dabbled just once in the narcotics market—"I don't intend to take this up as a trade"—and helped trigger the murder of his business associates, friends, and fiancée when a deal goes wrong, the narrative's namesake seeks the intercession of a businessman named Jefe who, not unlike Billy Parham's drifter, refuses to imagine a world unlike the neoliberal present. "At some point you must acknowledge that this new world is at last the world itself. There is not some other world," Jefe tells the Counselor over the phone:

> It is not for me to say what you should have done. Or not done. I only know that the world in which you seek to undo your mistakes is not the world in which they were made. You are at a cross in the road and here you think to choose. But there is no choosing. There is only accepting.[115]

In the Counselor's case, suggests the fatalist Jefe, the accepting in question is that all the world is a marketplace; that drugs, diamonds, human bodies, endangered species, and nation states are all for sale; and, in the end, only the best and most ruthless players of the game—presently Cameron Diaz's Malkina—are left alive to shape the world to their material benefit. Reminding readers who thought that Billy's drifter's line in 1998 was that character's reasoning only, McCarthy repeats in his screenplay more than a decade later that there is not some other world than the one organized "spontaneously" to kill everything we hold dear and that any efforts to suggest or strive for an alternative are the real delusion.[116] Or, as McCarthy told one journalist as early as 1992, "I think the notion that the species can be improved in some way, that everyone could live in harmony, is a really dangerous idea."[117]

Although *The Counselor* and its cognates do *identify* the frayed social fabric and decline in traditional morality—the "breakdown in mercantile ethics"[118]—that seem to have accompanied neoliberalism's forced competition and commodification of life, McCarthy's leading men and women routinely *stop* at this glancing identification or reinforce neoliberal reason, having internalized it seems Margaret Thatcher's maxim and thus never speculating on collective pathways *out* of the cultural and moral senescence, social fragmentation, and ecological collapse wrought by political economy. Or, if they do disrupt political economy, they die.

The Passenger and *Stella Maris* only extend such reasoning. Having explored in the former novel Bobby Western's lonely efforts to escape both the world and himself—an abandoned house in Idaho, the offshore oil rig, a remote Spanish island—McCarthy's final novel describes Alicia's fantasy of surpassing even Bobby's isolationism by absconding to Romania to live among the animals. In her final therapy session at the isolating institution into which she had committed herself, Alicia describes for Cohen her desire to withdraw to her "ancestral lands" alone and there become not simply nothingness but an object to be consumed less by the market than Nature:

> I'd burn everything I owned. My passport. Maybe I'd just put my clothes in the trash. Change money in the street. Then I'd hike into the mountains. Stay off the road. Take no chances . . . wrap myself in the blanket at night against the cold and watch the bones take shape beneath my skin and I'd pray that I might see the truth of the world before I died. Sometimes at night the animals would come to the edge of the fire and move about and their shadows would move among the trees and I would understand that when the last fire was ashes they would come and carry me away and I would be their eucharist. And that would be my life.[119]

As the prologue of *The Passenger* makes clear, the reader should understand this romantic picture of the desire for isolation as the last Alicia would paint before hanging herself in a Wisconsin wood. Gorgeous in its imagery, and its ontology, this final page of McCarthy's final novel puts a capstone on a career's worth of narratives which posit that the subject's only reasonable response to social fragmentation and Foucault's enterprise society is not social or political engagement, not organized resistance or the imagining of an alternative, but a resigned lone-wolfism followed by an isolated and typically premature death.

Although it's possible that McCarthy was consciously identifying-critiquing neoliberalism's snuffing out of his characters' radical potential, its theft of their voice and agency within a marginalizing socioeconomic and political system—what Jacques Rancière called the "part of no part"—he nevertheless seems to capitulate to the impenetrability and permanence of that system time and again.[120] So it is that even if McCarthy had read nothing of Foucault beyond *Madness and Civilization*—not the latter's *The Order of Things*, the anthropological, economic, linguistic, and taxonomic musings of which Judge Holden would have found compelling, and not his four-volume "neoliberal" history of Western sexuality that includes the titles *The Use of Pleasure* (1984) and *The Care of the Self* (1986)—we can say with confidence that despite what seem to be various comments upon late capitalism in McCarthy's novels, his fiction, intentionally or not, ultimately reaffirms rather than challenges the socioeconomic and political status quo that was emerging in the 1970s and after. Alicia Western, that much anticipated female protagonist from an author typically focused on male subjectivity, ends up as antisocial and atomized as any male character McCarthy has invented and seems incapable of envisioning a way out, other than suicide. Alicia is but the most salient example of her creator's predilection for the sort of stolid, misunderstood, noble, and independent *potential* dissident who, despite the fact that she knows better, effectively buys into neoliberalism's individuating logic and thus fails-refuses to imagine a future outside of the "real" world that may or may not include her horts. After all, "There is not some other world." The same goes for her brother: abandoning his mates, Bobby, not unlike Suttree, shows no interest in collective efforts to change the world, to complicate a political economy that produces state violence, surveillance, mental illness, and the poverty of his community; no organized activism that challenges Thatcher's foreclosure of thought (which Bobby has internalized); no solidarity or attempt to build intersectional structures. Only market economics, isolation, and flight in the wake of his schizophrenic sister's lonely suicide.

All of this is to say, McCarthy seems to be trying to have his cake and eat it too, sort-of-kind-of challenging the violence of neoliberal reason while both buying into it and endorsing it at the level of both aesthetics and institutional affiliation. Such hedging contributes to the fetishism of both McCarthy's increasingly commodified work (e.g., the tired and frequent online debates about who should play Holden in a film version of *Blood Meridian*) and complexity-as-ideology. McCarthy's "fetishism of misunderstood brilliance"—and individuation—"is a sort of Nietzscheanism, then, not the egalitarianism it first appears to be," argues Baker, whose "Nietzscheanism" I'd replace with "Foucauldianism." "At moments, it even has the flavor of Santa Fe Institute libertarianism. . . . For all the ways in which *The Passenger* and *Stella Maris* feel like a departure from the McCarthy we thought we knew, they also retrospectively illumine this throughline," in which there truly is no alternative to the order of things.[121]

So does the reader taking on McCarthy after the turn of the century witness the end of what David Holloway correctly called the "late modernism" of McCarthy's early fiction.[122] Ending his analysis of the novelist's project with *Cities of the Plain* (1998), Holloway's suggestion that McCarthy's work serves as "a laying of the ground" for "modernism's revival" encounters its limit in *The Road*, *No Country*, *The Counselor*, *The Passenger*, and *Stella Maris*, which, as commercial objects articulating an aesthetics of neoliberal reason, left their predecessors' modernism far behind.[123] Abandoning modernism as a category outright, rather, the late works are not only "dystopian" and fail to manipulate their respective genres as did, say, *Outer Dark*, *Suttree*, and *Blood Meridian*; they are actively *anti*-utopian products designed for commercial consumption. Rather, the atomized humans in these novels take little interest in challenging capitalism but simply slog through the brutal "Hobbesian" circumstances of their lives alone: individual actors seeking not solidarity or community but individualized and often ineffectual solutions to socioeconomic and political problems that were of course created by neoliberal political economy itself. Even if such narratives were intended to demonstrate the failures of neoliberalism, by taking his own "Operating Principles" to heart—"We have in general avoided becoming involved in matters of policy"—McCarthy's resignation in the face of politics proper too only serves to reinforce the inegalitarian structures that he writes into his narratives.[124] "It's compelling cosmology but bad social theory," concludes Baker, noting how the SFI's understanding of knowledge, power, political economy, and science suspiciously resembles that of Hayek and his followers, whose biases lead them to highlight only very specific bits of Darwin—competition over collaboration, individual interest over the common good, spontaneity over long-term planning, survival of the fittest—in their theorizing.[125] Adding that SFI "explicitly associates the name of Darwin with those of Hayek and [Adam] Smith," Li Vigni continues that the SFI exploits even as it reproduces complexity's "naturalization" of competition, "legitimizing a Darwinian and capitalistic view of the economy. At the same time, such a view has been embodied by the SFI administration in the very mode of functioning of the institute" which itself operates "by inscribing into digital tools [and science] a form of 'social Darwinism' . . . in a historical moment where this political economy began to be hegemonic internationally."[126]

The colonization of not only science but literary fiction by complexity—which is to say by neoliberal reason—as an ideological regime, on display in McCarthy's late fiction and elsewhere in the American arts since the 1980s especially, demonstrates just how ruthlessly Hayek and his allies have expunged from the collective unconscious the notion that either egalitarian-minded affinity groups or the public sector can improve the lives of individuals and communities. Fredric Jameson long ago noted how the "marked diminution in the production of new utopias over the last decades"—which is of course a direct result of the norming of neoliberal reason—ostensibly sealed the victory of late capitalism "over all imaginable, let alone practicable, alternatives," serving even as shorthand for anti-communism in the Cold War era and after.[127] As McCarthy's narratives suggest, such reason has effectively poisoned not just science but American literary fiction, political economy, and life itself for each of neoliberalism's abject subjects every day.

The refreshing materialism of not only Baker's and Li Vigni's but Jameson's analyses illustrate the problem of McCarthy's work that even some literary critics and McCarthy scholars seem unwilling to address. Recalling, for example, how SFI's emeritus board chair William H. Miller III, was "inspired" at SFI meetings "to invest in Amazon and Bitcoin, and the dividends of his stewardship have contributed to the health of SFI's endowments, fellowships, and campuses," Bryan Giemza almost celebrates SFI's economic pedigree, adding that the fact that SFI as an ideological concept—privately-financed interdisciplinary (social) science—has entered the mainstream must mean the institute is on the right path. "Fortunately for the financial health and repute of the Institute, some of its attendees found practical applications for its lessons in emergent economics," among them Miller, who "serves as the Institute's resident Warren Buffett," Giemza writes. "If a financial X-ray reveals the soul and prospects of an institution, SFI currently enjoys a good bill of health, and its new campus ensures another income stream as it offers educational retreats for corporations (think Google execs taking part in a seminar about the latest trends in collective behavior, self-organized criticality, and 'consciousness' as manifested in online social networks)." So it is that as SFI reaches middle age, Giemza concludes in something of a reiteration of Kushner and Krakauer, the neoliberal institute "faces the challenges of its own vindication."[128]

The twist in all of this in the context of the late McCarthy is that by exploring, in his intertwined final novels, Alicia's and Bobby's father's physics, which provided humans with a way of destroying the world in an instant, McCarthy misses the fact that the "complexity complex" produced by neoliberal reason became, retroactively, the twentieth century's alternate atomic moment: a long moment no less destructive than the bomb that has contributed to an unsustainable perpetual growth model of the economy and degraded humans, science, and art in all their forms by forcing art, science, and scholarship across disciplines into the entrepreneurial logic of competition and commodification—all while accelerating climate change. As Baker put it in his review of McCarthy's late novels, "Repudiating their father's Faustian science does not require Bobby and Alicia to repudiate science per se." It only encourages them "to seek, like the Santa Fe Institute, to develop an alternative, countercultural way of doing science."[129] In other words, this countercultural, "Foucauldian" alternative—the neoliberal econophysics that promotes competition over cooperation, private science over public solutions, self-care over solidarity, and individualized wins and losses over the collective—rather than rescuing guilt-ridden atomic scientists or saving these physicists' children from the sins of the father still ended up destroying the planet.

At the risk of seeming to censure a fish for getting wet as it swims upstream, my point here is not that McCarthy, an artist, should have provided readers with tangible answers to his own socioeconomic, historical, or epistemological questions, that he should have been more politically active in public or solved on paper the profound ontological mysteries he identifies, or that he should have himself gone off-grid to be a more "pure" artist—as pure in his late career as he was early on when he refused to give public readings or accept teaching offers, all of which forced McCarthy and his then-wife "to eat beans for another week."[130] My point is that, as we saw with Foucault, the conditions of cultural production matter. Even if McCarthy was attempting an archaeology of neoliberalism midcareer and commenting on complexity-as-ideology late-career, he was, in the last analysis, unable to escape the stranglehold that political economy has on the abject neoliberal subject, including himself and his work, and that the shifting conditions of production for McCarthy—his self-consciously self-imposed SFI residency and turn toward Hollywood (again, like Foucault)—affected both his aesthetics and, directly or indirectly, his political philosophy.

That's putting it charitably. A less charitable read is that notwithstanding neoliberalism's ubiquitous and totalizing logic, McCarthy was trying to have it both ways, lacking the courage of his convictions by critiquing late capitalism while simultaneously *cultivating* the endorsement of neoliberal reason late in his career and colluding with neoliberalism's architects and advocates as they reproduced and amplified its commodification of science, art, and the social. Recalling Kekulé's dream, McCarthy's SFI residency and the novels the residency helped produce demonstrate the degree to which the late McCarthy had become the ouroboros itself: a writhing creature eating its own tail.

The heartbreak of the late McCarthy, then, is that in repeating Foucault's mistakes—enabling the rationality and discourse that his earlier novels did such a marvelous job of undermining—McCarthy likewise seems to have ignored the advice of his friend Feynman. Speaking to graduating Caltech students in a 1974 commencement address, the year Hayek accepted the Nobel Memorial Prize in Economics, Feynman implored his audience to beware the pitfalls of "cargo cult" science. Its infantilizing narrative notwithstanding, Feynman's warning is worth quoting at length:

> In the South Seas there is a Cargo Cult of people. During [World War II] they saw airplanes land with lots of good materials, and they want the same thing to happen now. So they've arranged to make things like runways, to put fires along the sides of the runways, to make a wooden hut for a man to sit in, with two wooden pieces on his head like headphones and bars of bamboo sticking out like antennas—he's the controller—and they wait for the airplanes to land. They're doing everything right. The form is perfect. It looks exactly the way it looked before [when Allied air forces occupied the islands]. But it doesn't work. No airplanes land. So I call these things Cargo Cult Science, because they follow all the apparent precepts and forms of scientific investigation, but they're missing something essential, because the planes don't land.[131]

Following Popper's falsifiability thesis, Feynman offers a critique of the very thing that Hayek argued researchers of quantum theory, global economics, and complexity must come to embrace: the lack of repeatability and falsifiability in their work on dynamic and complex systems. Moving the goal posts for both himself and his colleagues—and perhaps for the SFI fellows Feynman and McCarthy would have known personally—Hayek, in his essay on complex phenomena, countered Feynman in advance by arguing that scientific inquiry had reached a point where it must necessarily "push forward into fields where, as we advance, the degree of falsifiability necessarily decreases. This is the price we have to pay for an advance into the field of complex phenomena."[132]

Speaking less to Caltech grads than his future SFI colleagues, Feynman responds to Hayek by arguing that although challenging those whose work has the form and air of science but none of its traditional rigor or demonstrability is never easy, it remains vital to the development of the disciplines—and the civilization. "It is not something simple like telling them how to improve the shapes of the earphones," Feynman muses, in something of an obvious lesson. Instead, the responsibility falls upon scientists with integrity to do the best science they can by way of example. "The first principle is that you must not fool yourself—and you are the easiest person to fool," says the physicist.

> We've learned from experience that the truth will out. Other experimenters will repeat your experiment and find out whether you were wrong or right. Nature's phenomena will agree or they'll disagree with your theory. And, although you may gain some temporary fame and excitement, you will not gain a good reputation as a scientist if you haven't tried to be very careful in this kind of work. And it's this type of integrity, this kind of care not to fool yourself, that is missing to a large extent in much of the research in Cargo Cult Science.[133]

My concern, ultimately, is that McCarthy, nearing the end of his career, fooled himself about economics, science, language, American power, and the politics of art under neoliberal reason. Sucked in by a version of Cargo Cult Science that worried Feynman in 1974, and which was by then already turning toward the market, McCarthy misunderestimated—to quote one American president—the neoliberal commitment to antagonism, inequality, atomization, and the commodification of art, science, and life as first principles, all of which was and is ongoing in Santa Fe. Or if McCarthy didn't underestimate the new capitalism and the new science, but eventually bought into them in a sort of shoulder-shrugging fatalism—"There is no otherwise"—so much the worse.

In either case, Cormac McCarthy, the "immortal" SFI fellow,[134] nonetheless began producing increasingly "neoliberal" novels and screenplays that while in some ways offering a critique of late capitalism and asking important questions about Being, evil, and the nature of reality, *also* carried water for the socioeconomic and political structures that, as he well knew, profited on death, exacerbated the abject subjectivity of his own characters (Joyce, Magdalena, Llewylen and Carla Jean Moss, Billy Parham, and so on), and produced the harried, institutionalized, marginalized, and precarious women and men in *The Passenger* and *Stella Maris*: the dead Alicia and Oiler, the petty thief and ex-mental patient John Sheddan, the clinically depressed Jeffrey, the off-the-grid Borman. Such abject subjects include those of us—scholars and scientists, authors and artists—who too are passengers on a jet that, as McCarthy intuits at the start of his last project, has not only failed to land but has crashed into the sea. The task of the scholar or scientist today thus remains: to dredge up the wreckage wrought by neoliberalism in an effort to find those missing passengers—to find ourselves—again.

Notes

1. F. A. Hayek, *Law, Legislation and Liberty*, vol. 1, *Rules and Order* (Chicago: Univ. of Chicago Press, 1973), 39–40.

2. F. A. Hayek, "Economics and Knowledge," *Individualism and Economic Order* (London: Routledge, 1949), 33–56.

3. Hayek, *Rules and Order*, 39–40.

4. Cormac McCarthy, "The Kekulé Problem," *Nautilus*, 17 April 2017, accessed 1 July 2024, https://nautil.us/the-kekul-problem-236574.

5. Albert Rothenberg, "Creative Cognitive Processes in Kekulé's Discovery of the Structure of the Benzene Molecule," *The American Journal of Psychology* 108, no. 3 (Autumn 1995): 419–38.

6. McCarthy, "The Kekulé Problem."

7. Ibid.

8. See Cormac McCarthy, "Cormac McCarthy Returns to the Kekulé Problem: Answers to questions and questions that cannot be answered," *Nautilus*, 27 Nov. 2017, accessed 1 July 2024, https://nautil.us/cormac-mccarthy-returns-to-the-kekul-problem-236896/: "I haven't read the William Burroughs book that several people mentioned in which apparently language is compared to a virus." See also, William S. Burroughs, *The Ticket That Exploded* (New York: Grove, 1962), 49.

9. Cormac McCarthy, *Stella Maris* (New York: Knopf, 2022), 30.

10. Ibid., 134.

11. Noam Chomsky, *Syntactic Structures* (London: Mouton & Co., 1957). It is worth noting that in his *Aspects of a Theory of Syntax* (Cambridge: MIT Press, 1965), Chomsky describes the recursive property in language as a "syntactic component" (137) of grammar that "specifies an infinite set of abstract formal objects" (16) that "provide infinite generative capacity" (225) in sentence construction. Readers of McCarthy recognize this concept, having read McCarthy's copious instances of recursion, including the following from *All the Pretty Horses* (New York: Knopf, 1992): "They rode up into the mountains trailing three horses apiece in their string with packhorses to

haul the grub and cooktent and they hunted the wild horses in the upland forests in the pine and madroño and in the arroyos where they'd gone to hide and they drive them pounding over the high mesas and penned them in the stone ravine fitted ten years earlier with fence and gate and there the horses milled and squealed and clambered at the rock slopes and turned upon one another biting and kicking while John Grady walked among them in the sweat and dust and bedlam with his rope as if they were no more than some evil dream of horse" (110).

12. Ludwig Wittgenstein, *Tractatus Logico-Philosophicus* (1921), trans. D. F. Pears and B. F. McGuinness (Routledge: London, 1961), 4.0311 and 5.6 (pg. 22, 56), emphasis original.

13. See McCarthy's interest in Wittgenstein in both Richard Woodward, "Cormac McCarthy's Venomous Fiction," *New York Times Magazine*, 19 April 1992: 28–31, accessed 1 July 2024, www.nytimes.com/1992/04/19/magazine/cormac-mccarthy-s-venomous-fiction.html; and Matthias Matussek, "Die Abendröte des Westens," *Der Spiegel*, 30 Aug. 1992, accessed 1 July 2024, https://www.spiegel.de/kultur/die-abendroete-des-westens-a-244c6734-0002-0001-0000-000009284806, trans. Ian Alexander Moore as "Cormac McCarthy's 1992 Interview with Der Spiegel," accessed 1 July 2024, https://www.academia.edu/21895511/Cormac_McCarthys_1992_Interview_with_Der_Spiegel.

14. McCarthy, "The Kekulé Problem."

15. See Bolhuis, J. J., Tattersall, I., Chomsky, N., and Berwick, R. C., "How Could Language Have Evolved?" *PLoS Biology* 12, no. 8 (2014): e1001934, https://doi.org/10.1371/journal.pbio.1001934. See also Noam Chomsky's and Robert Berwick's *Why Only Us? Language and Evolution* (Cambridge: MIT Press, 2017) and several of Chomsky's other papers, including Fitch, Hauser, and Chomsky, "The evolution of the language faculty: clarifications and implications," *Cognition* 97, no. 2 (2005): 179–210.

16. Steven Pinker and Paul Bloom, "Natural language and natural selection," *Behavioral and Brain Sciences* 13, no. 4 (1990): 707–84.

17. Christian Erbacher, *Friedrich August von Hayek's Draft Biography of Ludwig Wittgenstein: The Text and Its History* (Leiden/Boston: mentis/Brill, 2019), 28.

18. F. A. Hayek, "The Theory of Complex Phenomena," *Studies in Philosophy, Politics, and Economics* (London: Routledge, 1967), 22–42.

19. "The origins, evolution, and diversity of human languages," Santa Fe Institute, accessed 1 July 2024, https://www.santafe.edu/research/projects/the-origins-evolution-and-diversity-of-human-langu.

20. See Ciarán Dowd, "The Santa Fe Institute," *Cormac McCarthy in Context*, ed. Steven Frye (Cambridge: Cambridge UP, 2020), 33–44; Lydia Cooper, *Cormac McCarthy: A Complexity Theory of Literature* (Manchester: Manchester UP, 2021); and Bryan Giemza, *Science and Literature in Cormac McCarthy's Expanding Worlds* (New York: Bloomsbury Academic, 2023).

21. Jim Hilton, "Unsalvageable Parts: Diving into the Wreck with Cormac McCarthy," *The Quietus*, 3 Dec. 2022, accessed 1 July 2024, https://thequietus.com/articles/32424-cormac-mccarthy-the-passenger-stella-maris-review.

22. Hayek, "The Theory of Complex Phenomena," 26.

23. Bruce Caldwell, *Hayek's Challenge: An Intellectual Biography of F. A. Hayek* (Chicago: Univ. of Chicago Press, 2004), chap. 6–7.

24. Caldwell, *Hayek's Challenge*, chap. 7–8.

25. Hayek, "Economics and Knowledge," 50–51.

26. F. A. Hayek, *Law, Legislation and Liberty*, vol. 2, *The Mirage of Social Justice* (Chicago: Univ. of Chicago Press, 1976), 108.

27. Ibid., 54.

28. F. A. Hayek, "Friedrich August von Hayek—Prize Lecture," speech delivered 11 Dec. 1974, Nobel Prize Outreach AB 2023, The Nobel Foundation, accessed 1 July 2024, https://www.nobelprize.org/prizes/economic-sciences/1974/hayek/lecture/.

29. Hayek, *Rules and Order*, 44.

30. See, for example, F. A. Hayek, *Law, Legislation and Liberty*, vol. 3, *The Political Order of a Free People* (Chicago: Univ. of Chicago Press, 1979), 61: "Professor Milton Friedman's . . . [plan] for giving the parents vouchers with which they can pay for their children's education at schools of their own choosing seems to have great advantage over the prevailing system."

31. Hayek, "Use of Knowledge in Society," 79.

32. Hayek, *The Political Order of a Free People*, 165.

33. Ibid., emphasis added.

34. Hayek, *Rules and Order*, 31.

35. Hayek, "Use of Knowledge in Society," 87–88.

36. Hayek, *Rules and Order*, 23.

37. Hayek, "The Theory of Complex Phenomena," 42.

38. Thomas S. Kuhn, *The Structure of Scientific Revolutions* (Chicago: Univ. of Chicago Press, 1962), chap. 2–4.

39. Quinn Slobodian, *The Globalists: The End of Empire and the Birth of Neoliberalism* (New Haven: Harvard, 2020), 230.

40. Ibid., 257.

41. See Michel Foucault, *The Order of Things: An Archaeology of the Human Sciences* (1966; repr. New York: Vintage, 1973).

42. Hayek, "Facts of the Social Sciences," *Individualism and Economic Order*, 57–76.

43. Hayek, "Economics and Knowledge," 47–49.

44. Hayek, "Facts of the Social Sciences," 76.

45. Wittgenstein, *Tractatus*, 5.634 (pg. 58), emphasis added.

46. Michael Lynn Crews, *Books Are Made Out of Books* (San Marcos: Univ. of Texas Press, 2017), 85.

47. Michel Foucault, *Madness and Civilization* (1961; repr. New York: Vintage, 1988), 18–19; Cormac McCarthy, *Blood Meridian, or the Evening Redness in the West* (1985; repr. New York: Vintage, 1992), 282.

48. Foucault, *Madness*, 20–21.

49. Cormac McCarthy, *Suttree* (1979; repr. New York: Vintage, 2010), 456.

50. Foucault, *Madness and Civilization*, 8.

51. McCarthy, *Suttree*, 457–58; Foucault, *Madness*, 8.

52. Foucault, *Madness*, 203.

53. McCarthy, *Suttree*, 431.

54. Cormac McCarthy, *Child of God* (1973; repr. New York: Vintage, 2010), 193–94.

55. Michel Foucault, *The Archaeology of Knowledge* (1969; repr. New York: Pantheon, 1972), 16, 203.

56. Michel Foucault, *Politics, Philosophy Culture: Interviews and Other Writings 1977–1984*, trans. Alan Sheridan (New York: Routledge, 1988), 31.

57. Ibid., 262.

58. Foucault, *Archaeology*, 203.

59. Brian James Schill, "The Glanton Gang's Michel Foucault," *The Cormac McCarthy Journal*

20, no. 1 (2022): 23–43. See also, Dan Sinykin, *American Literature and the Long Downturn: Neoliberal Apocalypse* (Oxford: Oxford, UP, 2020).

60. McCarthy, *Blood Meridian*, 84, 239.

61. Ibid., 240.

62. Walter Benjamin, "Theses on the Philosophy of History," *Illuminations* (New York: Schocken, 1976), 256.

63. Terence Moran, "The Wired West," review of *Blood Meridian* by Cormac McCarthy, *The New Republic*, 6 May 1985: 37–38.

64. Foucault, *Archaeology*, 210–11.

65. Michel Foucault, "The History of Sexuality," trans. Colin Gordon, et al., in *Power/Knowledge: Selected Interviews and Other Writings, 1972–1977*, ed. Colin Gordon (New York: Pantheon, 1980), 193.

66. McCarthy, *The Passenger*, 298.

67. Ibid., 327–28.

68. McCarthy, *Blood Meridian*, 198.

69. James Miller, *The Passion of Michel Foucault* (New York: Simon & Schuster, 1993), chaps. 6, 9.

70. Michel Foucault, *The Birth of Biopolitics: Lectures at the Collège de France, 1978–79*, trans. Graham Burchell (London: Palgrave Macmillan, 2008), 19.

71. Ibid., 226.

72. Ibid., 131–32.

73. Ibid., 147.

74. Simeon Wade, *Foucault in California* (Berkeley: Heyday, 2019), xvii.

75. Jeffrey J. Kripal, *Esalen: America and the Religion of No Religion* (Univ. of Chicago Press, 2007), 4, 251–56, 338–44.

76. Ibid., 21–24.

77. Ibid., xvi–xvii.

78. Michel Foucault, *The History of Sexuality*, trans. Robert Hurley, vol. 2, *The Use of Pleasure* (New York: Random House, 1985) and *The History of Sexuality*, trans. Robert Hurley, vol. 3, *The Care of the Self* (New York: Random House, 1986). See also Michel Foucault, *The Government of Self and Others: Lectures at the Collège de France, 1982–1983*, trans. Graham Burchell (New York: Picador/Palgrave Macmillan, 2011).

79. Mitchell Dean and Daniel Zamora, *The Last Man takes LSD: Foucault and the End of Revolution* (London: Verso, 2021), 142. See also, *Foucault and Neoliberalism*, eds. Daniel Zamora and Michael Behrent (Cambridge: Polity, 2015).

80. Foucault, *Politics, Philosophy, Culture*, 170. On Foucault's support for a lower age of sexual consent and the Iranian Revolution, see Miller, *Passion of Michel Foucault*, 256–57 and 306–14.

81. Foucault, *Politics, Philosophy, Culture*, 170.

82. See "France: Defection of the Leftist Intellectuals," Central Intelligence Agency, United States Government, Dec. 1985, declassified 13 May 2011, accessed 1 July 2024, https://www.cia.gov/readingroom/docs/CIA-RDP86S00588R000300380001-5.pdf. As the report notes, "In the field of anthropology, the influential structuralist school associated with Claude Levi-Strauss, Foucault, and others performed virtually the same mission" of "challenging and later rejecting the hitherto dominant Marxist theories of historical progress."

83. Foucault, *The Birth of Biopolitics*, 305.

84. Ibid., 259–60.

85. Ibid., 305.

86. Thomas Picketty, *Capital in the Twenty-First Century*, trans. Arthur Goldhammer (Cambridge: Belknap/Harvard, 2013), 24, chap. 7–12. Picketty demonstrates the lie of Friedman's claim in 1969's *Capitalism and Freedom* (Chicago: Univ. of Chicago Press, 2002) that "capitalism leads to less inequality than alternative systems of organization and that the development of capitalism has greatly lessened the extent of inequality," 169.

87. "Quarterly Residential Vacancies and Homeownership, First Quarter 2024," U.S. Census Bureau, release number: CB24-62, 30 April 2024, accessed 1 July 2024, https://www.census.gov/housing/hvs/files/currenthvspress.pdf. In Fargo, N.D., for example, the percentage of housing units that were owner-occupied between 2018 and 2022 was a dismal 44.2 percent. See also "QuickFacts: Fargo city; North Dakota; Cass County, North Dakota; North Dakota," U.S. Census Bureau, accessed 1 July 2024, https://www.census.gov/quickfacts/fact/table/fargocitynorthdakota,casscountynorthdakota,ND/PST045222.

88. "Union Members—2023," U.S. Department of Labor, Bureau of Labor Statistics, 23 Jan. 2024, accessed 1 July 2024, https://www.bls.gov/news.release/pdf/union2.pdf.

89. "About Human Trafficking," U.S. State Department, accessed 1 July 2024, https://www.state.gov/humantrafficking-about-human-trafficking.

90. See Anne Case and Angus Deaton, *Deaths of Despair and the Future of Capitalism* (Princeton: Princeton UP, 2020); Daniel Dawes, *The Political Determinants of Health* (Baltimore: Johns Hopkins UP, 2020); Richard Wilkinson, *The Impact of Inequality* (New York: The New Press, 2005); Anna Zeira, "Mental Health Challenges Related to Neoliberal Capitalism in the United States," *Community Mental Health Journal* 58 (2022): 205–12; and Stephen Nkansah-Amankra, et al., "Disparities in health, poverty, incarceration, and social justice among racial groups in the United States: A critical review of evidence of close links with neoliberalism," *International Journal of Health Services* 43, no. 2 (2013): 217–40.

91. See, for example, Christian Parenti, "A Match Made in Hell: Climate Change and Neoliberalism" in *Climate and American Literature*, ed. Michael Boyden (Cambridge: Cambridge UP; 2021), 315–32.

92. Hayek, *Rules and Order*, 41, chap. 2.

93. McCarthy, *Suttree*, 283.

94. See, among many econophysics publications, Jing Chen, *The Unity of Science and Economics: A New Foundation of Economic Theory* (New York: Springer, 2015); Franck Jovanovic and Christophe Schinckus, "The Emergence of Econophysics: A New Approach in Modern Financial Theory," *History of Political Economy* 45, no. 3 (Oct. 2013): 443–74; Peter Richmond, et al., *Econophysics and Physical Economics* (Oxford: Oxford UP, 2013); and Martin Shubik, "Building Theories of Economic Process," *Complexity* 14 (2009): 77–92.

95. Fabrizio Lillo, "Econophysics and the Challenge of Efficiency," *Complexity* 14, no. 3 (2008): 39–54.

96. McCarthy, *Passenger*, 205.

97. Ibid.

98. Ibid., 327.

99. Hayek, "The Theory of Complex Phenomena," 25.

100. McCarthy, *Passenger*, 326. See also, Benjamin, "Theses on the Philosophy of History," *Illuminations*, 254.

101. See Fabrizio Li Vigni, "The failed institutionalization of 'complexity science': A focus on the Santa Fe Institute's legitimization strategy," *History of Science* 59, no. 3 (2021): 344–69; and Erik

Baker, "The ultimate think tank: The rise of the Santa Fe Institute libertarian," *History of the Human Sciences* 35, no. 3–4 (2022): 32–57.

102. Fabrizio Li Vigni, "Hayek at the Santa Fe Institute: Origins, Models, and Organization of the Cradle of Complexity Sciences," *Centaurus* 64, no. 2 (2022): 443–82. See also, "Individual Freedom & Free Markets," John Templeton Foundation, accessed 1 July 2024, https://www.templeton.org/funding-areas/individual-freedom-free-markets.

103. Li Vigni, "Hayek at the Santa Fe Institute," 467.

104. David Kushner, "'If It Doesn't Concern Life and Death, It's Not Interesting': Cormac McCarthy's American Odyssey," *Rolling Stone*, 27 Dec. 2007, accessed 1 July 2024, https://www.rollingstone.com/culture/culture-features/cormac-mccarthy-reclusive-american-novelist-1234770602/.

105. Ibid.

106. Cormac McCarthy, "SFI's Operating Principles," Santa Fe Institute, accessed 1 July 2024, https://www.santafe.edu/about/operating-principles.

107. According to Li Vigni, "Hayek at the Santa Fe Institute," "government" constituted only 21 percent of SFI's reported revenues in 2013, a marked decrease in public funding reported by the Institute in the 1990s. The figure is likely lower today.

108. David Krakauer, "Beyond Borders," *Parallax* 2 (Winter 2017): Santa Fe Institute, accessed 1 July 2024, https://sfi-edu.s3.amazonaws.com/sfi-edu/production/uploads/publication/2017/02/07/Parallax_Winter_2017_FNL-4.pdf, emphasis added.

109. Li Vigni, "Hayek at the Santa Fe Institute," 463–64, emphasis original.

110. Eric Baker, "Reenchanted Science: How did Cormac McCarthy become a shill for libertarian utopianism?" *The Baffler*, 22 Dec. 2022, accessed 1 July 2024, https://thebaffler.com/latest/reenchanted-science-baker.

111. "About Valerie Plame," Valerie Plame, PeaceLoveWeb, accessed 1 July 2024, https://www.valerieplame.com/about.

112. Cormac McCarthy, *Cities of the Plain* (New York: Knopf, 1998), 285.

113. For early articles exploring neoliberalism in Cormac McCarthy, see: Lydia R. Cooper, "Diamonds, drugs, and the digital age: Global capitalism in Cormac McCarthy's *The Counselor*," *Critique: Studies in Contemporary Fiction* 59, no. 4: 445–58; David Deacon, "'Some Unholy Alloy': Neoliberalism, Digital Modernity, and the Mechanics of Globalized Capital in Cormac McCarthy's *The Counselor*," *European Journal of American Studies* 12, no. 3 (2017), accessed 1 July 2024, http://journals.openedition.org/ejas/12364; Jordan Dominy, "Cannibalism, Consumerism, and Profanation: Cormac McCarthy's *The Road* and the end of capitalism," *The Cormac McCarthy Journal* 13, no. 1 (2015): 143–58; Jonathan and Rick Elmore, "'Human Become Coin': Neoliberalism, Anthropology, and Human Possibilities in *No Country for Old Men*," *The Cormac McCarthy Journal* 14, no. 2 (2016): 168–85; Casey Jergenson, "'In what direction did lost men veer?': Late Capitalism and Utopia in *The Road*," *The Cormac McCarthy Journal* 14, no. 1 (2016): 117–32; and Simon Schleusener, "The Dialectics of Mobility: Capitalism and Apocalypse in Cormac McCarthy's *The Road*," *European Journal of American Studies* 12, no. 3 (2017), accessed 1 July 2024, http://journals.openedition.org/ejas/12296. See also Dan Sinykin, *American Literature*.

114. Cormac McCarthy, *No Country for Old Men* (New York: Knopf, 2005), 159.

115. Cormac McCarthy, *The Counselor: A Screenplay* (New York: Vintage, 2013), 145–46.

116. Worth noting is the exceptionally brief scene—one paragraph in the screenplay—late in *The Counselor* where the title character, whose fiancée Laura never made it to the couple's rendezvous, is described as participating in a "protest" walk in Juarez. "People are marching with signs

and with banners. They contain large full color portraits of the missing. The signs say: Desaparecido or Desaparecido with a date following," writes McCarthy. "A khaki-colored Army jeep with a soldier in battledress at the rear of a mounted machinegun fords its way through the crowd. The counselor is among the mourners, carrying a poster with a color photograph of Laura" (153). Perfunctory as it is, this token scene's very existence, arguably only serves to confuse the reader-viewer about the value of its origin and inclusion, highlighting the lack of any other such scenes in McCarthy's oeuvre and begging the question of the point if its inclusion.

117. Woodward, "Cormac McCarthy's Venomous Fiction."

118. McCarthy, *No Country*, 304.

119. McCarthy, *Stella Maris*, 190.

120. Jacques Rancière, *Disagreement: Politics and Philosophy*, trans. Julie Rose (1995; repr. Minneapolis: Univ. of Minnesota Press, 1999), chap. 1.

121. Baker, "Reenchanted Science."

122. David Holloway, *The Late Modernism of Cormac McCarthy* (Westport: Greenwood Press, 2002), 4.

123. Ibid.

124. McCarthy, "SFI's Operating Principles."

125. Baker, "Reenchanted Science."

126. Li Vigni, "Hayek at the Santa Fe Institute," 446.

127. Fredric Jameson, "An American Utopia," *An American Utopia: Dual Power and the Universal Army*, ed. Slavoj Žižek (London: Verso, 2016), 1–96.

128. Giemza, *Science and Literature*, 15–16.

129. Baker, "Reenchanted Science."

130. Woodward, "Cormac McCarthy's Venomous Fiction."

131. Richard Feynman, *"Surely You're Joking, Mr. Feynman!": Adventures of a Curious Character* (New York: W. W. Norton, 1985), 340.

132. Hayek, "The Theory of Complex Phenomena," 29.

133. Feynman, *Surely You're Joking*, 342.

134. No author, "Cormac McCarthy," Santa Fe Institute, accessed 1 July 2024, https://www.santafe.edu/people/profile/cormac-mccarthy.

CONTRIBUTORS

Julian Caradec is a high school English teacher in southern France who began doctoral training at the Université Aix-Marseille in 2024. His research focuses on the politics of child death in North American literature.

Christine Chollier is professor of American literature and text semantics at the University of Reims, France. She has published studies in literature and translation. After writing her PhD on McCarthy's earlier books, she edited *Uncharted Territories* (2003) after the third McCarthy Conference in Europe (2002) and coedited the Cormac McCarthy volume (no. 17, 2004) of the *Profils américains Review* with Edwin T. Arnold. Her critical studies include papers on F. Scott Fitzgerald, William Faulkner, Washington Irving, W. S. Merwin, Stephen Crane, Katherine Mansfield, and other writers.

Vernon W. Cisney is chair and associate professor of Interdisciplinary Studies at Gettysburg College in Pennsylvania. He teaches and researches at the intersection of philosophy, religion, film, literature, politics, and popular culture. He is the author of *Deleuze and Derrida: Difference and the Power of the Negative* (2018) and *Derrida's Voice and Phenomenon: An Edinburgh Philosophical Guide* (2014) and is the author or coeditor of a number of works in continental philosophy, political philosophy, and the philosophy of film. Most recently, he has written articles and chapters included in the anthologies *Deleuze and Guattari Studies* (2023) and *Theology and Batman* (2022). He is currently editing a monograph on the philosophy of Gilles Deleuze for Wipf and Stock tentatively entitled, *Reading Deleuze.*

Lydia R. Cooper is director of the university core curriculum and professor of English at Seattle University. The author of *Cormac McCarthy: A Complexity Theory of Literature* (2021), *Masculinities in Literature of the American West* (2016), and *No More Heroes: Narrative Perspective and Morality in Cormac McCarthy* (2011), Cooper has also edited *The Routledge Companion to*

Masculinity in American Literature and Culture (2021), along with articles on masculinity, trans and Two Spirit identity, trauma, and climate crisis in contemporary American and Indigenous North American literature in journals such as *PMLA*, *GLQ*, *Contemporary Literature*, *Modern Fiction Studies*, *Studies in the Novel*, *Studies in American Indian Literature*, and *Interdisciplinary Studies in Literature and the Environment.*

Jordan J. Dominy is an assistant professor of English at Auburn University at Montgomery (Alabama), where he teaches courses in composition and literature. His book, *Southern Literature, Cold War Culture, and the Making of Modern America*, was published by the University Press of Mississippi in 2020. His research interests include Cormac McCarthy and the contemporary US, Southern and American fiction, and popular culture.

Jonathan Elmore is associate professor of English at Savannah State University and the managing editor of *Watchung Review*. He researches and teaches composition, environmental humanities, and Cormac McCarthy Studies. His scholarship has been published in the *Cormac McCarthy Journal*, *Mississippi Quarterly*, the *British Fantasy Society Journal*, *Orbit*, the *Journal of Liberal Arts and Humanities*, *The Criterion*, and elsewhere. He serves on the advisory board of the EcoCritical Theory and Practice series with Lexington Books and the editorial board of the *Cormac McCarthy Journal*.

Rick Elmore is associate professor of philosophy at Appalachian State University and senior managing editor of book reviews at *Symposium*. He is the coeditor of *The Biopolitics of Punishment: Derrida and Foucault* (2022). His articles and essays have appeared in *Politics and Policy*, *symplokē*, *Symposium*, *Mississippi Quarterly*, the *Cormac McCarthy Journal*, and elsewhere.

David Holloway is associate professor of American thought and culture and academic lead for the Joint Honours Programme at the University of Derby. He is the author of *The Late Modernism of Cormac McCarthy* (2002) and *9/11 and the War on Terror* (2008), and is a contributing coeditor of *American Visual Cultures* (2005). He has written widely on Cormac McCarthy and modern US cultural and political history in a variety of peer-reviewed journals and edited collections. He is preparing a forthcoming book on twenty-first century American conservatism.

Casey Jergenson is an independent scholar based in Omaha, Nebraska. His research interests include utopian discourse, Marxist cultural theory, and speculative fiction. His work has been published in the *Cormac McCarthy Journal* and *Utopian Studies*.

A writer and researcher based at the University of North Dakota School of Medicine and Health Sciences, **Brian James Schill** is the author of the literary history of punk and postpunk subculture, *The Year's Work in the Punk Bookshelf, or Lusty Scripts* (2017). His scholarship and journalism have appeared in *Salon*, *Punk & Postpunk*, *Prairie Schooner*, *PopMatters*, *North Dakota Quarterly*, and the *Cormac McCarthy Journal*, among other venues.

INDEX

Numbers in **boldface** refer to illustrations

INDEX

www.ingramcontent.com/pod-product-compliance
Lightning Source LLC
Chambersburg PA
CBHW060627310726
48982CB00003B/701
9781621909378